Palgrave Studies of Entrepreneurship in Africa

Series Editors
Kevin Ibeh
Department of Management
Birkbeck, University of London
London, UK

Sonny Nwankwo
Office of the Academy Provost
Nigerian Defence Academy
Kaduna, Nigeria

Tigineh Mersha
Department of Management and International Business
University of Baltimore
Baltimore, MD, USA

Ven Sriram
Department of Marketing and Entrepreneurship
University of Baltimore
Baltimore, MD, USA

The Palgrave Studies of Entrepreneurship in Africa series offers an urgently needed platform to document, promote and showcase entrepreneurship in Africa and create a unique home for top quality, cutting-edge work on a broad range of themes and perspectives.

Focusing on successful African firms, small and medium sized enterprises as well as multinational corporations, this series will cover new and ground-breaking areas including innovation, technology and digital entrepreneurship, green practices, sustainability, and their cultural and social implication s for Africa. This series is positioned to eminently capture and energize the monumental changes currently taking place in Africa, well beyond the pervasive informal sector. It will also respond to the great thirst amongst students, researchers, policy and third sector practitioners for relevant knowledge and nuanced insights on how to further promote and institutionalize entrepreneurship, and optimize its benefits across the continent. The series will offer an important platform for interrogating the appropriateness and limits of Western management practices in Africa, examining new approaches to researching the fast-changing continent.

A diverse set of established experts and emerging scholars based in Africa and around the world will contribute to this series. Projects will also originate from entrepreneurship-themed tracks and Special Interest Groups at major Africa-focused conferences, notably the International Academy of African Business and Development, the Academy of Management Africa, and the Academy of International Business African Chapter. The foregoing breadth and diversity of themes, target authors and manuscript sources will produce a richly distinctive series.

More information about this series at
http://www.palgrave.com/gp/series/15149

Nasiru D. Taura • Elvira Bolat
Nnamdi O. Madichie
Editors

Digital Entrepreneurship in Sub-Saharan Africa

Challenges, Opportunities and Prospects

palgrave
macmillan

Editors
Nasiru D. Taura
Business School, Bournemouth University
Bournemouth, UK

Elvira Bolat
Business School, Bournemouth University
Bournemouth, UK

Nnamdi O. Madichie
Centre for Research & Enterprise
Bloomsbury Institute London
London, UK

ISSN 2662-1169 ISSN 2662-1177 (electronic)
Palgrave Studies of Entrepreneurship in Africa
ISBN 978-3-030-04923-2 ISBN 978-3-030-04924-9 (eBook)
https://doi.org/10.1007/978-3-030-04924-9

Library of Congress Control Number: 2019931008

This Palgrave Macmillan imprint is published by the registered company Springer Nature Switzerland AG.
The registered company address is: Gewerbestrasse 11, 6330 Cham, Switzerland

Nasiru D. Taura

My dedication goes to my wife (Aisha Abdulkareem) and my son (Al-ameen Nasiru). Without their support, patience, and help this project wouldn't have been possible.

Elvira Bolat

I dedicate this project to my family, husband (Mahmut Bolat), my incredible and everyday inspiring daughter (Elisa Bolat), and my mother (Ramilya Byanova), who believe in me and gave me the foundation to do what I do. Thank you for being my support, my guide, and my strength.

Nnamdi O. Madichie

I dedicate this project to my wife (Lynda Madichie) and my lovely kids (Obinna and Nnenna Madichie). You are the tripod of my current existence—nothing compares to you all.

Foreword

It is a real honour for me to write a foreword for this book. Africa is one of the most varied and richest continents in the world, yet the countries making up Africa often languish behind the rest of the world. This book is a timely reminder that there is much entrepreneurship taking place in countries such as Nigeria, Ghana, South Africa, and Kenya, to name a few. The book gives us an interestingly sweeping perspective that ranges from digital entrepreneurship in banks to agriculture and the development of games.

The digital networks in Africa have been greatly facilitated by the undersea cables that girdle most of Africa from the north to the south, the east and the west by groups such as Seacom, EASSy, TEAMs, WACS, ACE (Africa Coast to Europe), to name a few. This network provides immense possibilities for digital entrepreneurship in both coastal and landlocked areas in Africa. These possibilities allow large swathes of Africa to be part of the global economy. As someone who has written extensively about eCommerce and digital branding, I understand the value of first mover advantages when new technologies are adopted swiftly and effectively by businesses. The digital platforms have matured in the developed countries, but they are more nascent in Africa. This is both a boon and a curse. It is a boon because African businesses do not have to make the same mistakes that were made by businesses in Europe and the USA.

It is a curse because it could herald another form of colonisation by the digitally more powerful nations, in terms of infrastructure and knowledge, compared with countries that are still grappling with more basic systems, abilities, and knowledge. To open up the country to true digital entrepreneurship requires education growth, digital access, and home-made digital solutions. The book quite rightly points out the growth of innovation hubs has not necessarily led to successful digital start-ups.

This requires good software experts and developers that can transform certain areas of the economy in different countries in Africa. At the same time, for digital entrepreneurship to succeed there has to be a critical mass of early adopters of the digital solutions, as shown in banking. To have a mass of early adopters also needs better infrastructure, better incomes, and better education. Until these barriers are broken and addressed, digital entrepreneurship will be always difficult to grow in many countries in Africa. One of the reasons Japan succeed after the Second World War was because it had a sufficient segment of the population that were early adopters, who were well educated and had reasonable incomes, who could try new ideas and inventions ranging from the Walkman to PlayStation.

This enabled them to compete with the technologies in the West and to begin to even lead them, once enough knowledge and expertise had been gained and local innovations began to grow rapidly. In all digital start-ups it is always important for companies to realise that it is not always about technology but it is about understanding how the markets can be mobilised and made to use and accept digital solutions effectively and easily. The success of many digital enterprises rests on this premise and on the premise that they are quite market- rather than technology-oriented. In many of the media and software/digital sectors, there is cultural domination by the West of the film and entertainment industry, and the book does show how Nollywood is breaking down barriers. However, they are still substantial, and it is good that we have individuals who have succeeded in the West, trying to bring funds to a resource-starved film industry. Many countries in Africa were colonised once, and for them to grow more independent requires good management, governance, and technological grasp, fostering digital industries. Unless this happens there is always the danger of a new form of colonialism appearing around the corner. In many ways the lessons offered by this book need to be heeded and used by people in power.

Africa offers a rich tapestry of landscapes, abundant resources, and a variety of peoples that are resourceful and interesting. Their knowledge and heritage need to be harnessed effectively. I was particularly impressed with the way in which digital technologies have been used in Nollywood in Nigeria and how farmers in Ghana have transformed and enriched their collaboration through digital technology. In Kenya, the richness of the talent in computer technology has given rise to games and this is a growing area internationally. An African imprint with African characters on games would be a welcome addition to the current offers. The book is well written with some good empirical evidence and interviews with top entrepreneurs. The variety of views and authors creates a rich seam of knowledge that would be useful not only to academics, but also provide interesting ideas, the problems and constraints associated with digital transformation on the continent. I congratulate the editors for bringing together a good range of authors, ideas, and topics that will be very helpful to promote a more nuanced and sound growth in small to medium sized African businesses.

University of Southampton, UK Ashok Ranchhod

Ashok Ranchhod Obituary

Professor Ashok Ranchhod passed away recently after a long and distinguished career in the field of marketing and online gaming. Ranchhod was a principal teaching fellow in Marketing Communications within Winchester School of Art (WSA) at the University of Southampton.

Prior to his work in academia, he was the managing director of Microplants, a biotechnology company based in Derbyshire. He was also the CEO of the Mudra Institute of Communications Ahmedabad (MICA)—one the leading Communications Schools in India—between 1999 and 2011.

Ranchhod has written numerous books and articles and received prizes for his papers at the Academy of Marketing and The British Academy of Management. He has undertaken consultancy work for major organisations and written case studies on companies in several different sectors of industry for the Chartered Institute of Marketing. He has also made several media appearances.

In recognition of his services to business and marketing he was made a Fellow of the Chartered Institute of Marketing in 2000.

His research at WSA was primarily focused around e-commerce and corporate social responsibility. He led a team of research students in these areas. He was also interested in issues around sports marketing and online gaming behaviour. Indeed, he put together a multidisciplinary bid on looking at the role of serious games in higher education—bringing together academia, industry and students as the major stakeholders.

Besides working on a luxury branding project in India with MICA and looking at ethical food consumption and marketing, he was also supervising students on contemporary marketing topics ranging from nation branding, through luxury branding in China, to corporate branding and performance in the pharmaceutical industry.

Ashok has been an external examiner at Manchester Metropolitan University Business School, University of Westminster, Henley, and Ashridge Business School. He held visiting professorships at the University of Angers (France), Napier University (Scotland) and the University of Canberra (Australia). He has also been on the editorial boards of leading business and management journals such as the *Journal of Small Business and Enterprise Development*, *Journal of Electrical Commerce Work*, *International Journal of Mobile Marketing* and the *Journal of Information Technology and Case Research*.

He was also recently appointed emeritus professor at Southampton Solent University where he previously held the title of Professor in Marketing.

Overall, we are privileged to have had the opportunity to incorporate his distinguished endorsement in this book. May his soul rest in peace.

Nasiru D. Taura
Elvira Bolat and Nnamdi O. Madichie

Contents

Part I Introduction 1

1 **Introduction to African Digital Entrepreneurship** 3
Nasiru D. Taura, Elvira Bolat, and Nnamdi O. Madichie

2 **Innovation Hubs in Africa: What Do They Really Do for Digital Entrepreneurs?** 9
Nicolas Friederici

Part II Fin-tech: Trust, Legitimacy, and Digital Infrastructure—The Promise, Prospects, and Challenges 29

3 **Renegotiating Legitimacy in the Digital Age: Insights from Nigeria** 31
Nasiru D. Taura, Obiajulu Christopher Ede, and Oladokun Ogunniyi

Part III Media-tech: The Creative Destruction and Reconstruction of African Digital Media 65

4 The African New Media Digital Revolution: Some Selected Cases from Nigeria 67
Elvira Bolat

5 The Impact of New Media (Digital) and Globalisation on Nollywood 89
Nnamdi O. Madichie, Bamidele O. Ajakaiye, and Vanessa Ratten

Part IV Animation and Games: Unlimited Opportunities for Exploration 123

6 Shifting Cultural Capital: Kenyan Arts in Digital Spaces 125
Paula Callus

Part V Inclusive-tech: Gender Inequality, Poverty, and Digital Ecosystems 145

7 Technopreneurship: A Discursive Analysis of the Impact of Technology on the Success of Women Entrepreneurs in South Africa 147
B. N. O. Irene

8 The Nature of Corporate Digital Agricultural Entrepreneurship in Ghana 175
George Acheampong

9 Agri-tech Opportunities at the Bottom of the Pyramid: How Big Is the Opportunity and How Little Has Been Exploited? Some Selected Cases in Nigeria 199
Ali Muhammad Garba

10 What Next for Digital Entrepreneurship in Sub-Saharan Africa? 221
Nnamdi O. Madichie, Nasiru D. Taura, and Elvira Bolat

Index 241

Notes on Contributors

George Acheampong holds a PhD from the University of Ghana after completing coursework at the University of Copenhagen and is a past DANIDA Growth and Employment Scholar. He has held fellowships at the UNU-WIDER and DERG University of Copenhagen. His research interests are in how enterprise can lead to development in Africa utilising market-based approaches. George teaches entrepreneurship, international business, and marketing at the University of Ghana Business School. He is a member of the following professional bodies: the Academy of Management (AoM) Entrepreneurship Division, Africa Academy of Management (AFAM), International Academy of African Business and Development (IAABD), Development Economics Research Group (DERG-UCPH), and International Network of Social Network Analysts (INSNA). http://ugbs.ug.edu.gh/ugbsfaculty/profile-faculty_member/acheampong-george

Bamidele O. Ajakaiye is a Nigerian filmmaker based in the UK who started his career in filmmaking in 1986 in his home country, Nigeria. In his 30-plus years' career he has worked in different capacities from acting, to script supervising, production management, first assistant directing, editing, scriptwriting, and producing before focusing on directing. He has directed nine TV dramas, including *One 2 Much*, *Freeman's College*, *Super Story*, and *Dear Mother*. A TAVA awards Most Outstanding TV Drama Director winner (2010), he co-produced a Nigerian–British film, *The Assassin's Practice*, which won the African Movie Academy Award's Best Actor (2013). Dele Ajakaiye has a Master's degree in

Directing Film and TV from Bournemouth University and BA (Hons) in English and Education.

Elvira Bolat is a Senior Lecturer (Academic) in Marketing in the Business School, Bournemouth University (BU). After leading BU's first inter-faculty degree, BSc (Hons) Marketing for five years, Elvira is now Global Engagement Leader at the Department of Marketing—responsible for driving BU's and the Department's global agenda. She is Deputy Chair for the Academy of Marketing B2B SIG and has interest and expertise in researching and consulting SMEs within the creative B2B sector. Her work has been published in the *Journal of Marketing Management*, *Journal of Business and Industrial Marketing*, and *Journal of Customer Behaviour*. Elvira earned her PhD with a thesis titled "Mobile Technology Capabilities and their role in service innovation practices in creative SMEs" and is now supervising doctoral students in the fields of marketing and management with a focus on digital/interactive marketing. Her recent consultancy project has covered digital marketing planning and implementation for Dr Jackson's (as part of the Grads for Growth EU-funded scheme), a marketing communications campaign for Kudu Clothing, and digital marketing consultancy for Eat Pho Ltd.

Paula Callus is a Senior Lecturer in Computer Animation at Bournemouth University, UK (National Centre for Computer Animation). She holds a PhD from SOAS, London, in the field of Animation in sub-Saharan Africa. She moved to the UK in 2001 from Malta, where she worked in animated graphics at a television station. She then completed a Master's degree in Computer Animation at the NCCA Bournemouth University.

Obiajulu Christopher Ede holds a Master's degree in Business Administration from the University of Gloucestershire, UK. With an interest in business, especially SMEs in developing economies, he enrolled for a doctoral degree programme in Solent University. His research focused on Institutional Environment and SME Growth in Nigeria. Obiajulu is currently a lecturer in the School of Business, Law and Communications at Solent University and a Fellow of the Higher Education Academy (FHEA). Obiajulu's research interest has generated a number of outputs in the form of presentations at international conferences, as well as accepted and work-in-progress papers.

Nicolas Friederici is a postdoctoral researcher at the Oxford Internet Institute (Oxford University), working on the Geonet project. He studies how digital entrepreneurship works in environments that are far more challenging than

Silicon Valley or London. His comparative grounded research covers African cities including Nairobi, Lagos, Accra, Kigali, and Harare. Nicolas is interested in the interplay of environmental factors with entrepreneurial motivations and capacities. Ultimately, this work addresses the question how and why digital entrepreneurship flourishes in some places but not in others.

Ali Muhammad Garba is an Assistant Professor of Business Administration at Dangote Business School, Bayero University, Kano (Nigeria). He holds the following qualifications: MA (Kent), MSc (Heriot-Watt), DMS (CNAA), PhD (Bayero).

B. N. O. Irene is a Visiting Professor at Universidad de las Américas Puebla, Cape Town Area, South Africa. She was previously the Dean of the Faculty of Entrepreneurship and Economic Transformation at Cornerstone Institute—Cape Town (South Africa).

Nnamdi O. Madichie is Principal Lecturer and Director of the Centre for Research & Enterprise at the Bloomsbury Institute London. He is an expert on African business and management, having published several academic papers and book chapters on topics as diverse as entrepreneurship (by women, micro-enterprises, and ethnic entrepreneurship) and marketing (notably consumer behaviour and sports marketing). His paper "Cultural determinants of entrepreneurial emergence in a typical sub-Sahara African context", published in the *Journal of Enterprising Communities: People and Places in the Global Economy*, received the Emerald Highly Commended Paper Award in 2009. Madichie is also recent past Editor-in-Chief of the *African Journal of Business and Economic Research*.

Oladokun Ogunniyi is an academic with more than a decade of experience lecturing in Nigerian tertiary institutions. He holds a Master's degree in Sociology (Industrial Relations and Personnel Management) as well as a post-graduate degree in Education. He is currently a PhD candidate in Human Resources Management and Organisational Behaviour at the Business School, Bournemouth University, UK. His current research interests include work–life balance, employment relations, and strategic human resources management.

Vanessa Ratten is an Associate Professor of Entrepreneurship and Innovation in the Department of Management, La Trobe Business School at La Trobe University, Melbourne, Australia. She teaches Entrepreneurial Business Planning, Managing Innovation in Organisations, and Entrepreneurship. She has previously been on the business faculty of Duquesne University, the

University of Queensland, Queensland University of Technology, and Deakin University. She has a PhD from the UQ Business School at the University of Queensland, which focused on the role of organisational learning in an alliance context in the information and communication technology industry.

Nasiru D. Taura is a Lecturer in Entrepreneurship and Innovation at Bournemouth University, United Kingdom (Faculty of Management—Department of Leadership, Strategy, & Organisation). He is currently the unit leader for the following Master's programmes: Entrepreneurial Mind Option (MSc Innovation Management and Entrepreneurship); Managing Innovation, Creativity, & Design; and undergraduate Entrepreneurship in the Global Environment (online). Nasiru has a number of peer-reviewed publications in *Entrepreneurship & Regional Development* and *Journal of Small Business Management*, book chapters, as well as several papers presented at leading international peer-reviewed entrepreneurship and innovation conferences around the word, including in Denmark, Spain, France, Estonia, Portugal, and the USA. Nasiru is an Associate Fellow of the Higher Education Academy (AFHEA), UK. He is also a Fellow of the Royal Society for the Encouragement of Arts, Manufactures and Commerce (FRSA), UK. By way of giving back to society, Nasiru is developing a robust and integrated digital platform for supporting and stimulating innovation and entrepreneurship in Africa (The Pan African Innovation and Cluster Academy—PAICA—see: https://paica.info/).

List of Figures

Fig. 6.1 Young Jedi from the Congo, by Salim Busuru (2018) 133
Fig. 6.2 Poster for *We Need Prayers* (2018) by The Nest. Reprinted with permission from The Nest Collective 134
Fig. 7.1 The gender gap in mobile phone ownership, by region. Source: OECD (2017) 154
Fig. 7.2 (a and b) The share of females among start-up founders. Source: OECD (2017). Note: Percentage of females in the sample of founders of companies less than ten years old and for whom gender is known 157
Fig. 7.3 The gender gap in start-up funding and acquisition. Source: OECD (2017). Note: The graphs show results from Ordinary Least Squares (OLS) regressions of the three outcomes variables on a set of founders and firms characteristics, and country and sector fixed effects. Bars show the average predicted probability of receiving VC, the amount of funding conditional on getting VC, and the probability of acquisition for male- and female-led businesses. The advantage of this way of representing the data is that it gets rid of potential confounding effects such as education or prior experience of start-up founders 158
Fig. 7.4 Average skill levels for male and female workers, 31 OECD countries and partner economies, 2012 or 2015. Source: OECD (2017). Notes: ICT = information and communication technology; STEM = science, technology, engineering, and

mathematics. All skill indicators are rescaled to the interval 0–100. Averages across 31 OECD countries and partner economies are computed giving the same weight to each country. All differences in skill means between male and female workers are significant at the 5% level, except for Management and communication and Readiness to learn 160

Fig. 7.5 Labour market returns to skills by gender across 31 OECD countries and partner economies, 2012 or 2015. Source: OECD (2017). Notes: ICT = information and communication technology; STEM = science, technology, engineering, and mathematics. Labour market returns to skills are based on Ordinary Least Square (OLS) wage regressions (Mincer equations) using data from the *OECD Survey of Adult Skills (PIAAC)* (OECD 2017h) for 31 OECD countries and partner economies. The estimates by gender are obtained through including an interaction term of the skill variable and the gender variable. The figure shows the percentage changes in wages determined by an increase in skills by one standard deviation, holding other correlates of individual wages constant. Shaded diamonds indicate that the difference between men and women is not significant at the 5% level 161

Fig. 7.6 The average risk of automation, by industry and by gender. Notes: The chart shows the 20 industries with the greatest number of jobs at risk (measured as the average risk of automation weighted by the employment share of the industry), in descending order of overall risk of automation (left panel). The width of each bar in the left panel represents the average share of jobs at risk in each industry. The placement of each bar relative to the centre line depicts how that risk is shared between men (light blue) and women (grey). Values in the right panel represent the share of total employment held by each industry. Risk of automation values are based on likelihoods calculated in Arntz et al. (2016). Countries covered in this analysis include the 29 OECD countries that participated in the first and second rounds of the *OECD Survey of Adult Skills (PIAAC)* (OECD 2017h) 163

List of Tables

Table 3.1	Respondents' profiles	46
Table 4.1	Profile of case companies	77
Table 5.1	High-flying videos using digital formats	94
Table 5.2	The independent film value chain	100
Table 5.3	Respondent profiles	102
Table 7.1	Involvement in entrepreneurial activity by gender in South Africa	150
Table 7.2	ICT report on sub-Saharan Africa	152
Table 7.3	Examples of countries' efforts to reduce the digital gender divide	166
Table 9.1	Prime Wave Limited—questions and responses	206
Table 9.2	Al-Wabel Trading Company Limited—questions and responses	208

Part I

Introduction

1

Introduction to African Digital Entrepreneurship

Nasiru D. Taura, Elvira Bolat, and Nnamdi O. Madichie

There is a general tendency to believe that adverse geography, weak institutions, and general lack of resources have contributed to Africa's inability to develop and to be innovative (Acemoglu 2010; Naudé and Havenga 2007; Naudé and Krugell 2002; Rodrik and Subramanian 2010; Sachs 2010). However, despite the hostile environment of doing business in Africa, variations in firm performance do exist: some have regressed, some have progressed, and some have stagnated. The variations in performance increase with technological advances, but there is limited evidence documenting how digital enterprises approach the hostile business settings in Africa (Chakravorti et al. 2017).

N. D. Taura (✉) • E. Bolat
Business School, Bournemouth University, Bournemouth, UK
e-mail: ntaura@bournemouth.ac.uk; ebolat@bournemouth.ac.uk

N. O. Madichie
Centre for Research & Enterprise, Bloomsbury Institute London, London, UK
e-mail: nnamdi.madichie@bil.ac.uk

N. D. Taura et al. (eds.), *Digital Entrepreneurship in Sub-Saharan Africa*, Palgrave Studies of Entrepreneurship in Africa, https://doi.org/10.1007/978-3-030-04924-9_1

This book focuses on how some outstanding digital enterprises and sectors have dealt with the hostile business environment in Africa. It has been argued that the arrival of the dual effects of globalisation and digitalisation has contributed to increasing speed and shrinking distances—thus creating equal opportunities for entrepreneurs globally—but this needs to be illustrated with insightful case studies. We contend that, while on the one hand, digital platforms have created equal access, on the other hand many digital entrepreneurs in Africa still struggle with local environments replete with corruption and other economic inefficiencies.

The digital landscape in Africa is changing (IMD's World Digital Competitiveness Index 2017). Despite low scores in digitalisation, some African countries have demonstrated the potential to evolve rapidly. Although they are held back by relatively weak infrastructure and poor institutional quality, they have demonstrated their potential to become leaders in digital innovation in the future.

The variations in momentum among African countries are likely to generate more competition on the continent while stimulating economic growth and competitiveness. According to Chakravorti et al. (2017), when digital momentum zones are mapped out in Africa, "the two largest economies, Nigeria and South Africa, remain in Break Out and Watch Out zones, respectively, digitally savvy Kenya has picked up an impressive level of momentum by assembling a thriving ecosystem".

In view of the changes in the digital landscape of Africa, this book addresses new perspectives on doing businesses in the rapidly changing African digital climate. Our aim is to go beyond the conventional rhetoric of the entrepreneurial revolution, to provide insights about the challenges, opportunities, and prospects of digital entrepreneurship in Africa. Overall, the purpose of this opening chapter is to introduce the African digital entrepreneurship landscape and its changing dynamics, taking into consideration the interplay between new entrants and incumbents.

Following this opening chapter, Chap. 2, "Innovation Hubs in Africa: What Do They Really Do for Digital Entrepreneurs?" by **Nicolas Friederici**, provides a grounded perspective on Africa's most widely noted type of digital entrepreneurship support organisation: the innovation hub. This is vital given the explosion of innovation hubs across Africa and the claims being made regarding how they facilitate entrepreneurship, including digital entrepreneurship, in Africa.

Chapter 3, "Renegotiating Legitimacy in the Digital Age: Insights from Nigeria" by **Nasiru D. Taura, Obiajulu Christopher Ede, and Oladokun Ogunniyi**, discusses how African enterprises are dealing with the challenging issue of establishing legitimacy from the perspectives of both new entrants and incumbents. The chapter begins with an interview with a successful African digital entrepreneur, **Olalekan Olude**, of Jobberman. The chapter also addresses how incumbent banks deal with the legitimacy challenge in a digital age that requires them to reposition themselves, drawing on legitimacy theory to examine how African incumbent banks have responded to the wave of digital enterprises (fin-techs) elsewhere referred to as a revolution. This is vital, since previous work mainly focuses on the "attacker's advantage" with little or no insight on entrepreneurial incumbents who have applied a range of strategies to successfully renegotiate their legitimacy despite challenges posed by the new order.

In Chap. 4, "The African New Media Digital Revolution: Some Selected Cases from Nigeria", **Elvira Bolat** explores the historical timeline of and changes in the media landscape and presents an empirical investigation of small and medium-sized new media enterprises, reflecting on their journeys in establishing technological enterprises, the media used, and the resources that were critical to manage and run these businesses, as well as general commentary on enablers and barriers.

Chapter 5, "The Impact of New Media (Digital) and Globalisation on Nollywood" by **Nnamdi O. Madichie, Bamidele O. Ajakaiye, and Vanessa Ratten**, investigates the Nigerian movie industry in the light of digitalisation of the sector. The chapter examines and highlights how two major forces—new technologies and globalisation—have impacted (and are still impacting) upon the Nigerian film industry (also known as Nollywood), drawing on theories of value chain in production, distribution, and marketing of cultural products (i.e. movies), and its internationalisation.

In Chap. 6, "Shifting Cultural Capital: Kenyan Arts in Digital Spaces", **Paula Callus** examines the impact of digital technology on cultural capital that is associated with curatorial practice, the gallery, and the marketplace. The chapter draws from the theory of cultural capital and illustrates how digital art challenges notions of authenticity in the discourse on African art.

In Chap. 7, "Technopreneurship: A Discursive Analysis of the Impact of Technology on the Success of Women Entrepreneurs in South Africa", **Bridget Irene** provides a discursive analysis of the impact of technology on the success of women entrepreneurs in South Africa. The chapter is a thematic synthesis of current literature on technopreneurship and the impact of technology on women entrepreneurs with a view to providing a basis for understanding the implications for the business strategy of women in the era of Gen Y and Z. This is vital given the opportunity that arises for inclusive-tech to reduce the equality gaps in the African business context.

In Chap. 8, "The Nature of Corporate Digital Agricultural Entrepreneurship in Ghana", **George Acheampong** takes the reader through an equally interesting research area on corporate digital entrepreneurship from the Ghanaian perspective. Likewise, in Chap. 9, "Agri-tech Opportunities at the Bottom of the Pyramid: How Big Is the Opportunity and How Little Has Been Exploited? Some Selected Cases in Nigeria", **Ali Muhammad Garba** examines closely the rise of a distinctive form of entrepreneurship at the bottom of the pyramid interfaced with digital technology, illustrating the massive opportunities that could potentially be exploited.

The book concludes with some thoughts on the subject of digital entrepreneurship in Africa and its many facets. In this final chapter, **Nnamdi O. Madichie, Nasiru D. Taura, and Elvira Bolat** present a synthesis of the ideas discussed in the book.

References

Acemoglu, D. (2010). Root Causes: A Historical Approach to Assessing the Role of Institutions in Economic Development. In G. Secondi (Ed.), *The Development Economics Reader*. New York: Routledge.

Chakravorti, B., Bhalla, A., & Chaturvedi, R. S. (2017). 60 Countries Digital Competitiveness Indexed. *Harvard Business Review*.

IMD's World Digital Competitiveness Index. (2017). [Online]. Retrieved October 18, 2018, from https://www.imd.org/globalassets/wcc/docs/release-2017/world_digital_competitiveness_yearbook_2017.pdf.

Naudé, W. A., & Havenga, J. J. D. (2007). An Overview of African Entrepreneurship and Small Business Research. *Journal of Small Business and Entrepreneurship, 18*(1), 101–120.

Naudé, W. A., & Krugell, W. (2002). African Economic Growth: Wrong to Rely on Small Businesses. *Journal of Small Business and Entrepreneurship, 16*(2), 21–44.

Rodrik, D., & Subramanian, A. (2010). The Primacy of Institutions (and What this Does and Does Not Mean). In G. Secondi (Ed.), *The Development Economics Reader*. New York: Routledge.

Sachs, D. S. (2010). Institutions Matter but not for Everything: The Role of Geography and Resource Endowments in Development Shouldn't Be Underestimated. In G. Secondi (Ed.), *The Development Economics Reader*. New York: Routledge.

2

Innovation Hubs in Africa: What Do They Really Do for Digital Entrepreneurs?

Nicolas Friederici

2.1 From Internet Access to Impact: The Promise of Digital Entrepreneurship

The global diffusion of the Internet continues unabated. The year 2017 marked a historical milestone: according to the best available estimates, the number of unique Internet users on earth outgrew the number of non-users at some point during the year.[1] While challenges remain, affordability and bandwidth have also improved in the world's poorest nations (Deichmann and Mishra 2016). Such drastically improved and truly globalized connectivity has led to an expectation of significant

[1] Cf., http://www.internetworldstats.com/stats.htm.

N. Friederici (✉)
Oxford Internet Institute, Oxford University, Oxford, UK
e-mail: nicolas.friederici@oii.ox.ac.uk

N. D. Taura et al. (eds.), *Digital Entrepreneurship in Sub-Saharan Africa*, Palgrave Studies of Entrepreneurship in Africa, https://doi.org/10.1007/978-3-030-04924-9_2

development potential for the Global South and especially on the African continent (Ndemo and Weiss 2017).

Digital entrepreneurship in particular has started to be seen as a powerful driver of local innovation, and thereby of structural economic transformation and development (Ndemo and Weiss 2016). It can be defined as the creative production and distribution of digital software and applications by skilled and opportunity-oriented individuals and ventures. As such, digital entrepreneurship depends on local availability of digital technologies in a dual sense: individuals and enterprises need digital infrastructures (such as browsers, social network sites, software development kits, open source code, etc.) to create digital products (Tilson et al. 2010), while users require the Internet to access those products.

It is clear that Africa is experiencing a boom in digital entrepreneurship (Bright and Hruby 2015). Following a few African success stories of digital businesses in the early 2000s, hundreds of fledgling technology start-ups have recently been created. Policymakers, corporations, development organizations, consultancies, and the media soon began to frame domestic digital economies as a significant source of economic transformation and revival (Ntale et al. 2013; Manyika et al. 2013; Drouillard et al. 2014).

Yet it is also true that digital entrepreneurship is still a new economic field in Africa, and rigorous research is extremely scarce. Reliable evidence is lacking both about the extent to which digital entrepreneurship is contributing to economic development, and about the mechanisms through which this happens. The defining questions are where and how entrepreneurial opportunity arises and is exploited following the advent of "the digital".

On the aspirational side, the key contention is that digital entrepreneurs face extremely low entry barriers, which allows entrepreneurs located in resource-scarce environments to catch up or do just as well as those in affluent contexts. Digital artefacts can be created everywhere and by anyone with a computer and Internet access, upon which they can be distributed to anywhere else in the world, to any other individual with an Internet connection. This idea is captured in recent scholarship that has depicted digital entrepreneurship as boundary-less, aspatial, and global in nature (Autio et al. 2017; Nambisan 2017; Sussan and Acs 2017). In combination with Africa's youthful population and robust economic growth, this digital potential has led many to proclaim that Africa is about to be transformed and revolutionized by digital technologies and entrepreneurship (Ndemo and Weiss 2016; Draper 2017; Kanza 2016).

More cautious arguments come from digital economic geographers. These scholars have begun to show that Africa's globally peripheral economic status does not seem to have been altered by digital technologies (Malecki and Moriset 2007; Foster et al. 2018; Murphy and Carmody 2015). Instead, Africa appears to have fallen further behind rather than catching up to the rest of the world when it comes to the economic impact of Internet connectivity or the quantity of digital production (Ojanperä et al. 2017; Friederici et al. 2017).

Just how large the market opportunities are for African digital entrepreneurs is thus still uncertain. The "mobile phone revolution" (Etzo and Collender 2010) that has swept the African continent is usually illustrated by means of rising mobile penetration and, at best, usage figures for widely used social networking and communication applications, such as Facebook and WhatsApp. Mobile money applications such as M-Pesa in Kenya represent another popular use case: their widespread adoption has been praised for increasing welfare (Munyegera and Matsumoto 2016). Yet these applications are produced and disseminated by mobile operators or Internet corporations with headquarters and research and development centres outside of Africa. Hence, at this point in time, it is safe to say that adoption of digital products originating from the Global North has expanded into vast swaths of Africa's user base and geography, while we have few use cases of technologies created by African digital entrepreneurs that are used by large numbers of people (within Africa or beyond). So far, the reach of digital software and applications created by African software developers and enterprises appears to be limited in scope and scale, at least when compared with solutions from the Global North.

Moreover, there appears to be a clear locational hierarchy of African digital enterprise clusters, with the most successful digital products emanating from Nairobi, Lagos, Johannesburg, and Cape Town, while enterprises from second-tier cities, such as Accra, Cairo, Kigali, or Kampala, usually remain confined to domestic markets.

Smaller cities and rural areas almost never host enterprises that produce scalable and financially viable digital solutions. This begets the question of how spatially unequal Africa's digital economy already is and how much more unequal it is likely to become. Going forward, scholars and other stakeholders will have to do more to probe into the hopes and ambitions that the rise of digital economies beyond Silicon Valley and Europe has inspired.

Research must determine, first, which kinds of entrepreneurial opportunities, practices, and processes have become possible or remained elusive, and, second, which actors in which places are involved or excluded.

2.2 Africa's Digital Entrepreneurship Boom and the Rise of Innovation Hubs

This chapter takes a step in this direction by providing a grounded perspective on Africa's most widely noted type of digital entrepreneurship support organization: the innovation hub (Toivonen and Friederici 2015). Hubs have proliferated rapidly across the African continent: depending on the counting method, in 2016, there were between 173 and 314 hubs on African soil (du Boucher 2016; Firestone and Kelly 2016). It is hard to say exactly when and where the hub phenomenon began, as traditional organizational forms such as incubators and science parks have been using the term "hub" as a brand name for a long time. For instance, the science and technology parks Botswana Innovation Hub (Gaborone, Botswana) and The Innovation Hub (Pretoria, South Africa) were both founded in 2002. However, it appears that the "hub" as a new type of organization has gained currency in Africa in particular between 2010 and 2016. During this period, iHub Nairobi became recognized as a role model, and international development funders and the media picked up on the promise of hubs (Friederici 2018b).

It is also not a trivial question why hubs have proliferated so quickly, but it is fair to say that hubs benefited from optimism and excitement about grassroots entrepreneurship, digital technologies, and social innovation in the international development landscape (Jiménez and Zheng

2017; Friederici 2018b). Organizations such as the World Bank (Kelly and Firestone 2016), the GSMA (du Boucher 2016), and the Institute of Development Studies (Sambuli and Whitt 2017) have since argued that hubs are essential enablers of digital entrepreneurship, functioning as powerful connectors of entrepreneurs and an array of partners (such as investors, mentors, governments, etc.). As with the rise of digital entrepreneurship, the emergence of African hubs in the 2010s has been framed as a direct consequence of the arrival of broadband Internet:

> Due to the increase in speed and affordability of connectivity, the sense of possibility the digital world has provided, and interest by investors, tech hubs, business incubators, hacker spaces, and maker spaces are providing places for the continent's young (and not so young) people to express their innate creativity and ambition, make up for disparity in educational opportunities, allow for the creation of wealth that is more sustainable than the resource extraction of the past, and help to produce products and services to address the needs of their communities. (Hopkins 2015)

Yet, following an initial wave of excitement, critical voices also began to surface, pointing out that start-up creation and development has been elusive for hubs. Aspirational voices across the donor landscape became pitted against a more hard-headed narrative, seeing hubs as nothing but ineffective incubators that have failed to develop successful digital start-ups (Essien 2015).

In line with the above-mentioned ambition to explicate the mechanisms of digital entrepreneurship in a grounded fashion, this chapter sidesteps the question of *whether hubs work* and instead tries to clarify *what work hubs do for African digital entrepreneurs.* Despite the great attention that a number of development organizations, governments, and technology corporations have paid to the phenomenon, little effort has been made to rigorously and clearly discern the opportunities and limits of hubs through empirical research (Littlewood and Kiyumbu 2017; and Jiménez and Zheng 2017 are recent exceptions). The chapter is thus an attempt at empirically grounding and testing both hopes for and criticisms of African hubs.

The chapter acknowledges both optimistic expectations of hubs as powerful connectors and dismissive assessments of hubs as failed start-up creators (cf., Friederici 2018b), but it begins with the premise that it is not obvious how hubs actually operate in a given context. The study therefore examines in more depth how hubs' supposed connection function plays out within the complex and challenging realities of African cities as contexts of digital entrepreneurship.

This chapter highlights in particular digital entrepreneurs' experiences with hubs. Previous work has tended to provide conceptualizations of hubs, or used interviews with hub leaders and select members as key data points (Friederici 2014; Gathege and Moraa 2013; Kelly and Firestone 2016; Sambuli and Whitt 2017; De Beer et al. 2017). The present chapter instead focuses on entrepreneurs as hubs' main constituents. Taking an entrepreneurial perspective is important to complement hub-centric analysis: this is a lesson from incubator research, which had to fundamentally revise its understanding of incubation once it discovered the important contribution of entrepreneurial agency (Bøllingtoft and Ulhøi 2005; Rice 2002). The study thus explicitly includes the perspectives of a wide range of entrepreneurs: from core hub members to entrepreneurs who avoided hubs, from hub proponents to those dismissing them outright, and from novices to experienced ones. This balanced and grounded approach is meant to do away with some of the confusion that arose during the early period of hype and excitement around hubs. The research questions are:

1. How do African hub organizations interact with digital entrepreneurs?
2. How do digital entrepreneurs participate in African hub organizations?

The research uses an embedded comparative case study set-up, studying six hubs in three African capital cities: Hub Accra and iSpace in Accra (Ghana), kLab and The Office in Kigali (Rwanda), and Hypercube Hub and Muzinda Hub in Harare (Zimbabwe).[2] A comparison between cases allows us to understand what is common and what is different across hubs operating in starkly different entrepreneurial contexts. The case study data includes interviews with 133 participants, roughly half of them digital entrepreneurs and half hub staff and other support actors. Further methodological detail and thick case study descriptions are available in Friederici.

2.3 Hubs Depend on Entrepreneurs but Participation Is Socially Complex

Unsurprisingly, the six hubs that were analyzed showed many idiosyncrasies. Yet there were also a number of commonalities in how entrepreneurs perceived and engaged with hubs. Here, a condensed and generalized account of patterns that applied across all six hub cases will be provided.

One apparent theme was the importance of iHub as an inspiration that initiated the founding of hubs. The founding team members of five of the six hubs analyzed (all except The Office) explicitly referred to iHub as their original role model. Yet, once hub implementations began, leaders quickly realized that they needed to adapt their vision to local conditions (Friederici 2018b; Jiménez and Zheng 2017):

> In our initial proposal, I think we were over-ambitious, a little bit, and I feel like Zimbabwe has its own context. When people think "tech hubs," everybody automatically thinks "iHub," or "Silicon Valley." But I think each country has its context and the hubs and the ecosystem were developed in a different way. (Hub manager)

Hubs struggled to move away from the broad goal of emulating iHub towards a consistent and specific mission of their own, and to translate

[2] Since this study was conducted, Hub Accra and The Office have become part of the Impact Hub network, rebranding as Impact Hub Accra and Impact Hub Kigali. Muzinda Hub became an impact sourcing and training provider, moving away from the innovation hub model as it is typically understood in Africa.

this mission into services. Many interviewed entrepreneurs worried that a “hub” was too fuzzy of an idea: often, neither hub members nor outsiders were able to determine what to make of hubs and how to engage with them. During implementation, the hubs’ multiple stakeholder groups also had different ideas of where hubs should direct their efforts, and how hubs could set in motion the kinds of catalytic effects that iHub was seen to have in Kenya. Oftentimes, hub board members were divided over priorities, and entrepreneurs often felt that hub visions were detached from their realities.

Ultimately, the particular organizational features of hubs, such as “openness” (Toivonen and Friederici 2015), resulted in three forms of organizational action: (1) services (such as events, desk rental, and training), (2) the establishment of spaces as social enclosures and locational fix points, and (3) the symbolization of an entrepreneurial purpose. These elements can be understood as the actions *of* hubs *towards* entrepreneurs: the actions came from hubs as organizational entities and were directed at entrepreneurs. Symbolization was a particularly rich and important form of hub action. By signalling a loosely defined purpose (such as kLab as “the place for tech entrepreneurship in Kigali”), African hubs compelled a wide range of actors, including most or all digital entrepreneurs in a given city, to associate meaning with the hub and consider participating (cf., Littlewood and Kiyumbu 2017):

> I didn’t understand that at that time, the importance of such a location in terms of being a central point where all the people interested in IT [can] come. If you would come to this country before kLab, and [Rwandans] claim [the country] is an ICT hub, you would run around and say “Where is IT here?” [It would seem like] there is nothing going on. You have small companies left and right, you don’t even know where they are, you don’t even have Yellow Pages here, right? … Everybody who comes to this country and has to do with IT, the first place they go to is kLab. We get some very famous people going there … Now you can say, “Yes, there is something going on in Rwanda.” Before, you could not. (Leader of a hub in Rwanda)

In turn, hubs rarely offered funding or other tangible resources directly, except for the provision of work space. Thus, digital entrepreneurs participated in hubs, in part to use free or cheap bandwidth and office space, but mainly to derive a cognitive benefit (e.g., knowledge, motivation, comfort, inspiration, ideas, etc.). Crucially, this benefit was derived, not directly from a hub organization's action or from interactions with hub leaders, but from *interactions with other entrepreneurs* that were members of a given hub. Ultimately, digital entrepreneurs participated in hubs when they expected to derive a total benefit (service and cognitive value) that outweighed the perceived cost. This cost can be defined broadly, including social, affective, and normative aspects (e.g., travel cost, usage fee if any, perceived social obligations, invested time and effort, opposition to hubs out of principle, etc.).

Based on their perception of the benefit, digital entrepreneurs participated more or less intensely in hubs. Since hubs imposed few if any limitations on participation other than nominal usage fees (i.e., hubs did not select or recruit entrepreneurs), it was up to entrepreneurs to decide "how much" to participate.

Different digital entrepreneurs made different choices, but there were some systematic variations. Specifically, novices, who had not yet started a venture and did not have their own office space, typically frequented hub spaces more than advanced entrepreneurs. Moreover, non-entrepreneurial support actors (such as mentors or investors) only had frequent interactions with others within a hub space if their regular workplace was co-located to the space. In other words, for support actors, the cost of participation (e.g., travel, time, etc.) needed to be very low for them to participate regularly and continuously, because interactions with novice entrepreneurs did not usually have a tangible and immediate benefit for them. On the contrary, the range of actors attending networking events or occasionally visiting hub spaces was much broader and included individuals who loosely felt that they had a stake in the hub's purpose and/or that they could access instrumental information.

Entrepreneurial participation also appeared to depend on the level of optimism or scepticism about hubs that existed in a given city among a given group of entrepreneurs. For instance, digital entrepreneurs in Kigali felt that hubs had shortcomings but were generally an important addition to the country's quest to become an "ICT nation". In contrast, many entrepreneurs in Accra felt that hubs lacked relevance, and participants in Harare complained that hubs wasted precious resources on the wrong things:

> Respondent: Hubs are trying to build Silicon Valley .... I don't know where they got ... their things mixed up.
>
> Interviewer: Why are they getting it wrong?
>
> Respondent: Because people who are leading the hubs have never been in the thick of things. [laughs] So it is sort of a loop. I mean how can they get it when they have never done it? ... Our hubs are run by ... anti-entrepreneurs ... But there's an entrepreneur who is struggling ... We have thirsty people here; they are dying from thirst ... The money used for [hub] meet-ups, actually 200 dollars could be enough to empower them to the next stage ... The final conclusion was: [the hubs'] resources would be better spent empowering entrepreneurs who are struggling to do things. (Digital entrepreneur in Harare)

Because the benefit of participation for a given entrepreneur depended in large part on other members, different entrepreneurs' choices influenced those of others, leading to group-level participation patterns that developed over time. Namely, *core communities*, composed of regular users of hub spaces, developed, while occasional space users, visitors of core community members, and attendees of events formed *peripheral communities*.

These communities were not formally but *fluidly bounded* towards each other and towards the hub's environment. Depending on the hub, core or peripheral communities contained substructures, ranging from team-based collaborations through role divisions and informal hierarchies to groups of friends.

These micro- and meso-level structures affected the perceived benefits for hub members:

> So that's why the idea of having communities is perfect. It works. When you have a community, this is something where it's on a need basis. So you have a community, you meet four times a month ... for example it's a community of Java, you say, "Monday we shall talk about object-oriented

> programming." If I'm a programmer and let's say ... I [already] know what is object-oriented programming, I won't come. But if on day two you talk about classes and I'm having a hard time with classes ... I'll show up. If on day three you talk about "loops," I know what is object-oriented programming, I know what is classes but I don't know what is "loops"—and I'll attend. So I think that's where you make it inclusive: you have community events, you have open events. I think 90% of events are open and then whoever is interested will come. (Digital entrepreneur in Kigali)

In sum, a given digital entrepreneur's participation decision thus depended on the hub's ongoing organizational actions, but also on other members' engagement choices and the social structures that formed as a result of these interdependent processes. The participation of digital entrepreneurs in African hubs was thus varied, dynamic, and emergent, depending on the gains that could be derived from the interactions that hub participation enabled entrepreneurs to have.

2.4 Do Hubs Make a Difference for Entrepreneurs?

Overall, the case studies showed messy processes that happened when hub visions met on-the-ground realities, ultimately leading to adjustments (kLab, Hub Accra), reshaping (Hypercube, iSpace), and in one case drastic reorientation (Muzinda Hub). Clearly, the case studies confirmed that a dyadic view is necessary to understand hubs: the unilateral and controlled action of hubs only determined in small part what happened. Entrepreneurial agency and participation in hubs mattered just as much—or even more so—than the services that hubs implemented.

More concretely, entrepreneurs saw hubs as an interesting idea and many were excited about them early on, but they rarely felt that hubs had helped them progress with their start-up project. Of the 57 interviewed digital entrepreneurs, only a handful reported that they had formed start-up teams "at the hub", that is, after meeting team members in the hub space.

Hubs appeared to make only a very small direct contribution to start-up creation and success, and most entrepreneurs reported that they would have pursued their start-up even if the hub in question did not exist. Entrepreneurs sometimes pointed out that the vagueness of hubs' purposes led to a degree of disorganization and inconsistency, especially in the early implementation stages.

The promise of hubs instead appeared to lie in creating "communities", and indeed, in cases such as kLab, The Office, and Hub Accra, entrepreneurs felt that a community existed and provided them with benefits, such as learning opportunities and emotional or motivational support. Yet hubs appeared to be faced with difficult balancing acts in nurturing active communities of practice that could support self-employment and entrepreneurial ventures (cf., Friederici 2018a). Both entrepreneurs and third parties (such as mentors, experts, or corporate partners) often merely "passed through" hubs, while sustained interactions that led to collaborations were rarer. Moreover, the idea that actors with different levels of expertise would interact through hubs was difficult to turn into a reality: more experienced entrepreneurs reported that they had little time to contribute, and that they did not expect benefits from engaging with others who were at or below their own level of skill. Hub spaces were sometimes too crowded (kLab, Hub Accra) and sometimes not crowded enough (Hypercube, Muzinda, iSpace). Hub communities were sometimes described as too stable (so that new influences were missing) and at other times as too dynamic (so that mutual familiarity was lacking). Similarly, entrepreneurs felt that hub visitors or partners (such as an expert giving a talk, or a development organization running an innovation competition) did not contribute to the hub community, given that they usually lacked real engagement and commitment to support the hub.

Ultimately, these issues meant that, in some cases, both hub leaders and members felt that more "process" (i.e., more hands-on services) was the right way forward (e.g., for iSpace, Hypercube, and to some degree kLab), even if this was equivalent to moving away from the openness that had originally been a defining feature of the hub. In other cases, hub leaders moved in the opposite direction, focusing on events to allow for more open-ended networking (The Office, Hub Accra).

2.5 Hub Practice Needs a Dyadic View, Away from Linear Thinking

In sum, the study highlights that African hubs trigger an entrepreneurship support process that is different from common understandings of incubation. If a support organization's actions are more facilitative than interventionist (like in hubs), digital entrepreneurs *together with* the organization shape the process. The capacity and willingness of entrepreneurs in a given geographical space to participate in hubs thus determine to a large extent what these organizations can and cannot do.

Based on this foundational insight, the study enables a clearer view of the outcomes that hubs can be expected to achieve, and how those outcomes can or cannot be measured. It should be clearly stated that the chapter did not conduct an impact evaluation of hubs, and so it cannot assess *whether* hubs work. This is important to note because "impact" has been a key concern and a difficult topic for hub funders and leaders. Especially in cases where development organizations or governments have funded hubs, hub leaders have faced pressure to justify how their expenses generate economic or social development.

While rigorous impact evaluations of hubs should indeed be attempted (see De Beer et al. 2017 for a useful start), the present research demonstrates that we first need to clarify how hubs work before we can answer whether they work. The study demonstrates that hubs are mainly directed at the creation of supportive social structures for digital entrepreneurs, specifically, entrepreneurial communities.

For instance, members of peripheral hub communities, even if they only attend events or visit hub spaces occasionally, can derive benefits from hubs that go beyond those of ad hoc networking. A hub's permanence gives peripheral communities an orientation point, for instance, to access novice entrepreneurs or to meet foreign actors who use hubs as a first point of contact when entering an African country. Such benefits can be substantial but largely go unassessed if funders focus on narrow output measures.

It is thus on the level of communities that hubs' most significant outcomes are achieved. Yet hubs rarely pursue "community" explicitly as a goal. Most hubs harbour visions of coordination, and "community" is an essential aspiration for any given hub's functioning, but hubs mainly employ simple quantitative targets, such as attendance of hub spaces, trainings, and events, membership figures, or number of start-ups created. The present findings show that hub leaders struggle to understand the impact chains of their organizations, and are tempted to cling to measurable statistics even if they are only crude proxies for notions such as "networking", "community building", or "ecosystem coordination". In contrast, this chapter makes clear that such metrics are entirely inappropriate to capture the social dynamics of community, which underlie hubs' complexity but also represent their greatest promise.

Instead, this chapter argues that vibrant entrepreneurial communities should be hubs' targeted outcome. Hubs make an impact mainly through a process that is interdependent with entrepreneurial participation: strictly speaking, hubs do not generate any socio-economic impact by themselves. For any given individual entrepreneur, a hub plays only a small role. Instead, they allow economic actors to reconfigure their relationships. Hub funders and leaders ought to acknowledge that this process is complex and fragile, and often beyond the comprehension and immediate control of hub leaders.

Measuring, for instance, a change in revenue for start-ups or the number of people attending an event is inadequate to assess the outcomes of hubs. Any rigorous assessment would have to account for hubs' nature as facilitators of entrepreneurial interaction. For instance, the cases of kLab, Hub Accra, and iSpace showed that desirable collaboration processes within communities are not well represented by the number of entrepreneurs that work in a hub space on a given day.

Moreover, hubs have to be measured against the environments in which they operate, as hub leaders might be powerless in the face of many constraints in African cities. Hubs are inherently limited by who and what is available in local contexts—specifically concerning the eagerness and capacity of local entrepreneurs to contribute. A hub without capable entrepreneurs cannot "create successful start-ups" irrespective of its service offerings. In turn, if a lack of facilitation and coordination of entrepreneurs is a palpable problem in a given city, and if hub communities allow entrepreneurs to collectively create more value, then (but only then) the hub can make a large positive contribution.

These insights may help us to move away from the somewhat unhelpful attempt to emulate iHub everywhere else in Africa: iHub worked well for Nairobi—a vast city with a large number of keen but fragmented digital entrepreneurs—but it is not a given that the same model will work in the same way in other places where actors do not lack coordination to begin with or where there are no, or not enough, actors to be coordinated.

Problematically, entrepreneurial communities and other social coordination outcomes of hubs might be difficult to measure in quantitative terms. It appears that an expectation of measurable socio-economic development as a direct outcome of hubs' action is unwarranted or nearly impossible to verify. In light of intricate community formation and self-selection dynamics highlighted in this study, hub funders and implementers should recognize that the impact of hubs is difficult to predict and assess. Hubs remain unattractive for funders that expect concrete "returns on investment", direct effects on start-up creation and development, or measurable social impact. Ultimately, hubs are not an intervention with effects that are measurable, linear, and predictable (cf., also Jezierski et al. 2014), but a facilitator for entrepreneurial interaction. There is a need to focus, not on planned impacts of hubs, but on outcomes that are "formally absent" (Ferguson 1994), such as the creation of purposeful core and peripheral hub communities.

While this study does not offer an immediate solution to the impact measurement problem of hubs, it highlights an issue that funders have to acknowledge and work on. Clearly, decision-makers should not continue to impose traditional frameworks that do not fit hubs. The research makes clear that a rush to judgement about hubs based on established evaluation methods (for instance, from incubators) might be well intended but ultimately risks perpetuating misunderstandings and misguided expectations about hubs. For instance, funders and leaders often expect hubs to achieve things they are inherently unable to achieve (such as the creation of start-ups or the development of a skilled labor force). In other cases, funders may establish quantitative targets for hubs that actually disrupt support processes more than they strengthen them.

2.6 Conclusion

This chapter took a step back from enthusiastically led practitioner debates about digital entrepreneurship and innovation hub organizations in Africa and sought to examine the purpose of hubs in the eyes of entrepreneurs. The study thereby offered a grounded perspective on what is otherwise a conversation marked by grand aspirations, conceptualizations, self-promotion, and at times erratic lines of argumentation.

Altogether, the chapter maintained that hubs represent a valuable and promising addition to African digital entrepreneurship, but also that they need to take seriously criticisms of their lack of effectiveness, exclusionary tendencies, and wastefulness. The study thus ultimately highlighted both the potentials and limitations of hubs.

Through a grounded empirical inquiry, the research showed that a rhetorical positioning of hubs as the "future of Africa" (Oxford and Jeffries 2013; Wakoba 2014) is certainly overblown. As iHub has demonstrated, hubs can be transformative and inspirational. Yet not every hub in every context will achieve such results, because *hubs are facilitators and not creators* of interactive, collaborative, and collective entrepreneurial value creation. Hubs depend on the active participation of their constituents and on a good fit with their local environments. For funders, leaders, and supporters of hubs, it is essential to keep this insight in mind, otherwise the misunderstandings and false expectations of hubs that have unfortunately become a staple in African technology and development discourse will be perpetuated.

References

Autio, E., Nambisan, S., Thomas, L. D. W., & Wright, M. (2017, September). Digital Affordances, Spatial Affordances, and The Genesis of Entrepreneurial Ecosystems. *Strategic Entrepreneurship Journal*. https://doi.org/10.1002/sej.1266.

Bøllingtoft, A., & Ulhøi, J. P. (2005). The Networked Business Incubator—Leveraging Entrepreneurial Agency? *Journal of Business Venturing, 20*(2), 265–290. https://doi.org/10.1016/j.jbusvent.2003.12.005.

Bright, J., & Hruby, A. (2015). *The Next Africa: An Emerging Continent Becomes a Global Powerhouse*. New York: Thomas Dunne Books.

De Beer, J., Millar, P., Mwangi, J., Nzomo, V. B., & Rutenberg, I. (2017). A Framework for Assessing Technology Hubs in Africa. *NYU Journal of Intellectual Property & Entertainment Law, 6*(2). Retrieved from http://jipel.law.nyu.edu/author/jeremydebeer/.

Deichmann, U., & Mishra, D. (2016). *World Development Report 2016: Digital Dividends*. Washington, DC: World Bank. Retrieved from http://www.worldbank.org/en/publication/wdr2016.

Draper, R. (2017, November 14). How Africa's Tech Generation is Changing the Continent. *National Geographic*. Retrieved from https://www.nationalgeographic.com/magazine/2017/12/africa-technology-revolution/.

Drouillard, M., Taverner, D., Williamson, C., & Harris, M. (2014). *Digital Entrepreneurship in Kenya 2014*. London: GSMA.

du Boucher, V. (2016, August 5). A Few Things We Learned about Tech Hubs in Africa and Asia. *GSMA Mobile for Development* (blog). Retrieved from http://www.gsma.com/mobilefordevelopment/programme/ecosystem-accelerator/things-learned-tech-hubs-africa-asia.

Essien, M. (2015, April 21). Startup Incubators in Africa and Why They Don't Work. *Venture Capital for Africa* (blog). Retrieved from https://vc4africa.biz/blog/2015/04/21/startup-incubators-in-africa-and-why-they-dont-work/.

Etzo, S., & Collender, G. (2010). The Mobile Phone 'Revolution' in Africa: Rhetoric or Reality? *African Affairs, 109*(437), 659–668. https://doi.org/10.1093/afraf/adq045.

Ferguson, J. (1994). *The Anti-Politics Machine: "Development," Depoliticization, and Bureaucratic Power in Lesotho*. Minneapolis: University of Minnesota Press.

Firestone, R., & Kelly, T. (2016, August 24). The Importance of Mapping Tech Hubs in Africa, and Beyond. *Information and Communications for Development* (blog). Retrieved from http://blogs.worldbank.org/ic4d/importance-mapping-tech-hubs-africa-and-beyond.

Foster, C., Graham, M., Mann, L., Waema, T., & Friederici, N. (2018). Digital Control in Value Chains: Challenges of Connectivity for East African Firms. *Economic Geography, 94*(1), 68–86. https://doi.org/10.1080/00130095.2017.1350104.

Friederici, N. (2014). *The Business Models of MLabs and MHubs: An Evaluation of infoDev's Mobile Innovation Support Pilots*. Washington, DC: infoDev, World Bank. Retrieved from http://www.infodev.org/mobilebusinessmodels.

Friederici, N. (2017). *Innovation Hubs in Africa: Assemblers of Technology Entrepreneurs*. Dissertation, Oxford Internet Institute, University of Oxford, Oxford, UK. Retrieved from https://ora.ox.ac.uk/objects/uuid:2e5c9248-15b4-450a-958a-0ce87cf6e263.

Friederici, N. (2018a). Grounding the Dream of African Innovation Hubs: Two Cases in Kigali. *Journal of Developmental Entrepreneurship, 23*(2), 1850012.

Friederici, N. (2018b). Hope and Hype in Africa's Digital Economy: The Rise of Innovation Hubs. In M. Graham (Ed.), *Digital Economies at Global Margins*. Boston, MA: MIT Press.

Friederici, N., Ojanperä, S., & Graham, M. (2017). The Impact of Connectivity in Africa: Grand Visions and the Mirage of Inclusive Digital Development. *Electronic Journal of Information Systems in Developing Countries, 79*(2), 1–20.

Gathege, D., & Moraa, H. (2013). *Draft Report on Comparative Study on Innovation Hubs Across Africa*. Nairobi: iHub Research. Retrieved from http://research.ihub.co.ke/uploads/2013/may/1367840837__923.pdf.

Hopkins, C. (2015, October 5). How Africa Grew More than 200 Local Tech Scenes. *The Daily Dot* (blog). Retrieved from http://www.dailydot.com/debug/africa-tech-hubs-hacker-spaces-incubators/.

Jezierski, E., Harvey, J., Hansen, L., Takeuchi, M., Sinha, R., Kieboom, K. M. M., et al. (2014). In H. Tiesinga & R. Berkhout (Eds.), *Labcraft: How Social Labs Cultivate Change Through Innovation and Collaboration*. London and San Francisco: Labcraft Publishing.

Jiménez, A., & Zheng, Y. (2017). A Spatial Perspective of Innovation and Development: Innovation Hubs in Zambia and the UK. In J. Choudrie, M. Sirajul Islam, F. Wahid, J. M. Bass, & J. E. Priyatma (Eds.), *Information and Communication Technologies for Development* (Vol. 504, pp. 171–181). Cham: Springer International Publishing. https://doi.org/10.1007/978-3-319-59111-7_15.

Kanza, E. S. (2016, May 4). Africa's Digital Revolution: A Look at the Technologies, Trends and People Driving It. *World Economic Forum* (blog). Retrieved from https://www.weforum.org/agenda/2016/05/africa-s-digital-revolution-a-look-at-the-technologies-trends-and-people-driving-it/.

Kelly, T., & Firestone, R. (2016). *How Tech Hubs are Helping to Drive Economic Growth in Africa*. Background paper for the World Development Report 2016: Digital Dividends. Washington, DC: The World Bank. Retrieved from https://openknowledge.worldbank.org/bitstream/handle/10986/23645/WDR16-BP-How-Tech-Hubs-are-helping-to-Drive-Economic-Growth-in-Africa-Kelly-Firestone.pdf.

Littlewood, D. C., & Kiyumbu, W. L. (2017, October). 'Hub' Organisations in Kenya: What Are They? What Do They Do? And What is their Potential? *Technological Forecasting and Social Change*. https://doi.org/10.1016/j.techfore.2017.09.031.

Malecki, E. J., & Moriset, B. (2007). *The Digital Economy: Business Organization, Production Processes and Regional Developments*. London: Routledge.

Manyika, J., Cabral, A., Moodley, A., Moraje, S., Yeboah-Amankwah, S., Chui, M., et al. (2013). Lions Go Digital: The Internet's Transformative Potential in Africa. McKinsey Global Institute, McKinsey & Company. Retrieved from http://www.mckinsey.com/industries/high-tech/our-insights/lions-go-digital-the-internets-transformative-potential-in-africa.

Munyegera, G. K., & Matsumoto, T. (2016, March). Mobile Money, Remittances, and Household Welfare: Panel Evidence from Rural Uganda. *World Development, 79*, 127–137. https://doi.org/10.1016/j.worlddev.2015.11.006.

Murphy, J. T., & Carmody, P. (2015). *Africa's Information Revolution: Technical Regimes and Production Networks in South Africa and Tanzania*. Oxford, UK: John Wiley & Sons.

Nambisan, S. (2017). Digital Entrepreneurship: Toward a Digital Technology Perspective of Entrepreneurship. *Entrepreneurship Theory and Practice, 41*(6), 1029–1055. https://doi.org/10.1111/etap.12254.

Ndemo, B., & Weiss, T. (2016). *Digital Kenya: An Entrepreneurial Revolution in the Making*. Palgrave Studies of Entrepreneurship in Africa. Basingstoke, UK: Palgrave Macmillan.

Ndemo, B., & Weiss, T. (2017). Making Sense of Africa's Emerging Digital Transformation and Its Many Futures. *Africa Journal of Management, 3*(3–4), 328–347. https://doi.org/10.1080/23322373.2017.1400260.

Ntale, A., Yamanaka, A., & Nkurikiyimfura, D. (2013). 2.2 The Metamorphosis to a Knowledge-Based Society: Rwanda. In B. Bilbao-Osorio, S. Dutta, & B. L. Geneva (Eds.), *The Global Information Technology Report 2013: Growth and Jobs in a Hyperconnected World*. Switzerland: World Economic Forum, INSEAD. Retrieved from http://www3.weforum.org/docs/WEF_GITR_Report_2013.pdf.

Ojanperä, S., Graham, M., Straumann, R., De Sabbata, S., & Zook, M. (2017). Engagement in the Knowledge Economy: Regional Patterns of Content Creation with a Focus on Sub-Saharan Africa. *Information Technologies & International Development, 13*(0), 19.

Oxford, A., & Jeffries, D. (2013, July 3). Why Tech Hubs Are a Key Part of Africa's Future | Forum for the Future. *Green Futures Magazine*. Retrieved from https://www.forumforthefuture.org/greenfutures/articles/why-tech-hubs-are-key-part-africas-future.

Rice, M. P. (2002). Co-Production of Business Assistance in Business Incubators: An Exploratory Study. *Journal of Business Venturing, 17*(2), 163–187. https://doi.org/10.1016/S0883-9026(00)00055-0.

Sambuli, N., & Whitt, J. P. (2017). *Technology Innovation Hubs and Policy Engagement*. Brighton, UK: Institute of Development Studies. Retrieved from https://opendocs.ids.ac.uk/opendocs/handle/123456789/12860.

Sussan, F., & Acs, Z. J. (2017). The Digital Entrepreneurial Ecosystem. *Small Business Economics, 49*(1), 55–73. https://doi.org/10.1007/s11187-017-9867-5.

Tilson, D., Lyytinen, K., & Sørensen, C. (2010). Research Commentary—Digital Infrastructures: The Missing IS Research Agenda. *Information Systems Research, 21*(4), 748–759. https://doi.org/10.1287/isre.1100.0318.

Toivonen, T., & Friederici, N. (2015, April). Time to Define What a 'Hub' Really Is. *Stanford Social Innovation Review*, no. Online article. Retrieved from http://www.ssireview.org/blog/entry/time_to_define_what_a_hub_really_is.

Wakoba, S. (2014, October 31). You Are the Hope of Africa |Ban Ki-Moon Tells IHub. *TechMoran* (blog). Retrieved from http://techmoran.com/hope-africa-ban-ki-moon-tells-ihub/.

Part II

Fin-tech: Trust, Legitimacy, and Digital Infrastructure—The Promise, Prospects, and Challenges

3

Renegotiating Legitimacy in the Digital Age: Insights from Nigeria

Nasiru D. Taura, Obiajulu Christopher Ede, and Oladokun Ogunniyi

3.1 Introduction

New entrant fin-techs, namely digital-only banks and lending platforms of various sizes, emerged as part of the new wave of creative forces shaping various industries in Africa. While this is an exciting opportunity for Africa as a whole, there are legitimate fears that the high number of new entrants may lead to congestion and subsequently negative growth and

---

N. D. Taura (✉)
Business School, Bournemouth University, Bournemouth, UK
e-mail: ntaura@bournemouth.ac.uk

O. C. Ede
School of Business, Law and Communications, Southampton Solent University, Southampton, UK
e-mail: obi.ede@solent.ac.uk

O. Ogunniyi
Business School, Bournemouth University, Bournemouth, UK
e-mail: oogunniyi@bournemouth.ac.uk

N. D. Taura et al. (eds.), *Digital Entrepreneurship in Sub-Saharan Africa*, Palgrave Studies of Entrepreneurship in Africa, https://doi.org/10.1007/978-3-030-04924-9_3

declining performance by incumbents (Sonobe et al. 2011; Yoshino 2011). The new entrant fin-techs have gained traction, equipped with 'attackers' advantage', which enables them to resort to various means to 'creatively destroy' the incumbents—while many of the incumbents are dealing with varying levels of inflexibility (organisational, managerial, and strategic) (Hill and Rothaermel 2003).

In view of the above, an emergent narrative in Nigerian print and electronic media promotes a dominant discourse in favour of the new entrants (Taura and Watkins 2014), while casting the incumbents as strugglers who must renegotiate their significant loss of legitimacy, currency, and relevance in a digital age (Fisher et al. 2016). The discourse has been somewhat silent about the liability of newness which arises when the new entrants attempt to raise funds (Fisher et al. 2016). Instead, the emphasis has been on promoting new entrants as a model of the future which enjoys lower cost structures and urban, youthful appeal to millennial customers (Raji 2017).

In the emerging discourse, the incumbents in Nigeria have fallen out of favour and have been faced with renegotiating varying levels of legitimacy, namely: *cognitive* (related to taken-for-granted products or services), *moral* (related to conformity with newer digital cultural norms and values), and *regulatory* (related to compliance with ICT infrastructure and rules and regulations governing them) (Aldrich and Martinez 2001).

We believe the tendency towards legitimacy erosion is *not* universal to all incumbents—thus, while some may have responded with reactionary measures by stigmatising the fin-techs (Hampel and Tracey 2017), more proactive ones are adopting a range of entrepreneurial strategies to remain relevant despite digital transformations of the industry. Thus, we take a different position in this chapter to the dominant discourse, arguing that some Nigerian incumbents have re-enacted and adapted their environment to reproduce their identities in the digital age.

Through multiple theoretical lenses, we develop our understanding of how legitimacy is being established, lost, renegotiated, and enacted in Africa's rapidly changing and competitive digital banking landscape (Hampel and Tracey 2017; Anderson et al. 2018). We integrate three key streams of literature—legitimacy, new entrant versus incumbents, and digital infrastructure.

The chapter is structured as follows. We begin with an in-depth interview with a successful African entrepreneur to set the scene for how new entrant African digital firms encounter and overcome the challenges of establishing legitimacy. We then proceed with a review of literature on incumbents' advantages in the digital age, challenges of developing digital infrastructure, and strategies for establishing legitimacy in the digital age. The literature review is then followed by a historical overview of the indigenous roots of Nigerian incumbent banks and the challenges of legitimacy in the pre-independence era. Next, a methodology for the chapter is presented followed by analysis and discussion of emerging themes. The chapter draws lessons from the rather unusual but intriguing case of Wema Bank Plc, an illustration of incumbent digital banking good practice. The conclusion generates insights for both new entrants and incumbents in a digital age. To set the scene for understanding the challenges for establishing legitimacy for start-ups, the next section presents an in-depth interview with a leading African digital entrepreneur.

3.2 "How to Start and Scale-up Digital Enterprises in Africa": The Challenges of Establishing Legitimacy—Interview with Olalekan Olude

Background of Olalekan Olude

Olalekan Olude is the Group Chief Operating Officer of Jobberman, a company he co-founded. Today, Jobberman is the biggest job site in sub-Saharan Africa by revenue, audience, and customers. Jobberman currently delivers services across Consulting, Testing, Advertising and Outsourcing. Olalekan oversees and provides direction for the company's operational and monetisation initiatives. He was responsible for growing the revenues of Jobberman from zero to millions of dollars on an annual basis. He is also responsible for the monetisation efforts of the group in new markets, including Ghana, Kenya, Tanzania, Uganda, Ethiopia, Angola, and Zimbabwe.

Olalekan helped to orchestrate the consolidation of the company into a holding company, One Africa Media, the largest digital classifieds company in Africa with a market capitalisation of ~US$200 million. He has domain expertise in running and scaling organisations across geographies with a focus on sub-Saharan Africa. He has over seven years of Operational and Project Management experience. Before Jobberman, he worked with Goldman Sachs & Co., London as a Network Strategist with a focus on Europe, the Middle East, and Africa. He is an alumnus of Obafemi Awolowo University, the Wharton School, and University of Pennsylvania, and has also participated in numerous courses at the Lagos Business School.

Interview Extract

Interviewer: I understand that you are a very busy person. I have looked up your profile from the Oxford Internet Institute. It is quite impressive what you have been able to do with Jobberman and we have a lot to learn from you. This is about digital entrepreneurship in Africa. There is a huge debate about the new entrant digital enterprise. Most people tend to look at it from success without looking at the challenges and failures one would have to encounter. Could you please share with us the personal experiences, the background story that gave rise to your digital enterprise and the role of motivation, passion, persistence you and the co-founders of Jobber had to endure?

Olalekan: For me JM started by what I will call a mistake. We have been friends and we have done some things together; most of them were not successful. Sometime in 400 level in school, there was an industrial strike. We then decided to try something that can be impactful. So, we have a number of mindsets: (1) something that can be impactful; (2) cost nothing to set up; (3) futuristic, that is it has something to do with the internet. We had about three options, which were jobs, news, and music. After checking it against what we wanted to achieve, we realise that we should go for jobs. We could get the jobs at zero cost, build a website, and we could generate some traffic. It was around the industrial action in school that we started JM. We set a target. The target was to have a certain number of jobs on the website and we were lagging behind, so we started hiring students to help us. When the industrial strike was called off, we decided to continue with the idea. We agreed to continue because we do not know where this would take us. Based on this, we set up a particular time on Tuesdays and Thursdays to discuss what we have achieved. This was opportunity for us to find out what has been achieved. We then divided the jobs amongst the three of us. For example, when it has to do with finance and strategy, I was in charge. The other person was in charge of IT and how we want to be seen from outside. On completion of studies, I had a full-time offer from Goldman Sachs, the other person was into web designing and the third person was still in medical school. We then had an offer from an angel investor from Lagos which we accepted. We then moved to Lagos, so I had to seek for one-year extension from Goldman, which they agreed. Ten months after we got our first funding from Tiger Global, New York.

Interviewer: Could you please elaborate more on why you chose jobs instead of the music and news? What are the other challenges that you encountered, especially as a start-up?

Olalekan: We chose jobs over other options because of exposures. It was really about the impact. We were confident that we will get a job given our pervious entrepreneurial exposures, although, they did not work out successful. We were still confident that we will get a job when we graduate. This was not the case for some of our classmates. They were asking where they can do internship, or can you help. This, I believe, helped influence our choice because we felt it might be able to help these people. Although everybody listens to music and reads news, we felt that job has more impact. In terms of how we were able to weather the storm, in retrospect, the hindsight is but ignorance was bliss. It was bliss in the sense that we did not have all the technical words and all the strategy. If we check the strategy with what we have today, I will say we were just having fun. If it were to be now, we ask ourselves if we are making progress or are we just deceiving ourselves. I will liken it to kids playing football with bare foot knowing that they stand the chance of hurting their legs. Turning professional footballer, someone now ask how you learnt to play football without kits. The truth is that there were no kits at the time. Ignorance could be disastrous, sometimes. But it also helps because you have not been in an industry and you don't even understand the challenges others have had in that industry—gives you some edge. You don't see challenges before you start. Yours will be, why can't it be broken?

Interviewer: Could that be the role of your capability to adapt and learn, because there would be a lot of people, like you said, ignorance could be a bliss and they couldn't get anywhere?

Olalekan: I wouldn't tie it to adaptability because we have tried some things that did not work, but not with reference to the internet. We have tried to organise seminar; that did not work. We could have been adaptable and done other things. Perhaps we would have been media mogul. I think what I will give to is a combination of luck and doing the right things at the right time. I will also give to the opportunity for *quick wins* that happened. For example, you want to put up the website in two weeks and that happens within the time. Again, we want to post 200 jobs and that happened within it. These are wins that are quick. Assuming it was something that was time intensive, say 8–12 months before we see a result, we would have probably moved on as students. Rather, we had quick wins in almost everything we do. These kept us going because we were seeing results in almost every step we took.

Interviewer: The next question relates more to start-up businesses with respect to legitimacy and trust. I have listened to your Oxford Internet Institute interview where you talked about a trend: "people now register businesses in developed nations, but the main focus of the business will be Africa". We know that Africa has a weak institution and accountability structure. What would you consider in selecting a country for registering an African digital business and why?

Olalekan: I think the first thing will be where you can attract the most funds. This is where you could easily list, where you could easily get technology and the skill. This is me being an entrepreneur. But if you take it to the person that is still in or just left school, he will probably register in Nigeria. Maybe as he brings in the first investor, the advice to register may be in the US or anywhere else will come into play. This will enable him to maximise the opportunity the business has. Whether it is set up in Nigeria or outside, it does not affect [or] remove the legitimacy. I think the legitimacy starts from when the business starts. The business legitimacy starts with your own legitimacy and credibility as a person. After a while, as you continue to hire more people, your staff will continue to talk about the business to prospective clients, the business will start to have credibility. The credibility of the business more often than not is built in a couple of ways. You either build the credibility through your board by attracting people that are outside the country; you can also build it through some level of partnership. For example, if you are a new business, say, in the UK and sign an agreement with T-Mobile, let's say the business has it on their website that they are the people that ensure T-Mobile website is up and running. This creates a level of credibility and legitimacy to your business because it shows you are serious with whatever you are doing. It does not matter the size of your business. It does not matter if the business is registered in Nigeria or not.

Interviewer: Is there anything that is specifically different in the African context from when you do it abroad in terms of creating legitimacy and credibility? For instance, here (UK), one can easily google 'credit reference agencies' if one wants to know about the credibility/legitimacy of a company. I guess in Africa, this is not quite the case. Are there African contextual ways to create credibility in the absence of these third-party agencies?

Olalekan: When trying to set up a business in Africa, the easiest way is for the business to rub off either on your own personal credibility or that of someone else. This could be the credibility of someone that is a mentor to you, or someone that you look up to. The person might refer you to someone who might be able to give you your first deal. Based on your first deal, you get your next referral. So, in Africa, your network and your relationship is extremely important. This relationship is more social than professional, the reason being that it is possible you can do the job but you are sloppy. It is also possible you are an expert but you cut corners to get the job done. Given the issue of corruption in Africa, though not only in Africa, many people will want to check the following:

- Can this person do the job?
- Am I safe dealing with this person?
- Can I sleep peacefully after giving this person the job?
- Do I need to chase him to do the job?

Apart from the professional integrity do get the job done, does this person have personal integrity? This is where the social connections come into play. In addition, it explains the reason why the potential client, before giving you a job, will call their friend to ask what they think of you. If the response is, they will probably go on with you.

Interviewer: On the issues of corruption, how does negative branding affect the company operating in such a country? How do you deal with it?

Olalekan: The negative brand of a country no doubt will affect your company. However, the client wants to do a certain business in your country. Therefore, they will. Thus, the client is not considering if he/she should get this from your country or country 'A'. This decision has nothing to do with you as a local business. It has to do with country information available and investment opportunities. Once the investor/client has decided that he wants to do business with your country, irrespective, the client will still do business with the country. The question should now be: how do you stand out from other companies in your country to be able to attract the client? This has a lot to do with, say, partnership. If, for instance, a client is sceptical about a company he is going to deal with, it is going to look at which companies are operating within the same space, that they need a contractor or are interested in. On this note, they will be comfortable dealing with companies that have partnerships with Tier 1 listed companies. The second, as I said earlier, is your board. They will likely know if those on the board of your company are also part of a public quoted company and if they can be trusted. At this level, business will come up. If we look at it from a macro level, for business to get to you, your country must be well positioned. As a small business, you should also be well positioned more than your competitors.

Interviewer: Why are companies that scaled up in Africa not scaling up in other continents?

Olalekan: We have a couple of companies that came from Africa to be big players in other markets (for example, Dangote, MTN), but there are reasons why we have not done more. First is the focus of the business/entrepreneur. He probably believes that he wants to cover Africa and invest in Africa. The downside is that the total number of business done is Africa is very small. Even if you control 60% of the business done in Africa, you are probably struggling to be at par with small business in the US.

Second, countries in Africa hardly do business with each other. They will do more business with external parties such as Europe. For companies that focus on Africa and Africa alone, they tend to face this challenge. Nevertheless, some people will look at it from another perspective, there are opportunities in Africa and that the market is untapped. However, the disposable income is low in Africa, which will naturally stunt the growth of any business within the continent. If we look at businesses that are successful within the continent, they are those that have to do with commodity that leverages on the scale of people. For example, if we look at telecom, that survives based on the population of the country, or Dangote (cement) because everyone wants to build a house. When we look at service and probably needed by a segment of the market, you will quickly realise that there is a strain on the business to be able to grow. Sometimes, businesses want to conquer Africa before going to a more developed market because they believe the market is saturated.

Interviewer: Are there reasons why you think African countries find it difficult to trade with each other?

Olalekan: I think there are reasons. If we look at inter-country trades, we can see it is very low. In terms of connecting between African countries, it is very poor. Thus, it is difficult to move from Nigeria to Cameroon—very few direct flights. You probably have to go on roads. If you might … say you actually want to set your business in a country, why are you thinking of the ease with which you can get to other countries? The truth is that all these will add up to your decision-making process. I would not leave Lagos to go set up business in the north, except it is extremely important, the reason being that I live in Lagos.

Other things include currency differentiator, language barrier, and education. The average education across Africa could be considered to be low. When you look at the countries in Africa, you will realise that there are few countries that you will quickly break even and make a profit. By the time you consider this, you are looking at a few countries like Nigeria, Ghana, Kenya, and Egypt. This also makes the African market extremely small.

Interviewer: Can you tell us the role of ecosystem and how this might have impacted positively or negatively in scaling up of business in Africa?

Olalekan: I think ecosystems are very important. There is transparency of skill and you have a common voice. It makes it a lot easier for what I describe as people looking at from 30,000 feet to be able to spot you. One of the things that has really worked for the internet industry in Nigeria is the ecosystem. This is because it allows the investors a very good opportunity to easily identify a starting point as they get into the country. I believe ecosystem is extremely, very important for any industry. I see the government trying to do a lot along that axis. This is not really about association. It is not about the association of internet business. It is really about clusters. Clusters are very important. If we look at it from the Chinese perspective, let's say I want to make a billion ball pens—not a single company in China can manufacture it. However, given the presence of a cluster, it can be broken down into pockets of contracts and I still get my billion pens.

Interviewer: In your opinion, how can African countries strengthen their ecosystems or clusters?

Olalekan: I think it is really through a concerted effort.

1. The government should develop the needed infrastructure for the cluster around a certain geographical region.
2. The government, through the help of the private sector, needs to market this cluster.
3. The thing about a cluster is that it makes employment creation a lot easier. For example, if I have a furniture cluster, I can easily determine the skills set gap in that cluster and then train people specifically to meet that need, unlike when they are dispersed across the nation. If dispersed across the nation and you cannot easily make all of them come together, gathering of data becomes expensive. Thus, you might have to do some guesswork.

It is basically seeing a country as a company. What product are you selling? If tourism is your product, let tourism be your cluster. This means you should have a good internet bandwidth, good roads for people to move around, let your people be friendly and make it easy for people to get the necessary visa. You need to understand what your product is and with that you can now position the country for investors. This is because you will need always investors.

Interviewer: This is about the future of digital entrepreneurs in Africa, taking into account prospects and challenges. Before this, I would like you to reflect on Jobberman. What would you have done differently?

Olalekan: If there is anything I would have done different, I would have done online to offline strategy. I think we would have committed more time doing that. If we look at the digital ecosystem in Africa, because bandwidth is still expensive, we still have a kind of barrier. Before, the story was that a lot of people do not have mobile phones; now it is a case of people not having data. Now we have a lot of cheap mobile phones; many still do not have mobile phones. For many that have mobile phones, they cannot afford data. It is in Africa that people turn off data because of the cost. They only turn it on at some point when they want to catch up with something. Based on this, you cannot set up a full digital enterprise. Even if it is set up, it means you are targeting a few people above the pyramid. Thus, if it is a business that is built on mass/scale, there will be a problem.

3.3 The Incumbents' Advantage and Strategies for Establishing Legitimacy

The literature is dominated by the persistent theme of the great difficulty experienced by incumbents (later entrants) when faced with disruptive innovations—leading to their decline as a result of the attacker's advantage (Lambkin 1988). When this happens, it is often preceded by a significant loss of industry-wide legitimacy and difficulty in raising finances for expansion and growth. Legitimacy could be defined as the perception that a venture is 'desirable, proper, or appropriate within some socially constructed system of norms, values, beliefs, and definitions' (Suchman 1995, p. 574).

The legitimacy challenge is confounding since digital models are characterised by low entry barriers and rapid disruptive innovations. While new entrants are known to benefit from their smallness in triggering gales of 'creative destruction' on their way to market dominance, it is possible for incumbents to adapt if they deploy a relevant strategic posture by reorganising (Hill and Rothaermel 2003). With an appropriate strategic posture, incumbent banks could engage in the 'creative reconstruction' of their digital spaces, thus avoiding the associated 'incumbent's curse' (Zook and Graham 2007). The already existing vast network of resources available to incumbent banks confer valuable advantage when facing threats of technological change (Mitchell and Singh 1991).

In so doing, they can engage in multiple forms of relationships, including strategic alliances and joint ventures with the new entrants they perceive as threats, thus consolidating their legitimacy and subsequently their competitive advantage (Hill and Rothaermel 2003). Incumbents whose relational strategy is based on a regular pattern of inter-firm interactions, allowing them to transfer, recombine, or create specialised knowledge with new entrants, are more likely to enjoy sustainable competitive advantage (Dyer and Singh 2004). They also could engage in knowledge exchange and sharing routines through cooperation and competition (Arikan 2009; Dyer and Singh 2004; Foss 1999; Grant 2010).

3.4 Digital Banking in Nigeria: Infrastructure, Trust, and Awareness Challenges

Africa suffers greatly from the impact of poor general infrastructure. Poor general infrastructure contributes to the high cost of doing business in Africa, subsequently affecting productivity levels and making African countries among the least competitive economies in the world (Blanke et al. 2013). It has been estimated that Africa loses at least 2% of its annual growth to poor infrastructure, further compounding the problems within the region (Ondiege et al. 2013; Blanke et al. 2013). The poor state of infrastructure, and in particular of 'digital infrastructure' negatively affected adoption of digital banking in Africa despite the emergence of a generation of digital-savvy Africans. Thus, according to Agbaje (cited in World Finance 2017):

> The lack of digital and electrical infrastructure, as well as lower levels of wealth than those found in more developed markets, means that there are some barriers to the full adoption of digital banking that are particular to Africa.

In view of the above, there are those who argue that, with adequate investment in digital infrastructure, Africa could lead the world in mobile banking. They contend that Africans exhibit a tendency and readiness to embrace new technology due to a peculiar African problem that prompted a large proportion of Africans to skip whole stages of traditional digital development all together—since for many their smartphone is their first computer (Agbaje cited in World Finance 2017).

The incumbent banks are especially well positioned to make the most of this opportunity, since many do not have a legacy that prevents them from trying new digital ways of banking (Agbaje cited in World Finance 2017). However, it is vital to be sceptical about the rhetoric arguing that all investments in digital infrastructure automatically lead to financial inclusion or inclusive development (Freiderici et al. 2017). Some claims are mainly rhetorical and are not supported by empirical evidence (Freiderici et al. 2017). Previous research on the visions of connectivity in Africa unveils how some powerful organisations promote certain discourses that are contrary to the available evidence (Freiderici et al. 2017).

Another pronounced barrier to digital banking in Nigeria is the perception of trust. Trust is the perception of the probability that other agents will behave in a certain expected way (Gambetta 2000). When digital banking emerged in Nigeria, many people were sceptical about adopting and trusting new models of e-consumption, due to concerns about security breaches (Accenture 2013). And rightly so, as research found direct links with online transactions and e-trust in the banking industry, sometimes involving third-party seals (Yousafzai et al. 2003;

Yap et al. 2010; Head and Hassanein 2002). To minimise the impact of high levels of mistrust, the Nigerian government played a key role through financial crime policing (Neegaard and Ulhoi 2006).

A number of government initiatives in Nigeria (e.g., the Economic and Financial Crimes Commission—EFCC) helped to restore some level of confidence and public trust about financial crimes in Nigeria. One can argue that such initiatives have improved public confidence, leading to increased digital banking adoption rates in Nigeria due to inter-organisational trust building (Neegaard and Ulhoi 2006). These initiatives police moral hazards and opportunistic behaviour (Gulati 1998). As such, the adoption rate of digital banking in Nigeria is growing rapidly (Accenture 2013; World Development Report 2016).

Although the level of trust arguably has improved, many Nigerians still do not engage with digital banking services, mainly due to lack of knowledge and awareness. Thus, while on the one hand it can be argued that for most unbanked Africans mobile banking provides great opportunities to go digital, on the other hand it can be argued that their lack of digital knowledge, previous experience, and awareness limits could limit their adoption rate and usage. This is taking into consideration that for many Africans the mobile internet is their first computer experience (Agbaje cited in World Finance 2017).

3.5 The Origins of Nigerian Banking and the Challenges of Legitimacy

Prior to independence, Nigerian traders were unsatisfied with the British and European banks of the time—which subsequently led to appeals and protests. For example, a letter of appeal was published in Lagos, which reads 'an appeal from native traders of Lagos to the financiers of Great Britain'. In 1916, Samuel Duncan led a delegation of traders to London to protest the monopolistic practices of the British Bank of West Africa (BBWA). The chain of events had given rise to Nigeria's indigenous banking system, which simultaneously developed alongside the colonial banking system (Uche 1996). However, these banks persistently failed to receive a seal of approval, and thus legitimacy, from the colonial administration of the day, which contributed to their collapse and their inability to raise finances from the public.

In the 1930s certain indigenous banks proliferated, but most were short-lived (Uche 1997). By 1960, out of the 27 indigenous banks established in Nigeria, 21 had already failed due to mismanagement, accounting incompetence, embezzlement, or an inability to comply with the strict banking guidelines issued in the 1952 ordinance (Newlyn and Rowan 1954 cited in Uche, 1997).

To combat the lack of legitimacy, the regional governments in Nigeria came to the aid of some indigenous banks with endorsements and financial support. For example, the African Continental Bank, established by Dr Nnamdi Azikiwe (then Premier of the Eastern Region), was supported financially by the government of the Eastern region. This was followed by a decision from the Western Regional government to support Agbonmagbe Bank (Uche 1997).

The Northern government supported the establishment of Bank of the North in 1952. Interestingly, not all indigenous banks supported by the regional governments succeeded. For example, despite extensive support from the Western Region government, the Merchant Bank still failed. Thus, while some indigenous banks continue to re-enact their environment to attract legitimacy, others have not enjoyed the same level of success.

3.6 Method of Data Collection and Analysis

We started by examining secondary sources such as PwC Journal Nigeria, Nigeria's FinTech Survey Report (PwC), McKinsey Report Nigeria, and World Economic Forum Report. We conducted semi-structured interviews with five seasoned bankers in Nigeria, focusing on questions which enabled the respondents to narrate series of events that unfolded as a reflection of their experience and knowledge as seasoned bankers—linked to renegotiating legitimacy in a digital age (Denzin 2000). The respondents are presented anonymously with pseudonyms in Table 3.1.

Table 3.1 Respondents' profiles

Respondent number	Profile
Respondent 1 (Green Bank)	Holds an MSc in Mass Communications with a tenure of eight years in the banking sector, primarily as a "customer-facing" employee. Within the 26–30 age bracket, her work experience cuts across two banks (one in Nigeria and the other in the United Kingdom). She currently heads the customer service unit and doubles as the assistant bank manager in a bank in Nigeria
Respondent 2 (Red Bank)	Holds a BSc in Accounting with tenure of 15 years in the Nigerian banking sector. Within the 36–40 age bracket, she has worked in different units across three banks, with the third bank being a product of 'merger and acquisition' of the second bank by another. She currently works as a customer relations officer, otherwise referred to as a 'marketer'. Her work is predominately 'market- facing'; holds responsibilities such as identifying and enlisting potential clients outside the bank as well as maintaining existing relationships, marketing the bank's products and services, and so on
Respondent 3 (Indigo Bank)	A computer engineer and certified software programmer within the 41–45 age bracket. Having worked previously as an IT and programme development consultant for several years in the Nigerian banking sector and beyond, he has a tenure of four years in the Nigerian banking sector, working basically as a 'back office' employee. He currently heads the IT unit in a Nigerian bank in an acting capacity. He oversees the IT infrastructures in the bank
Respondent 4 (Brown Bank)	Holds an executive MBA with a tenure of about 17 years in the Nigerian banking sector, predominantly as 'customer-facing' in the operations unit. Within the 41–45 age bracket, his work experience cuts across five banks in Nigeria. He is currently a regional operations manager in a Nigerian bank with responsibilities for overseeing bank operations of some branches in the region
Respondent 5 (Blue Bank)	Holds an MSc in Information Technology and Computer Science, with tenure of about six years in the Nigerian banking sector. Within the 31–35 age bracket, his work experience cuts across two banks in Nigeria. Currently he works in the IT, innovation, and cyber security unit in a bank in Nigeria

We then analysed the results of the semi-structured interviews by applying narrative analysis to underpin the narrative, and to elicit and scrutinise the stories the interviewees tell about themselves including antecedents and consequences of digital banking approaches in Nigeria (Sekaran and Boogie 2010). We conducted the analysis at two levels: conceptual and relational. For conceptual analysis we established the existence and frequency of concepts (such as words, themes, characters) in text (Sekaran and Boogie 2010). We then proceeded to interpret it by coding the text according to manageable content categories (Sekaran and Boogie 2010). Building on conceptual analysis, we examined the relationships among concepts and texts from the curated contents available to us (Sekaran and Boogie 2010).

In addition to the above, we also examined the emerging discourse specifically focusing on interpreting what is being implied and invoked in the discourse—due to its explanatory power (Anderson and Warren 2011). This interpretive form of discourse analysis, which emphasises the 'subject', not the 'object', offers numerous advantages in this study. We thus present a compelling case for dynamic incumbent banks in Nigeria, challenging the institutionalisation of an emergent discursive 'cultural milieu' that promotes negative stereotypes of them (Anderson and Warren 2011).

3.7 Findings and Discussion of Results

Barriers to Digital Banking in Nigeria: Willingness versus Relational Trust

Nigerian digital banks are still evolving and face a number of barriers that are preventing their full adoption. Our interviewees with seasoned bankers in Nigeria revealed a number of issues, namely: *availability*, *awareness*, and *trust*. The main barrier to digital banking often encountered by incumbent banks in Nigeria is the level of awareness and knowledge of how to use the available digital artefacts, products, or services. The problem is not whether the products or services are available, but to what extent Nigerians are aware of and ready to consume such products. This has been captured well by one interviewee:

> Will you give a trader POS? Their level of literacy has not gotten to that too, so all those affect things. You can't say you are going home with your ATM card and you are sure of buying everything you want with your ATM card. It is not possible, you must go with cash. So that is why most people also go with cash. (Respondent 2, customer relations officer, Red Bank)

The above reveals that, since most small business owners (traders) in Nigeria do not use POS, this forces customers to use cash, and hence they are not able to fully consume the services the banks are capable of providing. In addition, poor network provision and erratic power supply confounds the problem.

Unfortunately, most of the small businesses in Nigeria are not online, which reinforces the lack of motivation and demand-led digital market solutions. A lack of sophisticated demand side from customers often leads to unsophisticated provisions of digital solutions by the banks. In addition to the barrier identified above, one of the biggest challenges the incumbent banks are facing in Nigeria is that of trust. As a result of the strong lack of trust, many people prefer to physically go to the bank:

> So some people still believe coming to the bank. You must come to the bank, even if you want to withdraw your 1000, you must still come … (Respondent 2, customer relations officer, Red Bank)
>
> Hmmm, though the internet is faster and aids some transactions doing multiple things, but people still believe that in this system of ours in Nigeria, it won't work. Even people come to the bank to make complaints that they didn't book for certain things and their monies were deducted. So they believe they come to the bank hall to carry their transaction. They are more comfortable with the day-to-day bank hall transactions. They tell you anything online is another way of taking your money. (Respondent 4, operations unit, Brown Bank)

The above finding is alarming since relational trust is the glue that binds all economic transactions (Zahra et al. 2006). The lack of trust in digital banking in Nigeria, which customers perceive as a way to take their money away from them, has done huge damage to the digitalisation agenda and may have led to the erosion of equity. The deterioration of such relation-based trust could easily affect the level of acceptance of new digital solutions on offer (Zahra et al. 2006). Since a lot of Nigerian customers choose to use traditional banking, there is a need for Nigerian banks to embark on both online and offline strategies of establishing relational e-trust (Yousafzai et al. 2003; Yap et al. 2010). One would also expect the new generation of youth to have a different attitude, but our interviews revealed that the negative impact of perceived lack of relational e-trust actually cuts across all generations:

> Even some young ones still want to come to the bank because they tell you they have done a series of stuffs on their account and they make them allege fraud. That is one major thing they are afraid of. And also the facilities sometimes disappoint and cost so much for the bank to maintain. (Respondent 4, operations unit, Brown Bank)

Despite the challenges outlined above, Nigerian digital banking is evolving gradually and steadily. The next section discusses areas where progress is being made—albeit slowly.

Investment in Digital Infrastructure (Slow but Steady)

Progress has been made thus far, with a steady pace set in regard to general investment in digital infrastructure. Due to the infrastructural deficit inherited over time, most African countries are recognising that the best way to proceed is through public–private partnership (PPP), particularly in the banking sector (Luiz 2010). However, due to weak institutions, the investment in digital infrastructure has proceeded more slowly than anticipated (Rodrik and Subramanian 2008). One interviewee highlighted the slow but developmental nature of digital infrastructure in Nigeria's incumbent banks:

> IT generally in the entire banking sector needs to upgrade. Because there is no way we can just stop every transaction in the bank, everybody should go 'e'. They have not gotten to that level. In terms of network, their networks are not so strong like that. Today internet banking might be working but tomorrow they will tell you that they are under maintenance or something. (Respondent 2, customer relations officer, Red Bank)

Nonetheless, despite the slow progress made, as outlined below the need for system upgrades in most of these banks is imperative:

> Yeah, I think the bank has profited from the injection of technology and software to the banking process but they … as someone working as an IT guy in the bank, there is still a lot of equipment to facilitate this, it is still not enough in most of these banks. The bank might be vulnerable based on the information you have or you carry or based on the access you have. They are always very careful with them. Many customers also are very not comfortable to use these channels because of the challenges. There is the need for more upgrade of the banking system in many of banks. (Respondent 3, IT unit, Indigo Bank)

Digital Infrastructure: How Open Is Good Enough for Healthy Cooperation between Incumbents versus New Entrants?

Digital infrastructure has become a tool or interface that fosters rather than inhibits relationships between incumbent banks and fin-techs. Contrary to what the popular literature suggests—that incumbents and new entrants are in competition with one another—the dynamic in Nigeria is somewhat different. One interviewee made clear the idea of open EPI to foster healthy cooperation in the sector—however, the question is, how open does it need to be?

> I think many banks are working on an opened EPI connect so that fin-tech can readily plug into their own services. There is a regulation currently driving that now … so that every bank has an opened EPI that will allow fin-tech to consume your services wherever they are. It is a programme

interface that allows you to connect with a bank service. It is an interface through which you who is coming from outside can connect with bank services. There are EPI in every bank. One application connecting to another will connect through EPI. (Respondent 5, Blue Bank)

So, we are saying we want the EPI to be exposed so that it can be accessed from internet such that if anybody comes in, it will get to a level that individual comes … a lot of guys in Nigeria are doing some great things. We have some guys that are behind the open banking initiatives. Their services might just be to produce part of the digital banking journey, but banks should be in a position whereby they are ready to allow different services plug into theirs and the interface, the secured interface that will allow this needs to be readily available. (Respondent 5, Blue Bank)

It vital to note here that while investment in digital infrastructure as outlined above is leading to newer forms of positive relationships, there are other negative concerns. Some customers perceive digital banking negatively, concerned that it could be a mechanism which transfers risks to them, with no particular person to blame if things go wrong. They are used to the previous method, in which if anything goes wrong they can hold someone accountable:

Even while we have Mobile Banking, a lot of Nigerians are not ready to do it; if you have two people working, how one can leave it and because the banking system is still accommodating it and not enforced, some people prefer pushing that risk to somebody else instead of them doing it on their own. They prefer that you handle it; so as to say after all you did it for me. So as a result of that, a lot of people still troop to the banking hall instead of using the alternate channels. Instead of doing transfer on the ATM, doing it on their phones, doing it on the internet banking platform. They don't want to do it because they want somebody to lay hold on in case something happens. And as a result of that, we could not discourage it, if it is discouraged, we won't have as much crowd but because the system is still designed for them to walk in, queue and all those things, we just have to be there. (Respondent 1, customer service officer, Green Bank)

Digital Banking: The Preferred Approaches for Nigerian Incumbent Banks

Our research reveals three levels of digital banking favoured by Nigerian incumbents, namely: (1) outsourcing all digital services, (2) in-house fin-tech division in partnership with external providers, and (3) going fully digital. The emergence of these varying approaches is a testimony to the practices suggested in the literature:

> Incumbents have to proactively approach the FinTech challenge with a clearly articulated strategy rather than the current approach of adopting reactionary measures. Incumbents also need to identify the threats and opportunities that are most relevant to their business and explore ways they can build, acquire or partner with FinTech for the capabilities they lack. (PwC 2017)

Each of the outlined approaches has implications for how the banks are perceived in the digital age and hence their legitimacy. For example, the CEO of one of Nigeria's most dynamic new-generation banks, Guarantee Trust Agbaje (cited in World Finance 2017), stated:

> Our strategy is to take advantage of the new opportunities born from the digital revolution by moving beyond our traditional role as enablers of financial transactions and providers of financial products, to playing a deeper role in the digital and commercial lives of our customers. In pursuit of this strategy we have created our own in-house fin-tech division, while also actively seeking partnerships and collaborations with other fin-techs.

It appears that this approach, in which a bank establishes an in-house fin-tech division in partnership with external fin-tech collaborators, is gaining popularity. Understandably, the incumbent banks' strategy is often to leverage the trust they have with existing customers and clients, while at the same time tapping into areas where the fin-techs are strong (PwC 2017). The main challenge with such an approach, however, is that the fin-techs and the incumbent banks often have different operating strategies (PwC 2017). While new entrant fin-techs are good at the disruptive model of business, incumbents, on the other hand, tend to be held back by organisational rigidity that favours older ways of doing business (Hill and Rothaermel 2003; Taura and Watkins 2014):

> I want to believe digital banking is to a substantial extent still evolving. The fact is that because of the cost of the requirements, if you are fully digitising your banking activities it must be done on a smartphone and an internet-enabled device and you know the fundamental problem of power generation. It affects the cost of running to the equipment needed. (Respondent 5, Blue Bank)

For fear of the incompatibility which may arise in partnerships or collaborations with external fin-techs, it appears some incumbent banks such Wema Bank Plc preferred to adopt the approach of going fully digital.

Wema is proud of its creation of ALAT as one of the first fully digital banks in Nigeria, which provides more than other banks do through apps. Wema Bank claimed that, their ALAT is an independent entity sharing similar ethos with Wema Bank. Our interviewee shares a favourable outlook on what Wema achieved by creating ALAT, a fully digital bank:

> I think other banks will follow their footstep in future in going fully digital. It will eventually be the norm in Nigerian banking industry in years to come. Then we will have very few people going to the four walls of the bank to carry out their transactions. Because you will be able to consume all your banking services from your phone, even up to requesting for cheque book, requesting for loan, and so on. My understanding is that those were also digitised on the Wema Bank digital banking platform where you can also consume other services right from the application from your phone. (Respondent 5, Blue Bank)

Having described the favoured approaches gaining popularity among Nigerian incumbent banks, we now focus our attention on Wema Bank as one of the oldest Nigerian indigenous banks, as well as one of the few incumbents that have created a fully digital bank. In order to draw lessons from their approach, we trace their legitimacy journey over time in the next section.

Wema Bank Plc Nigeria: The Legitimacy Journey and Digital Footprints

Wema Bank, established in 1945, is one of Nigeria's longest-surviving indigenous banks. Wema Bank was incorporated as a Private Limited Liability Company (under the old name of Agbonmagbe Bank Limited) and commenced banking operations in Nigeria the same year. As it evolved, it acquired more "legitimacy" through earning public confidence and was later transformed into a Public Limited Company (Plc) in April 1987 and was listed on the floor of the Nigerian Stock Exchange (NSE) in January 1990.

During the deregulation (1980–90) that led to a general erosion of legitimacy in Nigeria's banking industry, Wema Bank responded by implementing an ICT-led organisational programme as well as Business Process Re-engineering (BPR). It appointed a multinational consulting firm to handle the project alongside members of Wema Bank Plc. By 1989, the team had come up with an initial strategic plan focusing on three key areas, namely: geographic spread, business focus, and image management (Bada 2002).

Notably, all three key areas are linked to legitimacy building. Wema Bank insisted on implementing the BPR change programme while still maintaining the internal stability of the workforce, known as the 'Wema family'. In essence, Wema Bank was changing but preserving a family of employees who had risen through the ranks (Bada 2002). This gave the bank an opportunity to focus on training the existing workforce and building employee legitimacy.

The BPR focuses on re-engineering by investing in state-of-the-art technology, banking software, and network interconnectivity in strategic banks (a small number of banks considered top earners) (Bada 2002). Redesigning involves redesigning the banks without heavily investing in technology—since they were considered less strategic than the former. Thus, existing software and hardware were upgraded (Bada 2002). The third layer of banks were put through a process of being 'streamlined' in which only the operations were restructured, without any change in IT infrastructure (Bada 2002).

The BPR implementation at branch level entails the adoption of efficient and effective computer-based controls with a semi-automated online approval system. The new authorisation system is believed to empower many customer-facing staff, such as tellers, giving them more autonomy to authorise cash up to 50,000 naira—and in so doing increasing customer satisfaction (Bada 2002). The idea is to empower the customer-facing staff so that the branch manager can scout for more clients through marketing and image making (Bada 2002).

While this was considered generally more efficient, conflicts arose when branch managers were out and a customer needing more than 50,000 naira arrived (Bada 2002). The response to the challenge had been to allow operations managers to override the authorisation power and reconcile it later with the branch managers (Bada 2002).

During the Universal Banking era (1990s–2000s), specifically on 5 February 2001, Wema Bank Plc was granted a universal banking licence by the Central Bank of Nigeria (CBN), thus allowing the bank to provide the Nigerian public with diverse financial and business advisory services. The granting of a licence by Nigeria's apex bank CBN further consolidated Wema Bank's legitimacy in Nigeria's banking industry and beyond. The bank now offers a range of services including retail and Small and Medium Enterprises (SME) banking, corporate banking, treasury, trade services, and financial advisory to its clients.

In 2009, the bank started taking advantage of its established legitimacy to strategically reposition, and by 2011 it has reached out to South-South, South-West including Lagos and Abuja Nigeria. Additionally, in 2015 the bank was granted a national banking licence by the Central Bank of Nigeria, enabling it to operate a network of over 140 branches and service stations across Nigeria, backed by a robust ICT platform. The origin of the bank's geographical spread can be traced to the 1997 CBN requirement to open rural banks—which were subsequently referred to as political branches due to inactivity (Bada 2002). Thus, "regional differences was one of the factors considered by almost all banks during that era, as it was an opportunity to integrate and spread geographically" (Interviewee 26, extracts, cited in Gomes et al. 2012).

During the consolidation era (2004), Wema Bank merged with National Bank of Nigeria to raise 35 billion naira (Gomes et al. 2012). In so doing, they created a coherent, legitimate identity in synch with their historic background. Wema Bank was careful in its approach by carefully selecting three banks from the same backgrounds. The origin of "the banks from the west and having a similar background" (Interviewee 15, extracts, cited in Gomes et al. 2012) contributes to their consolidated identity.

Illustrative Examples of Good Practices: What Can We Learn from Wema Bank's Digital Banking Strategy, the ALAT?

Having traced Wema Bank's legitimacy journey and its digital footprint in time in the previous section, it is clear that Wema's investment in technology infrastructure was pursued for a long time. In so doing, when the new waves of fin-tech emerged in Nigeria, they did not pose as much of a threat to Wema Bank as they did to others. Its investment in technology infrastructure over the years enabled Wema Bank to more easily create a fully digital bank—ALAT—in comparison with other banks. In so doing Wema was able to make a quantum leap, despite being an old-generation bank. One interviewee expanded on this point:

> For other banks, they do not go fully digital like Wema Bank. They only have just some part of the operation online, therefore have not gone fully digital. But most of the banks operate mobile banking. On the mobile banking platform, you can access your account through internet and still and carry out a lot of transactions. From your phone you can make transfers to other accounts, pay bills, top up your mobile phone credit. What Wema did is that they went ahead to create a banking app on which you can request cheques, you can even make withdrawals. To make the withdrawal, you will generate codes and go to a cardless ATM machine, put your code and retrieve your cash, you don't need a credit or debit card. On the Wema platform, you can apply for loan, you can apply for mortgage, you can carry out a full bank transaction. Those are just bank transactions made operational on an app which Wema Bank has done. Other banks

> have limited it. It is Wema Bank that has taken the quantum leap. (Respondent 5, Blue Bank)

The quantum leap had also proven worthwhile for Wema:

> Well, for Wema Bank, I believe that is the right thing for them to do because they were already losing market value because of their brand in terms of what people know them to do, like the status as old-generation bank, so to say. But from my understanding, they brought in a lot of new, creative and innovative guys together to look into the prospect of digital applications in the banking operations. And from what I hear, it has improved their own bottom line more so as they don't have so much presence across the country relative to other big-name banks. (Respondent 5, Blue Bank)

How Wema Bank Actively Uses the Digital Space and Social Media to Establish Legitimacy in a Digital Age

It is not enough to go fully digital—without investing in digital interactive technology to engage customers. We learnt that, unlike many other Nigerian incumbent banks, Wema has invested in interactive tools that engage the customers, as could be seen on their website as well as social media platforms such as Facebook and others. Wema's approaches, as outlined below, have helped them to stand out from the crowd and earn legitimacy.

Gamification: Wema adopted a very interesting interactive live game show called "Game show 945". The programme is hosted on the Wema Bank Facebook page, and it is based on an interactive live video game with customers. The programme uses the opportunity to interact with customers and educate them about Wema Bank Plc's services; customers can win a cash prize, which is then instantly transferred to their account.

The above is an example of how to use gamification to interactively engage with and educate customers (innovative approach). This justifies the literature which argues that gamification can be used as a tool for service marketing (Conaway and Garay 2014). One can argue that Wema

Bank's use of gamification on a social media platform such as Facebook has indeed embedded the features required for attracting customers, namely feedback and reward, social connection, and attractiveness of the site (Conaway and Garay 2014).

Video Contents: Wema Bank uses a range of other media to interact and engage with customers, especially videos on their website as outlined below:

(a) *Customer Service Week*: This is a video lasting a few seconds in which bank staff wish customers happy customer service.
(b) *My everyday hero*: This enables customers, in less than one minute, to talk about their everyday hero, including their families.
(c) *Where do you see yourself at 71?*: At Wema Bank's 71-year anniversary, Wema Bank partnered with a trendy TV station called Pulse TV to develop a video which engages members of the public with the question of where they see themselves at 71. This is interactive and provides an opportunity to educate the public about the Wema Bank brand.
(d) *Broadcast Interview with Senior Execs*: Wema broadcasts interviews with its senior executives to engage the public about their vision for the future. One example is an interview with senior executives at the 'World Finance London'.

3.8 Conclusion: Establishing Digital Legitimacy Is an Active Not a Passive Process

Based on the findings from this chapter, we can conclude that establishing legitimacy is crucial for both new entrant start-ups as well as established incumbents. Firstly, for new entrant digital start-ups in Africa, legitimacy starts when the business starts. However, there are at least three popular approaches to establishing legitimacy, mainly through (a) the credibility of the owner or their mentor, which serves as a magnet to attract and hire more credible people; (b) attracting high-profile people to the board of directors; and finally (c) signing partnership agreements with known and respected digital companies with international reputations. High net worth individuals and companies are comfortable dealing with digital start-ups in Africa that have partnerships with Tier 1 listed companies.

By actively engaging with the aforementioned, a digital start-up in Africa could create a level of credibility and legitimacy capable of sending a signal that they are serious in whatever they are doing. For African digital start-ups, the network of the owner or mentor is vital in the sense that, based on the first deal, you get your next referral.

On the other hand, a quick look at the websites and social media accounts of many incumbents reveals that they are static instead of interactive. For many, it is just a platform for one-way information sharing with little or no capacity for interactive engagement with customers. This affects any attempt to rebrand or reposition themselves to renegotiate their identity as modern and digital. Thus, many Nigerian incumbent banks would fail the test of renegotiating their identity in a digital age through discursive practices on digital media platforms (Clegg 1989).

Nonetheless, as we have seen in the case of Wema Bank Plc, some Nigerian incumbent banks have risen to the challenge by adopting a range of other complementary digital interactive tools and mechanisms such as gamification, interactive videos, and virtual money to engage customers, thereby scanning their environment and understanding the minds of the customers of the future. Such incumbent banks using interactive digital media have taken active rather passive roles (Taura and Watkins 2014), and have become discursive producers of their identity—thus demonstrating the power of technology and digital platforms in unleashing organisational as well as entrepreneurial action in ways not previously possible (Greenfield and Ribbins 1993; McMullen and Shephered 2006). The future is reserved for African businesses (new entrants or incumbents) that use digital spaces actively to produce their identity by telling their own story (Adeyemi 2017). We therefore conclude that establishing digital legitimacy (through interactivity and reconstruction of identity) is an active, not a passive, process for both new entrants and incumbents.

References

Accenture. (2013). The Future of Identity Banking [Online]. Retrieved March 13, 2018, from https://www.accenture.com/_acnmedia/Accenture/Conversion-Assets/DotCom/Documents/Global/PDF/Dualpub_9/Accenture-Future-Identity-Banking.pdf.

Adeyemi, A. (2017). "We Have to Tell Our Own Story": Semiotics of Resisting. Negative Stereotypes of Nigeria in the Heart of Africa Nation Branding Campaign. *Social Semiotics, 27*(2), 158–177.

Aldrich, H. E., & Martinez, M. A. (2001). Many are Called, but Few are Chosen: An Evolutionary Perspective for the Study of Entrepreneurship. *Entrepreneurship Theory & Practice, 25*(4), 41–56.

Anderson, A. R., & Warren, L. (2011). The Entrepreneur as Hero and Jester: Enacting the Entrepreneurial Discourse. *International Small Business Journal, 29*(6), 89–609.

Anderson, A. R., Warren, L., & Bensemann, J. (2018). Identity, Enactment, and Entrepreneurship Engagement in a Declining Place. *Journal of Small Business Management, 00*(00), 1–19.

Arikan, A. T. (2009). Interfirm Knowledge Exchanges and Knowledge Creation Capability of Clusters. *Academy of Management Review, 34*(4), 658–676.

Bada, A. O. (2002). Local Adaptations to Global Trends: A Study of an IT-Based Organizational Change Program in a Nigerian Bank. *The Information Society, 18*, 77–86.

Blanke, J., et al. (2013). Assessing Africa's Competitiveness in an International Context. *The Africa's Competitiveness Report* (pp. 3–37). World Economic Forum.

Clegg, S. R. (1989). *Frameworks of Power*. London: Sage.

Conaway, R., & Garay, M. C. (2014). Gamification and Service Marketing. *Springer Plus, 3*(1), 653.

Denzin, N. K. (2000). The Practices and Politics of Interpretation. In N. K. Denzin & Y. S. Lincoln (Eds.), *Handbook of Qualitative Research* (2nd ed.). Thousand Oaks, CA: Sage.

Dyer, J. H., & Singh, H. (2004). The Relational View: Cooperative Strategy and Sources of Inter-organisational Competitive Advantage. In J. J. Reuer (Ed.), *Strategic Alliances: Theory and Evidence*. New York: Oxford University Press.

Fisher, G., Kotha, S., & Lahiri, A. (2016). Changing with the Times: An Integrated View of Identity, Legitimacy, and Venture cycles. *Academy of Management Review, 41*(3), 383–409.

Foss, N. J. (1999). Networks, Capabilities, and Competitive Advantage. *Scandinavian Journal of Management, 15*(1), 1–15.
Freiderici, N., Ojanpera, S., & Mark, M. (2017). The Impact of Connectivity in Africa: Grand Visions and the Mirage of Inclusive Development. *The Electronic Journal of Information Systems in Developing Countries, 79*(2), 1–20.
Gambetta, D. (2000). Can We Trust in Trust. In D. Gambetta (Ed.), *Trust: Making and Breaking Cooperative Relations*. (Chap. 13) (pp. 213–237). Oxford: University of Oxford.
Gomes, E., Angwin, D., Peter, E., & Mellahi, K. (2012). HRM Issues and Outcomes in African Mergers and Acquisitions: A Study of the Nigerian Banking Sector. *The International Journal of Human Resource Management, 23*(14), 2874–2900.
Grant, R. M. (2010). *Contemporary Strategy Analysis* (7th ed.). Chichester, West Sussex, UK: John Wiley and Sons Limited.
Greenfield, T., & Ribbins, P. (1993). *Greenfield on Educational Administration: Towards a Humane Science*. London: Routledge.
Gulati, R. (1998). Alliances and Qualitative Methods in Management Research Networks. *Strategic Management Journal, 19*, 293–317.
Hampel, C. E., & Tracey, P. (2017). Hoe Organisations Move from Stigma to Legitimacy: The Case of Cooks Travel Agency in Victorian Britain. *Academy of Management Journal, 60*(6), 2175–2207.
Head, M. M., & Hassanein, K. (2002). Trust in E-commerce: Evaluating the Impact of Third Party Seals. *Quarterly Journal of Electronic, 3*(3), 307–325.
Hill, C. W. L., & Rothaermel, F. T. (2003). The Performance of Incumbent Firms in the Face of Radical Technological Innovation. *Academy of Management Review, 28*(2), 257–274.
Lambkin, M. (1988). Order of Entry and Performance in New Markets. *Strategic Management Journal, 9*(S1), 127–140.
Luiz, J. (2010). Infrastructure Investment and Its Performance in Africa over the Course of the Twentieth Century. *International Journal of Social Economics, 37*(7), 512–536.
McMullen, J. S., & Shephered, D. A. (2006). Entrepreneurial Action and the Role of Uncertainty in the Theory of the Entrepreneur. *Academy of Management Review, 31*(1), 132–152.
Mitchell, W., & Singh, K. (1991). Incumbents' Use of Pre-entry Alliances before Expansion into New Technical Subfields of Industry. *Journal of Economic Behaviour and Organisation, 18*, 347–372.

Neegaard, H., & Ulhoi, J. P. (2006). Government Agency and Trust in the Formation and Transformation of Inter-organizational Entrepreneurial Networks. *Entrepreneurship: Theory and Practice, 30*(4), 519–539.

Ondiege, P., Moyo, J. M., & Verdier-Chouchane, A. (2013). Developing Africa's Infrastructure for Enhanced Competitiveness. *The Africa's Competitiveness* (pp. 69–92). World Economic Forum.

PwC. (2017). Nigeria FinTech Survey Report [Online]. Retrieved August 31, 2018, from https://www.pwc.com/ng/en/publications/nigeria-fintech-survey-report.html.

Raji, R. (2017). Could Nigeria's Digital-Only Banks Conquer the Market? *African Business Magazine* [Online]. Retrieved March 13, 2018, from https://www.suntrustng.com/could-nigerias-digital-only-banks-conquer-the-market/.

Rodrik, D., & Subramanian, A. (2008). The Primacy of Institutions (and What this Does and Does not Mean). In G. Secondi (Ed.), *The Development Economics Reader*. New York: Routledge.

Sekaran, U., & Boogie, R. (2010). *Research Methods for Business: A Skill Building Approach*. Haddington: John Wiley & Sons Ltd.

Sonobe, T., Akoten, J., & Otsuka, K. (2011). The Growth Process of Informal Enterprises in Sub-Saharan Africa: A Case Study of a Metalworking Cluster in Nairobi. *Small Business Economics, 36*, 323–335.

Suchman, M. C. (1995). Managing Legitimacy: Strategic and Institutional Approaches. *Academy of Management Review, 20*, 571.

Taura, N., & Watkins, D. (2014). Counteracting Innovative Constraints: Insights from Four Case Studies of African Knowledge-Intensive Metalworking and Automotive Clusters—'The Akimacs'. *Entrepreneurship and Regional Development, 26*(3–4), 313–336.

Uche, C. U. (1996). The Nigerian Failed Bank Decree: A Critique. *Journal of International Banking Law, 11*(10), 436–440.

Uche, C. U. (1997). *Banking Development in Pre-independence Nigeria: A Study in Regulation, Control, & Politics*. Un-published (a thesis submitted for the degree of Doctor of Philosophy) [Online]. Retrieved May 1, 2018, from http://etheses.lse.ac.uk/1470/1/U105686.pdf.

World Development Report. (2016). Enabling Digital Development: Digital Finance [Online]. Retrieved March 15, 2018, from http://documents.worldbank.org/curated/en/896971468194972881/310436360_20160263021313/additional/102725-PUB-Replacement-PUBLIC.pdf.

World Finance. (2017). Digital Banking Holds the Key to Financial Inclusion in Nigeria [Online]. Retrieved August 30, 2018, from https://www.worldfinance.com/banking/digital-banking-holds-the-key-to-financial-inclusion-in-nigeria.

Yap, B. K., Wong, D. H., Loh, C., & Bak, R. (2010). Offline and Online Banking—Where to Draw the Line when Building Trust in E-banking? *International Journal of Bank Marketing, 28*(1), 27–24.

Yoshino, Y. (2011). *Industrial Clusters and Micro and Small Enterprises in Africa: From Survival to Growth*. Washington: The World Bank.

Yousafzai, Y. S., Pallister, J. G., & Foxall, R. G. (2003). A Proposed Model of E-trust for Electronic Banking. *Technovation, 23*, 847–860.

Zahra, S. A., Yavuz, R. I., & Ucbasaran, D. (2006). How Much Do You Trust Me? The Dark Side of Relational Trust in New Business Creation in Established Companies. *Entrepreneurship Theory & Practice, 30*(4), 541–559.

Zook, M. A., & Graham, M. (2007). Mapping DigiPlace: Geocoded Internet Data and the Representation of Place. *Environment and Planning B: Planning and Design, 34*(3), 466–482.

Part III

Media-tech: The Creative Destruction and Reconstruction of African Digital Media

4

The African New Media Digital Revolution: Some Selected Cases from Nigeria

Elvira Bolat

4.1 Introduction

Technological transformations are an inevitable part of globalisation, most often associated with the democratisation of societies and, therefore, opportunities for interactions and access to information that are free from geographical, institutional, and cultural boundaries (Dickel and Schrape 2017). Africa, like the rest of the world, has participated in the global new media digital revolution. However, unlike Western countries, Africa has taken an indigenous approach, mixed with integration and conflicts, to the adoption of information and communication technologies. This approach is often associated with authentic culture and creativity (Larkin 2018). This is certainly the case for modern Nigeria, where Internet connectivity, reliance on mobile technology, and use of social media networks have revolutionised the media landscape, specifically impacting on businesses and consumer experiences.

E. Bolat (✉)
Business School, Bournemouth University, Bournemouth, UK
e-mail: ebolat@borunemouth.ac.uk

N. D. Taura et al. (eds.), *Digital Entrepreneurship in Sub-Saharan Africa*, Palgrave Studies of Entrepreneurship in Africa, https://doi.org/10.1007/978-3-030-04924-9_4

Despite sub-Saharan Africa being "one of the least wired parts of the globe" (Poushter et al. 2018, p. 6), social media has increased the level of interest in Internet-enabled services and therefore triggered new business ventures. One such example is Farmcrowdy, Nigeria's digital business-to-business networking platform that connects investors and agricultural businesses in Nigeria (Farmcrowdy.com 2018). Another example is Wandieville Media, a communications agency based in Nigeria that focuses on global development projects around agricultural inclusivity and community development vis-à-vis the educative power of social media networks and new communications platforms (Wandievillemedia.com 2018). Despite catching the wave of crowdfunding businesses and new media agencies a bit later, major Farmcrowdy and Wandieville Media differ from their Western counterparts in their focus on sustainability and social benefits. Farmcrowdy and Wandieville Media aim to increase food production throughout the whole of Nigeria, but most importantly to create opportunities for young people, women, and less developed rural communities. The adoption of new digital media with a social purpose in mind is what differentiates Nigerian new media players.

This chapter reflects on historical changes in global, but mostly African, media, taking into account both business and consumer implications. Much has been written about the impact of new media on decolonisation, political systems and governance in Africa, particularly in Nigeria (Agboola 2014; Ikpe and Olise 2010; Musa 2012; Suntai and Targema 2017). More research has been undertaken in relation to individual media sectoral players, such as Nollywood (Ugor 2009), the press (Hassan and Azmi 2018), and advertising (Obukoadata 2017), as well as the application of new media digital technologies within education (Ogaji et al. 2017) and business (Rowland et al. 2017). The ways in which new media and digital technology have shaped new business practices and experiences of successful and influential African digital businesses have not received much attention in the academic literature. This chapter triangulates three different but interconnected phenomena: it provides a historical timeline of media evolution in sub-Saharan Africa, discusses the democratisation of media and the legitimate status of newest media, and assesses technological and micro entrepreneurship in Nigeria. The empirical part of this chapter explores the experiences of Nigerian new media business players, emphasising their adaptive strategies to global business practices but also the organisational mindset that differentiates these businesses.

Our findings are very much based on the notion of the fictional nation of Wakanda (McDow 2018), which possesses technological superiority with an aim to benefit societies. We discovered that culture and economic demands drive forms of technological entrepreneurship in Nigeria. Despite having made slower progress in the use of the Internet and mobile devices than the rest of the world, sub-Saharan Africa and in particular Nigeria are on a path to lead the new digital media application practices with strategic movements to train people in handling technologies that are not yet in use.

4.2 Historical Timeline of Media Evolution in Sub-Saharan Africa

Sub-Saharan Africa's media evolution can be split into four periods: the imperial era (1800s–1945), decolonisation (1945–1990s), liberalisation of media—phase I (1990s–2000s), and liberalisation of media—phase II (2000s onward) (Cage 2015). The imperial period was characterised by colonial censorship and dominance of the print press as the primary form of mass communication. Indigenous forms of print communication were still practised (from the 1930s), but they represent very much an underground part of the history; nevertheless, they had an impact on nationalistic pursuits across the sub-Saharan region later in the century. Typical stories featured in print are centred around evangelism and the promotion of Western, mostly European, business interests (Cage 2015). The advertising medium and the key messages were very much linked to the popularity of the press media outlets and main content features within the press. However, the advertising industry in the region has not followed the same evolutionary path and economic model as in the rest of the world. In sub-Saharan Africa, where newspapers received hardly any income from advertising, the corrupted state of the print media industry was not surprising. Moreover, the distribution of print media, which included a choice of communication language (not including any African languages) and a high price, historically was reliant on state support, limiting access to newspapers among the population (Cage 2015).

Another widely used and popular medium is cinema, which emerged during the imperial period (Cage 2015). Nigeria in particular was advanced in this field, with its film industry, Nollywood (the name first emerged in the early 2000s), and one of the most commercially savvy film industries globally today (Okome 2017). Nollywood today comprises different subdivisions linked to religious and ethnic groups. The Yoruba-language cinema, for instance, which represents the indigenous groups of the western part of Nigeria, originated in the 1960s during the decolonisation period. Today, with Netflix featuring large numbers of Nollywood films and with the proliferation of social media expanding global viewership, the film industry is increasing its impact, firstly to educate the world about the diversity and cultural differences within the sub-Saharan region, but secondly to improve the economic welfare of the region by seeking investments in training and technological developments for the production and commercialisation of films (Okome 2017). The developments and success of Nollywood are further discussed in the Chap. 5.

The decolonisation period was manifested by the rise of electronic mass media such as television and radio. These forms of media contributed to the spread of nationalism and the desire for independence. Moreover, these are perhaps seen as the most popular mass communication media, as in some countries within the region the colonial and state-owned newspapers were battling against nationalised and privatised radio stations that conveyed content on nationalisation. However, radio and TV still represent symbols of civilisation and power among the sub-Saharan political and institutional elite. TV in particular was used extensively as the main propaganda medium for states and the authorities. Their censorship policies and tactics, however, continued during the liberalisation of media—phase I, when electronic media emerged in the region. During this period most media outlets were either state-owned or at least largely governed by the states, while indigenous and privately owned media outlets that truly embraced political and institutional change remained underground (Cage 2015). During the post-1990s era, newly developed technological solutions such as media transmitting devices (i.e. players), mobile phones, and the Internet gave power and voice to communities that had not previously been heard due to state censorship. Nollywood is one the outputs associated with that period of technological liberalisation: "from its humble beginnings as a 'fetish art' of the jobless youth in the city of Lagos, the Nollywood industry has become one of the most formidable in the world today" (Cage 2015). Today it is the third-largest film industry in the world, with gross income of approximately US$50 million annually (Okome 2017). At the core of Nollywood products today is digital video technology and reliance on social media networks and subscription-based film services such as Netflix. This liberalisation of media—phase II period has enabled the film industry to become one of the mainstream economic contributors, as opposed to being seen as a "shadow economic sector" of media production in the past.

The media industry and players in sub-Saharan Africa have experienced significant transformations since the turn of the century. With historically two African media landscapes, state and indigenous, today we see how the new digital media revolution has created opportunities for authentic and commercially viable ventures that embrace the region's differences and uniqueness, but also connect it with the rest of the world. Media content has changed, moving away from state propaganda to critical and diverse conversations that cover interests and voices of different audiences (Nyamnjoh 2005). Access to international media streams and content is another contributor to the success of the media liberalisation. International radio, the Internet, satellite and cable TV, and social media networking sites such as Facebook have exposed the sub-Saharan population to different sources of information, enabling them to choose and form their own opinions. Wider access to media and content (although still lower than in the rest of the world—the average social media penetration rate for sub-Saharan Africa is 15%, as reported by Hootsuite (2018)) is also very much due to the emergence and use of mobile devices (Donner 2006). With personal and business purposes aligned in the handheld devices, the affordability of smart devices at reasonable prices, as well as the Internet public connectivity infrastructures, media enabled the emergence and growth of micro and technopreneurs who were able to drive historical change in the evolution of media (Bolat 2016).

Moreover, events receiving global coverage, such as the FIFA World Cup 2010, encouraged greater use of social media sites (SNSs) such as Twitter and Foursquare. Across the whole sub-Saharan African region, global digital media giants including Google, Facebook, Blogger, Yahoo, YouTube, LinkedIn, and Twitter are used by youth to share news and media, and to network and blog. This in turn has shifted the focus from state ownership and censorship of messaging and content to active participation by diverse audiences, and today such liberal media outlets are no longer seen as underground but are perceived as legitimate.

4.3 Nigeria's Digital Media Landscape

The historic evolution of media in the sub-Saharan African region is critical for understanding the contemporary dynamics and structure of the media environments. Today, however, with print, radio, and TV media being more and more pushed towards an online presence and content distribution, some countries, such as Nigeria and Senegal, are developing much more advanced advertising industries as well. Digital advertising investments represent half of the overall spending on advertising in Nigeria (Okusaga 2018). This in turn encourages traditional media outlets to diversify their journalism and content, becoming less reliant on state support vis-à-vis state-paid reporting and broadcasting. One of the most interesting phenomena evident in Nigeria is that most journalists today are operating on a freelance basis and distributing content via personal SNSs. Online stories are seen as more credible and exploratory. Needless to say, this credibility comes from authority, as with the emergence of the Internet the Nigerian media industry obtained its very first Audit Bureau, which audits the dissemination and scope of online news (CNBC Africa 2018).

Nigeria is one of the most developed nations in sub-Saharan Africa, and its modern media landscape is undergoing digitalisation with the creation of new opportunities as well as disruptions for long-time players, including newspapers (e.g., 234Next newspaper), TV (e.g., Ndani TV, featuring web-based video content), and advertising (e.g., Wowe Media), and the emergence of new players (e.g., Eskimi and 2go—Africa's own mobile social networking apps and sites) (Imaralu 2012). The first digital media outlets to emerge in Nigeria were blogs on topics ranging from lifestyle to technology to politics. The opportunity to react, comment on, and share blogging content converted social media platforms into a news source. Hence, most media firms in Nigeria operate via mobile apps or websites with chat functions, as these respond to demands for real-time and on-the-go access to news and the ability to react. The ability to react and participate is very much differentiated in the digital media landscape of Nigeria and the whole sub-Saharan African region. The co-creation of news is embedded within the digital media business models today, emphasising the adoption of the sharing economy principle, where We is at the centre of the operational model (Okusaga 2018). This approach has a historical basis in the culture of Nigerian tribes.

Other than news reading, sharing, and co-creation, digital media has created other Africa-specific media players that localise globally available digital services. Despite Facebook and LinkedIn being among the most popular SNSs in Nigeria, new players have emerged that understand the cultural nuances of the region as well as the developments around technological infrastructure such as access to broadband. The emergence of independent media companies and advertising agencies is due to the global nature of digital technologies. However, the growth of specific and localised forms of media practices is due to the domestication of digital technologies. An example of this is the development of Eskimi and 2go, Africa's own mobile social networking apps. They were developed as mobile applications first in order to cater to sub-Saharan Africa's high penetration rate of mobile devices, which were the primary source for Internet access; this represented a forward-thinking approach that was later followed by SNSs with global reach such as Facebook and Twitter. Nigeria is "the most mobilized country in the world with most of the internet traffic coming from mobile devices" (Ventures Africa 2018). In Sub-Saharan Africa we are witnessing the indigenisation of global media (Cage 2015). In Nigeria, Eskimi and 2go provide connection opportunities for largely disregarded groups of people such as ethnic minorities, youth, and women.

In total, 72% of Nigeria's 50 million Internet users regularly visit SNSs—in fact, this is the most popular activity among mobile phone users (Ventures Africa 2018). Using digital devices to search for services, people, and experiences is the second most popular form of new media consumption. However, the digital divide, still apparent across the country, has triggered innovative approaches to omni-channel communication and services provision. In Africa, including in Nigeria, many people own a mobile device but have no data services enabled. Hence it is critical to cater to this context while recognising that demand for digital services is growing. One example of an innovative firm that does support data analytics by incorporating an omni-channel approach is Terragon Group, often referred to as "Africa's digital powerhouse" (Nsehe 2017). Terragon is grounded in the use of its flagship software, Adrenaline, which uses a distinctive mix of Web and non-Web inventory to crunch data and enable access for advertising streams. Terragon essentially built an ecosystem of various media players, including mobile operators, advertising firms, and other media publishing companies, to enable omni-channel data analytics (Nsehe 2017). Partnership and collaboration across industries is also mentioned by Ventures Africa (2018) as underpinning the evolution of digital media and realising its great potential in Nigeria.

It is critical to note that popularity of SNSs shifts audience preferences from consuming centralised largely controlled media outlets (i.e. TV, radio) to using SNSs as main sources of media information. Today, online video is seen as the most accessible content form (Ventures Africa 2018). This and other changes available due to digitalisation are stimulating the growth of start-ups within the digital media domain. According to Karanja (2018), in Nigeria "start-ups raised a total of $63.3 million in 2017", more than in any other African nation.

4.4 Micro and Technological Entrepreneurship in Nigeria

Most start-ups in Nigeria today represent micro and technological entrepreneurial entities. These start-ups and technological businesses play a vital role in national cultural and economic development by enabling employment growth and economic recovery vis-à-vis new streams of innovative solutions that mostly focus on sustainability. According to

Goutam and Rishiraj (2015), technological entrepreneurship is the main driver of economic growth and cultural advances worldwide today. It entails both the application and production of technology. Today, most of Nigeria's micro businesses are heavy users of digital technologies and SNSs that enable them to curate resources and networks. Increasingly SNSs are seen as platforms for building businesses and brands (Goutam and Rishiraj 2015). This is particularly the case due to the accessibility of SNSs, the relatively low costs involved, and the opportunity they provide to scale business up based on the accumulation of network resources. This is in line with the definition of technological entrepreneurship provided in the literature, which according to Siyanbola et al. (2011) involves "identifying technology-intensive opportunities, efficient gathering of resources, such as capital and talents, adapting to rapid growth and changes".

Understanding the technology, but also possessing unique technological knowledge and the ability to forecast technological trends and uses (Nambisan 2017), is what truly sets technopreneurs apart. This is very much evident in the case of Terragon Group. The founder of Terragon Group, Elo Umeh, developed an understanding of mobile technology and digital data analytics and predicted that mobile connectivity alone could enable data gathering outside the Internet-enabled context (Nsehe 2017). This led him to produce Adrenaline and other similar programming software used by businesses not only in Nigeria but across the globe. Because of the technological nature of the business, Terragon Group was successful in diffusing its technological solutions (Giones and Brem 2017). Moreover, Terragon Group's digital solutions made advertising, marketing, and business research easier, widening access and wealth creation. In this example we witness the alignment of technological know-how and customer knowledge.

Despite softer skills being critical in running successful technological or any entrepreneurial business, "technology is the brain behind entrepreneurship development" (Goutam and Rishiraj 2015). However, to date Nigerian technological entrepreneurs' experiences are largely hidden. Hence research into understanding the context (barriers and enablers), with its unique consumption and cultural practices, as well as the resource implications of establishing and running a successful digital media business in Nigeria, is necessary.

4.5 Method of Data Collection and Analysis

Alongside secondary literature-based research, we applied a qualitative multiple-case study method to review six companies representing multiple industries within the Nigerian media sector. The qualitative approach to exploring the experiences and practices adopted by the Nigerian media businesses is applied due to the limited amount of empirical research. Literature around technological entrepreneurship and the adoption of digital media technologies evidences the contemporary nature of the phenomena, which fits well with the case study research methodology (Yin 2018). Moreover, complexity and diversity of media firms in the sub-Saharan region would challenge the conduct of investigation at a larger scale (i.e. via survey). Despite case studies being viewed as a softer research method, a detailed profiling of individual media players will allow us to develop a comprehensive understanding of Nigeria's modern media landscape and enable more generalisable research in the future.

Multiple sources in relation to the six cases have been collected in order to profile the businesses as well as to understand the experience of the people running and working within the selected companies. Technical documentation in the form of website and social media networking site information, companies' annual reports, and online PR content (which, according to Anderson and Warren (2011), shapes public understanding of new media businesses) serve as secondary sources for the research. The primary sources comprise Web-based (using LinkedIn and email) in-depth interviews with key decision-makers, where experiences and associated strategic challenges and gains are the central focus of interviews (key decision-makers provide an overview of the strategic position of the company).

Multiple case studies and accumulated sources of data have been described and analysed using a thematic approach (Fereday and Muir-Cochrane 2006), but following a three-stage coding process where initially scanned interview transcripts are broken down into empirical codes

Table 4.1 Profile of case companies

Case ID	Ownership	Industry	Representative interviewees	Number of employees	Business context	Founding period
C1	Privately held	Advertising	Founder—C11	1–10	B2B	After 2000
C2	Partnership	Games	Founder—C21 Marketing director—C22	51–200	B2C	After 2010
C3	Partnership	Data analytics	Managing director—C31	1–10	B2B	After 2010
C4	Privately held	Non-profit all-inclusive media production	Founder and managing director—C41	11–50	B2B	After 2010
C5	Partnership	Advertising	Creative director—C51	1–10	B2B	After 2000
C6	Privately held	Games	New product development director—C61	11–50	B2C	After 2010

which are then grouped into abstract categories of codes and eventually framed according to much more abstract, theoretical themes (Fereday and Muir-Cochrane 2006; Miles et al. 2013). The study follows a homogeneous sampling strategy geographically (Nigeria, primarily Lagos) and sectorally (media companies), which demonstrates sufficient compatibility of the cases to carry out a comparative cross-cases analysis. However, the heterogeneous sampling strategy is also employed in regard to business contexts (both business-to-business (B2B) and business-to-consumer (B2C)) and the portfolio of products and services (see Table 4.1).

All of the case companies were founded after 2000, with the majority, four out of six, having been created since 2008. Two of the companies (C1 and C5) are advertising agencies, and two (C2 and C6) are games companies, while one (C3) is a specialised company providing data analytics services and one (C4) is an integrated media agency that works with the non-profit sector. All of the companies qualify as small and medium-sized enterprises (SMEs), with three (C1, C3, and C5) being micro businesses. In the following sections, the journeys and experiences of these companies are explored, with the aim to understand the context in which they operate but also the internal resources structure that underpins their survival and success.

4.6 Findings and Discussion

Media Use: Profile and Perceptions

In line with reflections presented in existing academic and periodic literature, all case companies we have analysed deployed various media to develop their unique selling points (USP), meaning the use of technological solutions enabled the product innovations. This is apparent with C2, C3 and C6. All three companies have used mobile applications programming and data analytics software to create its own unique omni-channel management solutions that deliver services using mobile network connectivity. Most importantly, however, all of the companies have used media to build their business capacity, to gain access to resources such as networks and talent, and to promote their products and services—meaning the use of technological solutions stimulated the process innovations. This is in line with existing academic thinking (Goutam and Rishiraj 2015). All the companies have built a presence on SNSs for recruitment and branding purposes. For instance, a new product development director from C6 commented that the company's presence on Eskimi made it possible to search for game developers and programmers:

> It was apparent that traditional send me CV or let's recruit via agency could not work if wanted to build a team we have now. So we just used our everyday network to get access to like-minded people. Eskimi is what I use every day and of course, it made sense to use for talent hunting purpose. Honestly, it is easy, quick and so effective. No need to interview when you have the opportunity to learn about people almost everything you would not otherwise in the traditional job interview. (C61)

Both of the advertising agencies included in this study used SNSs for developing knowledge and conducting competition and product-related research. Social media is an integral resource in most operational activities of these companies. The founder of C1 commented:

> I would not envision our existence without social media. God, it is like flour for a cake without which you can't actually bake a cake—apologies for this parallel. As much as it sounds immature, we spend most of our time on social media searching for ideas, looking into what competitors are up to and of course get inspired. Most of the training today is accessible via social media. I am personally signed up to webinars two or three times a week. I do run my webinars too, occasionally. We no longer live in a competitive world but embrace working together. My agency operates on a freelance basis so I invite content writers for certain topics when needed. How if not with social media I could have pulled off all freelancers I have today. (C11)

Another critical digital technology highlighted by all of the interviewees is mobile solutions, both hardware and software. The founder of C1, commented that if she had not had a phone and all of her creative software next to her anytime, anywhere, she would not have been able to build the business she has today:

> My magic is in here, this small but huge device. I talk to clients, I find clients, I proof creative concepts with it, I pitch to investors and partners—it is amazing how much I can do with this one little box of magic. (C11)

It is interesting that despite the availability of mobile solutions at low cost, all six companies presented in this chapter have invested heavily in establishing their own systems of mobile connectivity-based sharing of data. C1 and C5 have purchased existing solutions, which were later reprogrammed to cater for their company-specific needs and processes, whereas the rest of the companies built their own in-house unique software and programmes.

"Mobile First" Mindset

Other critical comments provided by the interviewees in regard to mobile technology deployment concern the whole mindset of the organisation. In the existing Western literature this is referred to as organisational culture (Zhang and Tansuhaj 2007). Mobile technology is seen as at the heart of new media solutions in Nigeria. The marketing director of one of the games companies (C2) noted:

> Nigeria, as the whole central and South Africa, is not as advanced in terms of Internet penetration. I am referring to a number of users. We are not very much realistic about that but then look at the revolution of mobile tech. Quite frankly I know no other place like Nigeria to be so mobile connected and doing so much with mobile phone—paying bills, talking, sending messages, learning about the weather—even though it is all done via SMS [author's note: SMS stands for short messaging service] or MMS [author's note: MMS stands for multimedia messaging service]. So all we do is to have this in mind. All our product ideas start with mobile in mind, mobile devices, mobile content, and mobile connectivity. (C22)

Continuous learning, embracing technology, focusing on clients' needs, and the flexible and adaptive process of creative thinking and responding to the external environment were particularly stressed as being part of this mobile-first organisational mindset. Within that, a technological orientation is seen as the foundation of individual attitudes towards embracing mobile technology and seeing new ways of catering for the local context in Nigeria.

It was apparent from the interviews that Nigerian media businesses today embrace new media with two elements in place: integration and collision. Integration is driven by the globalisation of the media landscape and businesses' desire to align their own practices to global standards, for example using global SNSs such as Facebook and Twitter, but also to enable business expansion opportunities. Although this was not mentioned specifically by any of the case studies, the cases of Terragon and Wandieville Media demonstrate that practices of using indigenous media present novel solutions for the rest of world, evidencing that technological entrepreneurship is a strategic option for creating a 'born global' business. Collision, of course, is evident in all six case companies, particularly in the adoption of mobile-first thinking. As the scalability of Internet-enabled services and media use is limited, globally adopted technologies and business models have forced Nigerian new media companies to think of localised appropriations and domestication of social and digital media solutions. This is how the mobile-first mindset emerged.

Technological Entrepreneurship as an Enabler of Innovation

All of the companies included in the empirical study can be classified as cases of technological entrepreneurship. As has been shown in the previous two sections, in the context of Nigeria technological entrepreneurship entails both technology application (C1, C3, C4, and C5) and technology production (C2, C3, C6). The integration and collision of media application and usage approaches demonstrate that in the Nigerian context technological entrepreneurship enables both demand-driven innovation (penetration of mobile-enabled services and products) and technology-driven innovation (proliferation of mobile-enabled services and products).

The most interesting characteristic of technological entrepreneurship in Nigeria is its ability to survive without substantial external investments. In fact, all six companies studied mentioned that internal funding opportunities were utilised first and that they were heavily reliant on minimal financial resources at the start. However, the scalability of the business and its further development was made possible by crowdfunding (C3 and C4 used crowdfunding platforms to raise further finances for business growth) and by institutional investors (which C1, C2, C5, and C6 utilised to access the resources needed for strategic growth).

In addition to investments, the following enablers of technological entrepreneurship were listed by all of the interviewees:

- *Technological knowledge* (both generic and specialist skills);
- *Networks*—all of the interviewees commented on the value of extended business and institutional networks due to the historical nuances of media evolution as well as the partnership culture that enables greater benefits for Nigerian society and economy;
- *Talent*—all interviewees commented that available skills are located within Nigeria, with many young specialists obtaining foreign degrees and qualifications and returning to Nigeria to create innovative solutions;
- *Culture*—a common goal embraced by all six companies studied in this chapter is the sustainable and economic growth of Nigeria that brings in better services, provides opportunities to access quality entertainment and media content, and enables development opportunities for youth. This is a unique side of Nigerian businesses—that despite being commercial entities, they embrace social causes as driving forces of the business.

In terms of barriers, the following common themes emerged:

- *Technological infrastructure*—this barrier is inevitable, with Nigeria and the whole sub-Saharan region lagging behind on technological advancements and Internet penetration rates. Moreover, the quality of mobile network connectivity varies throughout the country, leaving many rural areas inaccessible and reliant on fixed network connectivity;
- *Funding*—although the number of funding opportunities is much greater now than a decade ago, the amount of funding available, and

the largely foreign sources of funding, limit the freedom of Nigerian SMEs, creating an atmosphere of tension and corruption;
- *Corruption*—a historical characteristic of most Nigerian business environments (Cage 2015), corruption remains a key concern among the new generation of technological entrepreneurs who, as a result, choose not to accept certain types of funding and therefore miss out on chances for further growth.

The list of enablers and barriers highlighted by the interviewees demonstrate that although the softer side (skills, partnerships, and networks) of entrepreneurship is well established in Nigerian new media SMEs, a key element—technological infrastructure—prevents further growth. However, a particular mindset of integration and collision in turn is the outcome of Nigeria's less developed technological infrastructure, meaning it is this particular barrier that shapes today's Nigerian new media companies, forcing them to think outside the box and deliver frugal mobile-based innovations.

4.7 Reflections on Prospects

New media companies in Nigeria have pioneered technological transformations within a given technological landscape that, with its limitations, presents opportunities for unique and different solutions that set Nigeria's media industry apart from global competitors. The selected companies studied in this chapter have embraced a culture of experimentation, continuous learning, and partnership. Mobile technology is very much at the heart of media businesses in Nigeria, due to its rate and scope of adoption, and revolutionary new media solutions are being translated into innovative practices in the agriculture, oil, and education sectors (Cage 2015). In fact, this raises questions about the impact that technological infrastructure has on technological entrepreneurship, when limitations empower much-needed cost-effective and inclusive services and products.

It is critical to devote more attention to and enrich our understanding of the complexity and structures of the ecosystems within which the explored case companies operate. This has not been done within the remit of this chapter. The interrelation of barriers and enablers can be explored further within the wider ecosystem of the business environments in which Nigeria's new media companies operate.

Collision and integration were identified as complimentary behavioural and cultural strategies employed by Nigerian new media players. This raises the question of how increasing interest from global companies, and therefore requests and pressure for standardised practices, will change the dynamics and media landscape of Nigeria as well as other sub-Saharan nations. The historical period of colonisation brought little technological innovation, economic growth, or political stability to the region. It is critical to reflect on the historical timeline and to ensure that the indigenous approach is given priority in individual privately owned entities and state-owned organisations. Secondary and empirical evidence indicates that only by following this trajectory will the sub-Saharan media revolution generate positive impacts for the people of the region and the globe.

References

Agboola, A. K. (2014). The Influence of New Media on Conventional Media in Nigeria. *Academic Research International, 5*, 105.

Anderson, A. R., & Warren, L. (2011). The Entrepreneur as Hero and Jester: Enacting the Entrepreneurial Discourse. *International Small Business Journal, 29*, 589–609.

Bolat, E. (2016). Business Practitioners' Perspectives on the Value of Mobile Technology. *Journal of Customer Behaviour, 15*, 31–48.

Cage, J. (2015). The Economics of the African Media. In C. Monga & J. Y. Lin (Eds.), *The Oxford Handbook of Africa and Economics: Volume 2: Policies and Practices* (pp. 605–625). Oxford: Oxford University Press.

CNBC Africa. (2018). This is How Many Internet Users Nigeria has and How it Plans to Grow This Figure. *CNBCAfrica.com*. Retrieved September 1, 2018, from https://www.cnbcafrica.com/news/technology/2018/07/04/internet-users-nigeria/.

Dickel, S., & Schrape, J.-F. (2017). The Logic of Digital Utopianism. *NanoEthics, 11*, 47–58.

Donner, J. (2006). The Use of Mobile Phones by Microentrepreneurs in Kigali, Rwanda: Changes to Social and Business Networks. *Information Technologies & International Development, 3*, 3–19.

Farmcrowdy.com. (2018). About Us. Retrieved May 1, 2018, from https://www.farmcrowdy.com/media/team.html.

Fereday, J., & Muir-Cochrane, E. (2006). Demonstrating Rigor Using Thematic Analysis: A Hybrid Approach of Inductive and Deductive Coding and Theme Development. *International Journal of Qualitative Methods, 5*, 80–92.

Giones, F., & Brem, A. (2017). Digital Technology Entrepreneurship: A Definition and Research Agenda. *Technology Innovation Management Review, 7*, 44–51.

Goutam, S., & Rishiraj, S. (2015). Role of Technology in Entrepreneurial Development: Facilitating Innovative Ventures. *International Journal of Emerging Technology and Advanced Engineering, 5*, 239–244.

Hassan, I., & Azmi, M. N. L. (2018). Readers' Preferences for Print and Online Newspapers in Northwestern Nigeria. *International Journal of Academic Research in Business and Social Sciences, 18*, 965–974.

Hootsuite. (2018). Digital in 2018. Retrieved June 1, 2018, from https://www.slideshare.net/wearesocial/digital-in-2018-in-southern-africa-86865907.

Ikpe, E. H., & Olise, F. P. (2010). The Era of New Media Technologies and the Challenges of Media Relations Practice in Nigeria. *Journal of Communication, 1*, 59–68.

Imaralu, D. (2012, September 27). Meet the Co-founders of Africa's Hottest Mobile App, 2go. *Ventures Africa*. Retrieved June 1, 2018, from http://venturesafrica.com/interview-with-the-co-founders-of-one-of-africas-hottest-app-2go/.

Karanja, M. (2018, February 13). Insights from TechPoint Build 2018 and Nigeria's Tech Ecosystem. GSMA (London). *Techpoint*. Retrieved from https://www.gsma.com/mobilefordevelopment/programme/ecosystem-accelerator/insights-techpoint-build-2018-nigerias-tech-ecosystem/.

Larkin, B. (2018). *Signal and Noise: Media, Infrastructure, and Urban Culture in Nigeria*. Durham, NC: Duke University Press.

McDow, T. (2018, February 15). Searching for Wakanda: The African Roots of the Black Panther Story. *Origins: Current Events in Historical Perspective Blog*. Retrieved May 15, 2018, from http://origins.osu.edu/connecting-history/searching-wakanda-african-roots-black-panther-story.

Miles, M. B., Huberman, A. M., & Saldana, J. (2013). *Qualitative Data Analysis*. Thousand Oaks, CA: Sage.

Musa, A. O. (2012). Socio-economic Incentives, New Media and the Boko Haram Campaign of Violence in Northern Nigeria. *Journal of African Media Studies, 4*, 111–124.

Nambisan, S. (2017). Digital Entrepreneurship: Toward a Digital Technology Perspective of Entrepreneurship. *Entrepreneurship Theory and Practice, 41*, 1029–1055.

Nsehe, M. (2017). How Nigerian Tech Entrepreneur Elo Umeh of Terragon Group is Building an African Digital Powerhouse. *Forbes*. Retrieved August 24, 2018, from https://www.forbes.com/sites/mfonobongnsehe/2017/07/06/how-nigerian-tech-entrepreneur-elo-umeh-of-terragon-group-is-building-an-african-digital-powerhouse/#639c26943487.

Nyamnjoh, F. B. (2005). *Africa's Media: Democracy and the Politics of Belonging*. London: Zed Books.

Obukoadata, O. P. (2017). The Challenges and Prospects of the Internet and Interactive Media in Nigeria Advertising Scene. *International Journal of Communication, 9*, 397–412.

Ogaji, I. J., Okoyeukwu, P. C., Wanjiku, I. W., Osiro, E. A., & Ogutu, D. A. (2017). Pattern of Use of Social Media Networking by Pharmacy Students of Kenyatta University, Nairobi, Kenya. *Computers in Human Behavior, 66*, 211–216.

Okome, O. (2017). Nollywood: Spectatorship, Audience and the Sites of Consumption. In S. Monteiro (Ed.), *The Screen Media Reader: Culture, Theory, Practice*. New York, NY: Bloomsbury Academic.

Okusaga, B. (2018). The Nigerian: Evolution, Trends and Projections for 2018. *The Cable*. Retrieved September 1, 2018, from https://www.thecable.ng/nigerian-evolution-trends-projections-2018.

Poushter, J., Bishop, C., & Chwe, H. (2018). Social Media Use Continues to Rise in Developing Countries but Plateaus Across Developed Ones. *Pew Research Center, 22*.

Rowland, W. E., Ifunanya, A. V., Oluwaseun, O. O., Shina, I. A., & Kehinde, A. O. (2017). *Social Media and Entrepreneurship Growth in Nigeria: A Conceptual Perspective*. Paper presented at the 1st Covenant University International Conference on Entrepreneurship (Cu-Ice) 2017, Covenant University, Ota, Nigeria, June 12–14.

Siyanbola, W. O., Aderemi, H. O., Egbetokun, A. A., & Sanni, M. (2011). Framework for Technological Entrepreneurship Development: Key Issues and Policy Directions. *American Journal of Industrial and Business Management, 1*, 10.

Suntai, D. I., & Targema, T. S. (2017). New Media and Democracy in Nigeria: An Appraisal of the Opportunities and Threats in the Terrain. *Brazilian Journal, 2*, 198–209.

Ugor, P. (2009). Small Media, Popular Culture, and New Youth Spaces in Nigeria. *The Review of Education, Pedagogy, and Cultural Studies, 31*, 387–408.

Ventures Africa. (2018). Terragon Releases 2018 Digital Trends Report for Nigeria. Here's What You Need to Know. *Ventures Africa*. Retrieved August 24, 2018, from http://venturesafrica.com/terragon-releases-2018-digital-trends-report-for-nigeria/.

Wandievillemedia.com. (2018). About Us. Retrieved May 1, 2018, from http://wandievillemedia.com/#.

Yin, R. K. (2018). *Case Study Research and Applications: Design and Methods*. Los Angeles: Sage.

Zhang, M., & Tansuhaj, P. S. (2007). Organizational Culture, Information Technology Capability, and Performance: The Case of Born Global Firms. *Multinational Business Review, 15*, 43–78.

5

The Impact of New Media (Digital) and Globalisation on Nollywood

Nnamdi O. Madichie, Bamidele O. Ajakaiye, and Vanessa Ratten

5.1 Introduction

The purpose of this chapter is to contribute to a broad understanding of digital entrepreneurship in Africa from the perspective of the largest film industry on the continent. The chapter traces and highlights the development of the sector over the years and situates that development in the context of digitalisation and entrepreneurship. The Nigerian movie industry (also known as Nollywood) is used as a case illustration of digital

N. O. Madichie (✉)
Centre for Research & Enterprise, Bloomsbury Institute London, London, UK
e-mail: nnamdi.madichie@bil.ac.uk

B. O. Ajakaiye
DNA MediaWorks Nigeria Limited, London, UK

V. Ratten
Department of Management, La Trobe Business School, La Trobe University, Melbourne, Australia
e-mail: v.ratten@latrobe.edu.au

N. D. Taura et al. (eds.), *Digital Entrepreneurship in Sub-Saharan Africa*, Palgrave Studies of Entrepreneurship in Africa, https://doi.org/10.1007/978-3-030-04924-9_5

entrepreneurship in Nigeria. The chapter's contribution takes a holistic perspective, bridging the divide between theory and practice in the sense that the contributors approach the subject through divergent but complementary lenses—that is, academic versus practitioner. From an academic standpoint, the chapter builds upon a paper published in 2010 in which some of the key challenges facing the emergent movie industry were outlined—albeit from a marketing perspective (see Madichie 2010).

Considering the manner in which technological advancements have been made since 2008, the chapter builds upon the limitations and challenges derived from the technological advancements in the sector—with particular emphasis on the creative industry in general, and the film industry in particular. Indeed, this has been one of the key sectors that propelled the country back to the number one spot in a rebased GDP (gross domestic product) exercise a few years ago (see Adibe 2014; Madichie 2015). This chapter, therefore, highlights the impact of new and/or digital media on the sector, spanning three core stages of the film value chain advanced by Bloore (2009) and picked up on by Kehoe and Mateer (2015)—ranging from production, distribution, and marketing of the products (i.e., movies), to the internationalisation of the same. Consequently, the chapter is split into three broad sections—notably digital production, digital distribution, and digital marketing of Nigerian movies targeting both domestic and international (including the Nigerian diaspora) audiences (Akoh 2014; Arthur 2016a, b).

The pioneers of the Nigerian film industry struggled from the late 1950s to the late 1980s to develop a viable and sustainable indigenous film industry, but without much success. The main constraints to developing a viable film industry included at least five key elements, notably (1) the cost of shooting on celluloid and editing, (2) lack of government support, (3) limited investment in the production of films, (4) competition from foreign films, and (5) unwillingness by foreign-owned cinemas in Nigeria to exhibit locally produced films.

The late intervention of the government was not enough to save the film industry from marginalisation in the global film landscape. As Bisschoff (2015) has pointed out, "this economic climate made film-making on celluloid prohibitively expensive, and created a fertile ground for other, more affordable methods to develop". One notable example in this regard is the direct-to-video approach, which cuts out the time-consuming aspects of the film value chain and underlines the short life cycle of movie production that has come to characterise the industry. When the film industry eventually collapsed, television became the only technology-driven platform where dramas could be consumed. In the case of Nigeria, the state, rather than the private sector, owned the TV stations. For example, the Nigerian Television Authority (NTA)—the equivalent of the British Broadcasting Corporation (BBC)—owned by the federal government, was the only national broadcasting network in the country from independence in 1960 right through to the early 1990s. Indeed, the management structure of NTA was initially modelled after the BBC, but was changed when the Nigerian military took over the government in 1985. From personal observations and encounters with Professor Stoller at Bournemouth University, the views expressed in a previous article (Stoller and Wray 2017) seemed to hold sway—that is, that while the BBC is funded "by licence fee and grant-in-aid", the funding structure for and operation of the NTA is completely different, as the latter receives its funding from the Federal Government of Nigeria and generates supplementary revenue from the sale of air time to corporate organisations, independent producers, and advertisers (see Horst et al. 2018 on legacy broadcasters). In collaboration with in-house producers and some independent producers, NTA churned out captivating and engaging TV dramas in the 1970s and 1980s—notably *The Village Headmaster*, *The Masquerade*, *Ichioku*, *Hotel De Jordan*, *Cock Crow at Dawn*, *Mirror in the Sun*, *Ripples*, *Checkmate*, and *Fortunes*, among others. These TV dramas were the equivalent of British TV dramas such as *EastEnders*, *Coronation Street*, *Some Mothers Do 'Ave 'Em*, and *Fawlty Towers*, to mention just a few.

However, it was not long after that the relationship between the NTA and independent producers became strained when the producers demanded better deals. A stand-off with major independent producers led to the wresting of *Mega-Fortunes*, which was the only very popular drama series in Nigeria in the early 1990s. Igwe (2015), for instance, observed and reported, "when NTA made a decision in 1990 to stop producing media content, it released its in-house talent—and, most importantly, its audiences to other operators." These new players included the likes of AIT (Africa Independent Television).[1] It is against this backdrop that the current business model of independent filmmaking (Ferrer-Roca 2014; Kehoe and Mateer 2015) emerged, and this emergence was further accentuated by the dual forces of globalisation and digitalisation. This chapter will address digital production, digital distribution, and digital marketing of Nigerian movies to these diverse and disparate audiences.

5.2 Digital Production

The advent of the Video Home System (VHS) technology was a game-changer following its initial teething problems. The film industry worldwide has always been dependent on and influenced by technology. According to Hayes (2015), "the esteemed Austrian economist Joseph Schumpeter coined the term 'creative destruction' in the 1940s to describe the way technological progress improves the lives of many …" From the 1980s onwards, home video entertainment via video players and VHS tapes started growing with the influx of used imported video players from the Western world to Nigeria, and consequently a significant number of Nigerians started embracing home video entertainment. This new consumerism based on film and digital media-enabled consumption prompted entrepreneurial responses and created a "new breed" of first-movers or early adopters who started shooting home video movies in the country.[2] Indeed, due to the institutional void of quality TV dramas on the NTA's network, audiences gravitated towards home video movies made possible by the introduction of VHS technology. As Jedlowski (2016) points out:

[1] Africa Independent Television, also known by its acronym AIT, is a Nigerian satellite television station based in Lagos. AIT is a subsidiary of Daar Communications Plc, available throughout Africa, and via Dish Network in North America. Raymond Dokpesi. Official website. www.aitonline.tv/news Official Website: http://www.aitonline.tv/.

[2] One of the authors of this paper was a first assistant director for one of the early video movies, entitled *Cocaine Connection*, in 1986.

> The introduction of VHS technologies in the late 1970s and the early 1980s radically transformed the landscape of media production, distribution, and consumption throughout sub-Saharan Africa.

In this context, film production emerged as an affordable and attractive economic activity for an increasingly large section of the local population, and myriad low-budget video film production ventures joined the bandwagon (see Jedlowski 2016, p. 175). However, unlike the government-backed NTA (as with the BBC), the breakaways or digital entrepreneurs had to resort to financial bootstrapping (Lam 2010; Jonsson and Lindbergh 2013; Grichnik et al. 2014; Rutherford et al. 2017) in order to survive and compete for a viewing audience. Indeed, Barnard and Tuomi (2008) described this in terms of demand and supply sophistication, but the advent of the VHS as a "new" consumption medium was only one of the multifaceted technological advancements that characterised the period. Other video technologies that impacted on the Nigerian film industry include Super VHS cameras and tapes, U-Matic video cameras and tapes, the Betacam, and the DV cameras and tapes used for recording movies. In addition to camera technologies, editing technologies also had an impact on Nollywood. When Nollywood started, some NTA producers and editors rendered editing services using the last generation of analogue editing equipment. Soon video equipment rentals and video editing companies were established to cater for the young film industry's post-production needs. With the coming of non-linear video editing software such as Canopus, Adobe Premiere, Apple's Final Cut, Avid editing, and audio effects software and hardware, post-production work greatly improved the quality of Nollywood films.

At the turn of the twenty-first century, Nollywood moved to the Sony DVCAM camera experience, and again one of the authors of this study was among the first Nollywood film directors and producers to use it, to shoot a film entitled *Infidelity* in 2000. Prior to 2000, many Nollywood fans complained about the poor quality of Nollywood films (see Madichie 2010). With the introduction of digital cameras such as DVCAM, Digibeta cameras, and HD camcorders, however, the picture quality of Nollywood films improved, and the audience increased. As Bisschoff (2015) points out, "the industry captures the entrepreneurial spirit of

Nigeria using affordable and accessible technology such as small-scale digital cameras, desktop editing software, and distribution primarily on DVD and video compact disc". The quality of these films could not, however, compare with films produced in the West. The drive to catch up with the West, coupled with the desire to get on the global stage, propelled Nigerian filmmakers to take the next step. Improved video technologies, for example high-end digital cameras such as Red One, Red Epic, and Scarlet, Red weapon cameras, high-end Arri's Alexa camera, Panasonic Varicam 35, Black Magic, and Sony F65 and F55 cameras, which are used in film and TV industries in the West, are now also commonly used in the production of Nollywood films. The most technologically adept Nollywood movies have been produced since 2009. As illustrated in Table 5.1, the quality of films produced from 2009 onwards has made it possible for Nollywood films to break out onto the global stage. Indeed, Bisschoff (2015) further highlights that "these films are seen more widely than standard Nollywood [films] and are accessible to non-African audiences".

Omanufeme (2016) also notes that:

Table 5.1 High-flying videos using digital formats

Count	Title	Year of production
1	The Wedding Party	2016
2	The CEO	2016
3	93 Days	2016
4	76	2016
5	A Trip to Jamaica	2016
6	Fifty	2015
7	Dazzling Mirage	2014
8	30 Days in Atlanta	2014
9	October 1	2014
10	Half of a Yellow Sun	2013
11	Phone Swap	2012
12	Last Flight to Abuja	2012
13	The Assassin's Practice	2012
14	Tango with Me	2010
15	Ije	2010
16	Figurine	2009

> The spread of digital technology has been identified as a growth driver for the film industry and will continue to play that role as domestic and foreign consumption continue to rise. Greater Internet access, increased Smartphone use, and improved bandwidth are also contributing to a production boom.

Regrettably, however, this has only happened recently despite the age of the industry. The next element of the marketing mix is distribution, which has been among the most contentious issues for Nollywood—besides the issue of piracy in the supply chain, there are challenges to the reach for a global audience.

5.3 Digital Distribution

In the second area explored in this chapter—digital distribution—it is worth noting the changing socio-economic environment in the country under investigation. Just like technology, human interactions and movement from one place to another for trade and other socio-cultural activities have continued to evolve. Globalisation has changed the face of the media world in many parts of the globe, including Nigeria, but the Nollywood film industry still has some catching up to do, especially in the context of production. There is also anecdotal evidence that the process of globalisation seems to have only impacted positively on the distribution element of Nollywood films. Interestingly, the opening up of foreign distribution networks for the industry has been driven mostly by Nigerians and Africans in the diaspora, who perceived these films as a means of connecting with their roots and therefore sought to play their part in addressing the distribution challenges of the industry. A case in point is the British-born Nigerian entrepreneur Jason Njoku, owner of iRoko Partners, who helped broaden the distributional base and audience of Nollywood films across the world online. As aptly captured by Soroczynski (2012):

> iRoko Partners, an online distributor of Nigerian movies and music, is working with Nigerian producers and artists to bring their content to the

digital world. The company is the brainchild of Nigerian internet entrepreneur, Jason Njoku.

Addressing the issue of distribution of Nollywood films, Omanufeme (2016) reiterates the above commentary, quoting yet another Nollywood producer and actor, Lilian-Amah Aluko, as follows:

> the rise of Internet use on the continent has helped bridge a little of the distribution problems, as content is also now available online.

Besides Nollywood films "going global"—thanks to Nigerian Internet entrepreneurs—some Nigerians in the diaspora especially in the UK, US, Canada, South Africa, Caribbean, and other investors in other parts of the world are taking advantage of the benefits of globalisation to establish TV stations where mostly Nollywood films are legitimately screened (Onookome and Matthias 2013; Uzo and Mair 2014; Haynes 2016; Zoe 2016; Madichie and Madichie 2018). Examples of these stations include Nollywood Movies UK, ROK TV UK, African Channel UK, Cable channel operators such as M-NET South Africa, and a recent entrant, Chinese-owned StarTime cable channels, to mention a few. Furthermore, Soroczynski (2012) points to the collaboration between iRoko partners and YouTube, "Nollywoodlove", which pumps US dollars into multi-year contracts that go straight to the production houses. This business partnership between a Nigerian film distribution company and a giant American company could be likened to the partnerships between Hollywood studios and British film and TV companies.

Indeed, such border crossings have been attributable to the whole process of globalisation and the cultural exchanges that have accompanied this movement, such that Nollywood films were beginning to enjoy cinema screenings and film premieres in top UK cinemas and other Western countries. Indeed, Nollywood fans had begun to benefit from the opportunity to consume films in the cinemas at least once every two months in London. Nollywood films which hitherto had been restricted to the Nigerian and African communities are now watched by Europeans, Americans, Caribbeans, and Asians—thereby breaking out of their ethnic enclaves. While the positive impact of globalisation is acknowledged, it should also be noted that there are some negative sides to it. This is primarily because of the unintended consequences of the information and/or power asymmetry between behemoths such as YouTube and their local and/or domestic partners. Indeed, anecdotes seem to highlight that YouTube does not deal with Nollywood film production companies directly, but rather goes through the likes of iRoko TV as agent or cyber-mediary. This arrangement does not allow producers to receive royalties for their films. Hence, there is a need to revisit the business model (see Ferrer-Roca 2014; Kehoe and Mateer 2015).

In Nigeria, British and Hollywood films are screened daily in cinemas, but Nigerian filmmakers in Britain have to resort to hiring halls or other venues to screen films. This skewing in favour of the Western world vis-à-vis Nigeria tends to invalidate claims that the "world of films" has become more globalised due to technological advancements (Soroczynski 2012; Madichie 2010, 2013; Chapain and Stachowiak 2017). Indeed, technological advancements, especially in the form of the "D-cinema", an emerging data-driven digital projection standard, have accelerated the business approach of exhibitors who now have greater programming flexibility, having bypassed logistical bottlenecks associated with the physical distribution of 35 mm film reels (see Kehoe and Mateer 2015, p. 98). Evidently, cinema is a supply-led market where exhibitors play the role of gatekeepers for curating entry into the theatrical retail value chain. Over the ten-year period between 2003 and 2013, UK exhibitors increased supply by 40%, with 423 films theatrically released in 2003 (UK Film Council 2004)[3] compared with 698 in 2013 (BFI 2014, p. 14).[4] Annual admissions generally declined during this period, with cinema attendance of 167.3 to 165.5 million between 2003 and 2015 (UK Film Council 2004; cf. Kehoe and Mateer 2015, p. 98).

Furthermore, revenue generated from admissions tended to favour the big-budget films, with the top 100 releases in the UK over each of the

---

[3] The Film Council was set up in 2000 to promote the UK film industry, but was abolished in 2011. https://www.gov.uk/government/organisations/uk-film-council.

[4] Founded in 1933, the British Film Institute is a charity governed by a Royal Charter. It combines cultural, creative and industrial roles, bringing together the BFI National Archive and BFI Reuben Library, film distribution, exhibition and education at BFI Southbank and BFI IMAX, publishing and festivals. The BFI awards Lottery funding to film production, distribution, education, audience development and market intelligence and research. Retrieved from: https://www.bfi.org.uk/about-bfi.

five years to 2013 having taken an average of 91% of gross revenue. Therefore, a greater number of films are now competing for a limited cinema audience, resulting in a squeeze of revenues for independent distributors, and further constraining the commercial viability of these players (Kehoe and Mateer 2015, p. 98). The home video window has likewise become increasingly challenging for distributors. This market's emergence in the 1980s led to it developing into the most profitable segment of the film value chain. However, the home video market peaked in the UK in 2004 with video retail worth over £1.4 billion (BFI 2014). Since 2008, revenues have fallen year-on-year and by 2013 the market had shrunk by 33%, valued at £940 million, its lowest point since 2001 (BFI 2014). A primary force behind this decline is digital piracy (discussed in more detail later in the chapter), which has been driven by increased consumer demand for readily available products led by advances in new media technologies, such as broadband Internet and Web-enabled devices. The trend of declining sales and the impact of piracy are being felt on the high street, as exemplified by the closure of Blockbuster and HMV entering administration (cf. Kehoe and Mateer 2015, p. 98).

Traditional distribution systems are being reconsidered, with questions raised concerning the viability of release windows and, more fundamentally, the appropriateness of exclusivity and timing, upon which these windows are constructed (Ulin 2010, p. 299; cf. Kehoe and Mateer 2015, p. 99). These questions have arisen in response to the rising popularity of new technologies such as broadband Internet and connected devices that play movies (including iPads, Internet-connected TVs, and mobile phones). The release of Sony's PS4 and Microsoft's Xbox One is also significant, as both consoles have repositioned themselves not just as gaming devices but also as home entertainment centres that can live-stream content. Online habits are evolving as individuals spend more time accessing the Internet and consuming content online.

Video-on-demand (or VOD) is a key part of this evolving expansion of entertainment delivery. The UK online VOD market is considered the most mature in Europe, with numerous platforms competing for consumers including Netflix, Amazon Instant Video, and iTunes. There is evidence of this translating into market growth when analysing revenues. This market was estimated to be worth £193 million in 2013, up from an estimated £55 million in 2011 (BFI 2014; Kehoe and Mateer 2015, p. 99). While £193 million is a small return when considered against more profitable windows such as theatrical (£1.1 billion) and home video (£940 million), the doubling of revenue in such a short period suggests there is significant market traction occurring (BFI 2014). Furthermore, the television-based VOD "catch-up" market—where scheduled content can be subsequently watched again for a limited period, as offered by Sky, Virgin Media, and British Telecom services—has risen steadily, increasing by 16% from an estimated £112 million in 2012 to £130 million in 2013 (BFI 2014). Because of these emerging digital technologies, the independent film distribution value chain is being affected by two interrelated movements: (1) a changing relationship with a new type of consumer (known as "active audiences"); and (2) the opportunity to explore new business models that these technologies facilitate. The term "Active Audience" (Gubbins 2012, p. 37) refers to the emergence of a new group of technology-savvy consumers who primarily consume media products via the Internet. This demographic demands personalised online entertainment content—music, movies, TV shows, video games—that entails greater freedom of choice, flexibility, and portability in their media consumption (Pardo 2015, p. 330).

5.4 Digital Marketing

Adopting the definition of Parsons et al. (1998), digital marketing refers to leveraging unique capabilities of new interactive media to create new forms of interactions and transactions between consumers and marketers, as well as integrating interactive media with the other elements of the marketing mix—product/production, place/distribution, pricing, and promotions. It also includes strategies for competitive advantage and value-chain optimisation (see Bloore 2009; Finney 2010; Kehoe and Mateer 2015). Taking the study of Bloore (2009) as the starting point, and as illustrated in Table 5.2, the film value chain encompasses six primary activities (development; financing and pre-sales; production: shoot and post; international sales and franchising; international distribution; and exhibition), and one secondary activity (marketing).

Table 5.2 The independent film value chain

Element	Development	Finance and pre-sales	Production: shoot and post	International sales and licensing	International distribution	Exhibition and exploitation	Consumption
Players	The development stage often lasts longer than other stages and is high risk	This is the most complex stage, where multiple stakeholders (e.g. national subsidy/finance, equity financiers, etc.) have to be made to commit	This is the process of actual filmmaking. There is cost reduction due to digitalisation of production and post-production	Actual selling takes place through film festivals and sales agents	Territorial rights holders, merchandisers, and other distributors	Windows of exploitation include DVD sales, pay TV (satellite and cable), free TV, cinema, video on demand (VOD), etc.	Film critics influencing consumers, Internet and streaming services, online downloads, etc.
Support services	←→ Marketing, Lawyers and Accountants and Consultants						
	Potentially higher risk, long period to return				Potentially lower risk investment, closer to consumer		

Source: Adapted from Bloore (2009). Redefining the independent film value chain. *UK Film Council*

The first stage, *development*, often lasts longer than the other stages and involves a high level of risk. A report in 2007 found that only 18% of films developed in the UK reach production. The money is repaid on the first day of shooting out of production finance, and funders do not usually share much in the final revenue. Some development funding is available from public subsidy bodies, especially in Europe. The second primary activity is *financing and pre-sales*, which is described as the most complex stage of the process, where multiple stakeholders have to be made to say "yes" simultaneously. This period includes "soft pre-production", recces, and casting. The third activity is *production (shoot and post)*—the process of actually making the film. There is some reduction of costs due to digitisation of the entire production and post-production. The fourth activity is *international sales and licensing*, which is the selling of the completed film, and the delivering of it to those who pre-purchased it. International film markets and festivals (Cannes, AFM, Venice, Berlin, MIP, Sundance) provide platforms and sales opportunities for sales agents. The fifth primary activity is *international distribution*, with territorial rights holders. Some distributors only buy a portion of rights for that territory or buy them all and license some to third parties. They may pay for the territory rights (advance), pay for prints and advertising, and then keep a proportion of exploitation revenues to recoup those costs. The distributor in each territory then controls the marketing (a secondary activity) and release of the film, not the producer. In the US studio system, for instance, local national distributors are often owned by the studio, and marketing control is retained. However, there are "spin-off" secondary products and/or merchandising activities, which allows other companies to sometimes acquire these rights, the production of which may have their own value chain. In another study, Crissey (2010, p. 1) describes the "film value chain" paradigm as arguably the most prominent commercial analytical concept to emerge in the global motion-picture industry since 2008. In the context of Nollywood, this chapter observes the next decade from 2010. The film value chain comprises a chain of connected companies and individuals, all working on different elements of the film production and distribution process. Before rearticulating these interactional dynamics, however, it is worth first stating the research approach/design/method guiding the chapter.

5.5 Methodology

This chapter is based on a qualitative enquiry drawing upon a documentary analysis of various secondary sources such as media reports and analyses, a review of the literature, personal/participant observation, and a purposively selected set of elite interviews (see Table 5.3 for a profile of

Table 5.3 Respondent profiles

Respondent number	Elite qualification
Respondent #1	A retired Professor from the University of Nigeria, Nsukka and an external collaborator to the French National Centre for Scientific Research. She is also author of the first Igbo–French dictionary as well as numerous books, including two on Nollywood. She is an expert on cinema and translation
Respondent #2	A broadcast media manager and filmmaker. He has about 30 years' experience in the media in Nigeria, working in both the print and electronic media before studying filmmaking and media at Sheffield Hallam University with a PGD. He is presently engaged as Editorial Adviser to the government-owned Aso Radio and Television Service in Abuja
Respondent #3	Comes from a family of one of the founding producers of the Nigerian movie industry that has come to be known as "Nollywood". A graduate in Dramatic Arts from one of the leading universities in Nigeria, he studied under Nobel Laureate Wole Soyinka and has been a practising audio-visual consultant for over 20 years and exhibits a high level of professionalism, dedication, and commitment. A producer, writer, editor, and director. He also produced and directed the highly acclaimed TV drama series *Bachelors*. He is the initiator of the acting talent hunt programme: Class Act UK. He holds an MBA in Human Resources Management and a PRINCE2 Project management certificate
Respondent #4	A screen writer/producer and a Nigeria Media Merit Award winning journalist. Frontline filmmaker, critic, and former National President of Association of Movie Producers, AMP, he predicted that the Nigerian movie industry would witness a bumper year in 2018, despite the prevailing economic depression in the country
Respondent #5	An independent moviemaker based in the UK. He holds an HND and BA in Media Production and an MA in Audio Visuals, and is currently working on producing a Nollywood feature film

respondents). For the purpose of the elite interviews (Richards 1996; Goldstein 2002; Harvey 2011; Mikecz 2012; Madichie 2013; Darbi and Hall 2014) four broad questions were posed as follows:

1. How would you describe movie making in Nigeria in the last decade?
2. To what extent has digital technology impacted on the sector to position it as a product with a more global appeal?
3. What are the challenges (production, distribution, and/or marketing) for a digital Nollywood revolution? Please elaborate on the most impacted phase, that is: (a) Production, (b) Distribution, and (c) Marketing.
4. What are your suggestions on the way forward?

The respondent profiles are presented in Table 5.3 and the responses to these discussion points were checked against the data from the literature as discussed in the next section—starting with the historical background and running all the way through to what the next decade might look like in the face of globalisation and digitalisation of the sector.

5.6 Discussion of Findings

In this section, four broad areas are covered and the views expressed in the elite interviews are checked against the broader literature on the topic, tracing the trends in the sector since 2008 and culminating in the challenges for the next decade—especially in the face of globalisation and digitalisation.

Description of Movie Making in Nigeria Since 2008

The Nigerian movie industry has evolved since 2008, as the quality of production has noticeably improved. One of the recurring themes from the discussions about the development of the sector was quality. As one respondent pointed out:

> When it started, we were content to film with any sort of camera and without much regard to the quality of filming. But in recent years, there has been a conscious shift to getting the best of available digital equipment. It is my opinion though, that where the industry has gained in technological advancement, it has suffered from lack of adequate stories. Most of the stories from the last decade are more engaging than the stories being told now. (*Respondent #3*)

A similar concern is raised by another expert on the subject who uses terms such as "pedestrian" and "mediocre" in describing the script-writing and production respectively. This respondent describes the development of the Nigerian movie industry as:

> Adventurous, exciting, challenging and growing with inevitable ups and downs like the grave issue of piracy that solution looks hopeless. It is adventurous because the home video era started like an accident, no preparation for it, no training. It was like a plunge into the unknown with sheer optimism. Naturally as it turns out with promises and possibilities, it became exciting. But then the challenges of pedestrian script, mediocre production and the depressing issue of marketing and cinema followed. But today, hopes are still aglow, and Nollywood is marching forward as more cinema theatres spring up. (*Respondent #4*)

> The movie industry in Nigeria … started as an experimental approach to filmmaking, using the home-movie style (direct to video) opportunity [which] has blossomed into a multi-million-dollar industry. The last ten years has seen more job opportunities, more income and less art … That was almost twenty years after it all started with the adventure of *Living 'n Bondage* directed by television producer Chris Obi-Rapu. (*Respondent #2*)

Some interesting themes emerge from the above—accidental development is identified alongside production, marketing, and training challenges. However, the sector seems to have been growing organically, with some notable (or perhaps a handful of) examples having been cited as internationally competitive—such as *The Wedding Party*—and thereby changing perceptions:

> I believe that movie making has improved considerably within the last decade and some of the initial problems such as lighting and poor sound has been tackled. The past decade has produced high grossing films such as *The Wedding Party* (2016) … which grossed 450 million naira locally, so the appeal of Nollywood has increased and is reaching even the "Yuppy" generation, who used to look down on the industry, because the storylines are now dealing with stuff that they can relate to. (*Respondent #5*)

Interestingly, however, the issue of content, rather than language, receives some mention as a main barrier. As one respondent put it:

> the verbal language is usually not a barrier: people are more interested in the content and use the body language of actors and their surroundings as a substitute in order to follow the story. Their keen interest in Nollywood movies greatly helps them to stay tuned to the film, and ensures they continue watching those movies. The public watching films in English/Igbo is usually Igbo, but those from the diaspora or allies without a knowledge of either, usually end up getting some basic understanding of the language (English/Igbo). (*Respondent #1*)

While agreeing that language takes on a lesser significance, another respondent highlights the challenges this creates for marketing:

> The cast and crew of Nollywood are cashing in on their fame in the country, within the English-speaking African countries and Africans in the diaspora. They have helped create a booming industry, which now turns in more foreign exchange than any other commodity apart from oil to Nigerians. Yet, it is faced with exploitation from disorganized marketing approach that leaves the entire industry in the hands of opportunists. There has been improvement in visual qualities helped by the DSLR revolution. However, Nollywood movies are yet to be cinematic. (*Respondent #2*)

From the above, it is evident that the sector has "gone global" against the odds—a manifestation of the duality being explored and highlighted in this chapter—notably, globalisation and digitalisation.

Impact of Digital Technology on Nollywood

Digital technology in the movie and filmmaking sector has had a global impact, and Nollywood is clearly no exception, as was expressed in the elite interviews undertaken for this study. In two specific cases, both involving the production side of the film value chain, the advent of the digital single-lens reflex (DSLR) camera is mentioned:[5]

> The digital evolution has greatly impacted the filmmaking industry in a very positive way. Film equipment has become more readily available in terms of cost and user-friendliness as well as improved quality. With the advent of digital cameras, especially the DSLR range and the use of soft and LED lights, there has been a massive transformation of the filmmaking. Mention should also be made of digital editing. In the days of analogue editing, there was a lot that could not be achieved at a budget rate. (*Respondent #3*)
>
> Digital technology has been the driving force behind the growth of the industry; starting from the first film that was shot on digital video, Nollywood has embraced the changes in the digital world and used it to its advantage. The use of DSLR cameras and other digital means of production brought the ability to make films to the common man, by bringing down the cost of production, and this enabled more people to enter the industry and created other jobs associated with production. (*Respondent #5*)
>
> Nollywood is thriving on the digital train. All aspects of the productions are based on the digital technology, from production to post-production. Nollywood is yet to shoot a movie on the traditional 35 mm film stock. Until a couple of years back, Nollywood was unable to participate competitively in the world-acclaimed African Film Festival—FESPACO—in Ouagadougou, Burkina Faso, because of the direct-to-video approach to production. This has been overcome with the introduction of digital/video workflow at the cinemas there. (*Respondent #2*)

[5] A digital single-lens reflex camera is a digital camera that combines the optics and the mechanisms of a single-lens reflex camera with a digital imaging sensor, as opposed to photographic film.

Nollywood Challenges (Production, Distribution, and Marketing)

The challenges confronting Nollywood are varied and cut primarily across production and distribution. As one respondent pointed out:

> There is still a lot to be achieved in the realm of production, from the storylines to casting and actors, to higher production values. A lot has to be considered before Nollywood can get to its desired place. Distribution is still a major challenge. With the era of cinemas coming back to Nigeria, the ratio of cinema houses to viewers is alarmingly small. Even the DVD or video on demand outlets are inadequate. The lack of proper marketing is a reflection of the general lack in Nollywood. Most productions do not have a serious budget for marketing. They rather rely on basic online presence in Facebook, YouTube, and other social media outlets. Even these social media outlets are not maximised. (*Respondent #3*)

Distribution posed a key challenge as far as digitalisation is concerned. As one respondent noted:

> I think the greatest challenge right now is distribution. No question, Nollywood digital home video production may not be like a Hollywood movie, but the bar is being raised with each day passing. The marketing too is not a critical issue. But it enjoys little investment in Nollywood because of the perpetual attempt to keep cost as low as possible to ensure return on investment and this is essentially due to caprices of distribution. (*Respondent #4*)

Another respondent confirms the above observation:

> The problem facing filmmakers is how to distribute and market before their movie is pirated. Some filmmakers have opted for taking their movies abroad to show in small cinemas before officially releasing it in Nigeria; that way they get to get some of their money back before their movie is pirated. Filmmakers try to get their movies out by cinema screenings, online streaming, and DVD sales. (*Respondent #5*)

To cap the frustrating distribution issue, the sharing formula, which is 50–50% first week, 60–40% second week (in favour of distributor), seriously fractures survival of the producer. Because the number of screens is so few, and the movie is not running for so long, plus the sharing formula skewed in favour of the distributor, the filmmaker lives with a blinking hope. Finally, the online distribution almost ridicules the producer as the pay is pittance and these distributors ask for EXCLUSIVE despite the ridiculous pay. (*Respondent #4*)

In the diaspora, the main challenge at the moment is the supply: kiosks which used to sell VCDs may not be there any more, replaced with TV channels (Nollywood TV). In the UK, the cost of subscription is low, but you cannot choose the films—they are given on a daily programme, and their quality is highly variable. In France, Nollywood films are part of a package which is attached to a particular provider. (*Respondent #1*)

The challenges are many. The biggest distribution line within the country is uncoordinated. It is through bootlegging by shop owners who buy the movies packaged in DVDs from all avenues. The piracy law in Nigeria is not enforced and it is difficult to ascertain who handles distribution in the country. Most major marketers acquire movies from producers and directors through a package deal of bulk purchase. Whatever is done or distributed through unauthorised multiplication is unaccounted for. (*Respondent #2*)

The Internet is not reliable either: after a blackout period, many films have become available, but the choice is not completely open. Then, there is a big security problem: some Nigerian websites offer Nollywood subscriptions, but they may not always be safe, and I personally would not recommend using your debit/credit cards on those sites. American websites are not safe either—I already got debited for items I did not get/approve and stopped transactions with USA. (*Respondent #1*)

Sites like YouTube also provided a platform to reach millions of people, who would have never heard of Nollywood. Today there are streaming sites like iRoko TV, which can be accessed online through paid subscription. We also have social networks, which has revolutionised the way news is distributed. Nollywood filmmakers have become experts at using sites like Facebook, Twitter, and Instagram to promote their films. Digital technology has been hugely responsible for the ability of Nollywood to reach a much wider market. (*Respondent #5*)

There are quite a few other challenges—notably that of training. This is irrespective of availability of requisite equipment. As one respondent pointed out:

> Nigerian crew, mainly derived from the well-trained Nigerian TV background, entered the trade with knowledge of digital components for programme making. It came as a training base for future filmmakers to learn on the job. The opportunities of digital technology, which enabled TV producers in Nigeria to work round the clock producing TV programmes within 24 hours, was extended to Nollywood. Digital technology could be said to have been made for Nollywood and it has advanced its comfort in fire-brigade approach to filmmaking, without the traditional storyboards and others. (*Respondent #2*)
>
> The problem in Nigeria is not that of poor equipment—some of the best filmmaking equipment are in Nigeria—but the best can only be gotten if people are trained properly to make the best use of the equipment. (*Respondent #5*)
>
> The impact of technology is almost unquantifiable. It has inspired more training by practitioners to ensure we keep tempo with cameras, editing, light, and sound equipment. This in turn has raised the quality of production as Nollywood aspires to meet international benchmarks. (*Respondent #4*)

Indeed, there are other learning requirements involved, such as more structured instruction that highlights some historical and scholarly context to filmmaking. Some of these are captured in the discussion around the way forward for the sector, which is the focus of the next section in this chapter.

Suggestions on the Way Forward

There are numerous suggestions for how the Nigerian movie industry should look going forward. These tend to range from making the most of the Internet, support from government, development of cinema houses, and co-production initiatives, as well as formal instruction (courses on filmmaking). Starting with the need to more fully embrace the Internet, one respondent stated:

> More films should be made available on the Internet. If there were secure websites, a subscription would be good. TV channels should offer a wider choice. Lastly, more films should be offered for purchase on DVD, which would ensure quality viewing. At the moment, very few directors/producers agree to sell DVDs of their films, as they fear piracy. (*Respondent #1*)

In terms of the role of government and its much-needed support, another respondent pointed out:

> Nollywood is a big money earner for the country and has done a lot towards promoting the image of the country, and all of this has been achieved with little or no government backing, and I believe that government has to invest in the industry, it has to back the introduction of filmmaking degrees in the universities, it has to crack down on piracy and make the environment hostile for pirates; it can also give tax breaks to companies that fund movies, it can also create film funds that can be accessed by filmmakers. (*Respondent #5*)
>
> I also believe that for Nollywood to develop it has to tell universal stories that everybody can relate, then it can become global; a good story with high production value and universal appeal will always travel. (*Respondent #5*)

However, the role of the private sector is equally as important as any anticipated government support:

> Nollywood will go nowhere unless some critical issues are addressed … Involvement of the organised private sector, OPS, through investment in production and in particular distribution. But they need to see hope and potentials of profit to spur this investment. And this is where distribution comes in. Nollywood also desperately needs more viewing avenues to cut down what is looking like a monopoly now by the very few distributors. (*Respondent #4*)
>
> Regulatory agencies need to wake from their slumber. Pirates are having a wild time and popping champagnes because the agencies are not doing enough, and this has had disastrous effects on such movies as *30 Days in Atlanta*, *Half of a Yellow Sun*, and *Wedding Party 1*, among others. (*Respondent #4*)
>
> Funding … is one of the biggest challenges facing filmmakers all over the world and Nigeria is no exception; the only problem is that in Nigeria

most films are funded by marketers who sometimes impose actors who are not suited for roles on directors, because they believe that they can sell movies. (*Respondent #5*)

A third key element, which is worth highlighting, is related to audience engagement through exhibitions such as cinematic experiences. As one respondent points out:

There are few cinema houses in Nigeria. More than 20 of the 36 states in Nigeria have no cinema houses at all. Perhaps about ten states can boast of cinema presence and yet Lagos with the most of them cannot boast of more than 50. There is the need for industry support from both public and private sector financiers. The entire Nollywood has been driven by adventurous Nigerian youth with little or no help from corporate Nigeria. There is need for investment in the industry. (*Respondent #2*)

On a positive note, the future of Nollywood is very bright. The film world has taken notice of the baby steps that have been taken by Nollywood. The Marvel movie—*Black Panther*—is a positive commentary on the role of Nollywood. There was a determined and deliberate effort to have the actors speak like Nigerians, as well as having a lot of the production design being influenced by Nollywood. Also, there has been some movement in terms of co-production with Hollywood. Once these arrangements kick off, Nollywood will then take its rightful place in the global world of film. (*Respondent #3*)

The greatest challenge which affects both production and marketing is distribution. The number of screens in Nigeria is less than 100. This means that you need your movie to run for a fairly long time to break even. Unfortunately, the competition for space in the theatre is choking. Some movies are therefore easily yanked off less than a week or two after the first day of showing. This apart, it takes more than sometimes five months after producing to find a space at the theatres to show your movies. (*Respondent #4*)

When talking about production, we are referring to pre- and post-production. When talking about pre-production, we refer to everything that happens before the camera starts to roll to the rolling of the camera. The problems still facing Nollywood in terms of production are numerous, but I will elaborate on a few. One of them is acting: a lot of actors in Nollywood tend to over act, forgetting that film is visual, and the reason for this is because at the universities acting for the cinema is not taught,

> what is taught is acting for the stage and because the stage actor, because of the limitations of the stage, has to be vocal and express himself more vocally using dialogue to pass information and sometimes even use exaggerated action, the result is that we have good actors, who are very good on stage but are bad in cinema. (*Respondent #5*)
>
> Another problem is that the universities do not teach film studies or media production and most filmmakers have to learn privately and as a result lose out on a lot of vital information. Most filmmakers have no knowledge of film history and know nothing about great African filmmakers like Ousmane Sembene, or even how certain shots might mean certain things. (*Respondent #5*)
>
> Screenwriters in particular, and other professionals in Nollywood, need more serious and regular training, much more than it is now. Training will do Nollywood a lot of good in terms of exposure and professionalism. (*Respondent #4*)

Ultimately, and based on the above comment, it is clear that training—be it in the use of digital technology or acting for the screen—is imperative for the development of the film industry in Nigeria.

Other Challenges

With the widespread availability of VHS tapes and video recorders, video piracy became an insurmountable challenge for Nollywood filmmakers. While the advent of video compact disc (VCD), digital video disc (DVD), and later the Internet were welcome advancements in technology, they were accompanied by challenges that were not envisaged—that is, the absence of robust copyright laws. This has had consequences, as identified by Professor Dinusha Mendis in her lecture on "An Introduction to Copyright Law and its Application within Media Production"—notably the violation of incentives by unscrupulous elements.[6] Indeed, Bamgbose (2015) reports that:

[6] Professor Dinusha Mendis is Professor of Intellectual Property and Innovation Law and Co-Director of the Centre for Intellectual Property Policy and Management (CIPPM). Dinusha's research focuses on the digital aspects of copyright, copyright licensing, and digital copyright policy

Ironically, pirates have always been ahead in Nollywood because of their dexterity with the technology. It gave them a start on other people's work when the CD and DVD technology came onto the scene in the early 2000s.

The other category of Nollywood film pirates are the ones that operate online. According to Soroczynski (2012):

> Online pirates are uploading content to their sites without permission or payment of due royalties to the producers. They don't charge viewers for access to the hosted movies but make their money off Google Ads that result from traffic generated to their website.

If Nollywood filmmakers, the Nigerian government, and those responsible for drafting and enforcing intellectual property laws work collaboratively, the issue of piracy can be curtailed—thereby redressing the negative impact on the revenue generated through piracy. Indeed, the video technologies that were introduced to Nigeria brought about disruption in Nollywood. According to Kehoe and Mateer (2015, p. 105):

> The impact of digital technology on distribution and consumption value chain activities is transitioning the independent market from supply-led to demand-led. But it is not just the technology that is challenging the value chain since few technologies are intrinsically disruptive. Rather, it is the business models that these technologies enable that create the disruptive impact ...
>
> As new business strategies are adopted, the market may develop in two directions: one for independent distributors based around multiplatform releases, the other for Hollywood studios that continue to use models centred on traditional mechanisms.

However, such traditional mechanisms and/or business models seem to have passed their sell-by date, and especially so in the context of devel-

as well as considering the challenges to intellectual property rights (IPRs) arising from emerging technologies. Her profile is online at: https://staffprofiles.bournemouth.ac.uk/display/dmendis.

oping world economies such as Nigeria, thus prompting the need for optimality as far as business models are concerned. As Kehoe and Mateer (2015, p. 106) point out:

> The search for optimal business models in this new digitally driven market will undoubtedly continue for some time as the market evolves. The film value chain provides an effective framework for firms to re-examine their tactical and strategic operations in a dynamic business environment. In this case, it has acted as a stimulus to identify[ing] the impact of emerging digital technologies on distribution and consumption processes, arguably revealing the beginning of a fundamental shift toward a demand-led independent market.
>
> Consequently, film distributors can now develop alternative release models best suited to satisfying consumer demand, breaking away from the constraints of traditional distribution systems and transforming the relationship between key segments in the film value chain in the process. (Kehoe and Mateer 2015, p. 106).

With regards to the film value chain, the issue of production remains a challenge for Nollywood. As Madichie (2010, p. 632) points out:

> Sound quality is another major product attribute to contend with. While … consumers of Nollywood are not particularly concerned about the quality of the movies, which includes the imagery and sound effects, participants in the focus group tended to indicate otherwise. From the discussions, there seems to be a lurking feeling that the industry needs to "move with the times" and improve on such basic attributes such as sound management.

Another key element of the value chain is that of actually making the film, where time constraints have been mooted as a key factor. As Madichie (2010, p. 634) reported in his findings from 2010, "over 90 percent of respondents rated production as an area of high priority—compared with 70 percent and 67 percent for marketing and distribution, respectively". It was also pointed out that "the good movies did not have to be restricted to only those made in English and a second in the diaspora who still seemed connected" (Madichie 2010, p. 637). Reflecting on the views expressed by the interviewees in that study, two are worth highlighting. The first is the view expressed by a Nigeria-based fan:

> suggestive of the fact that there still exists an interested audience in the domestic market of industry: Let me add that I have also seen some that can be considered nice. I think most of Tade Ogidan's works are quite good, e.g. "madam dearest." Tunde Kelani's works (saworo ide, magun, agogo ewo) are also quite nice although you might not appreciate them because they are Yoruba films (some if not all are subtitled). These films are representative of the rich Yoruba culture and you even have Akinwunmi Ishola (a Professor of Yoruba) featuring in some of them. "O le ku" is another nice one. (Banker, Lagos, Nigeria)

The second provides some indication of the appreciative posture of diasporic audiences towards the improving production quality of some Nigerian movies. According to this US-based Nigerian movie insider (see Madichie 2010, p. 637):

> It seems like most of us have the same mind set on Nigerian Movies. I also do not really watch them, but since my wife is a Nigerian Movie watcher I cannot help but watch every now and then. One particular one that stood out for me was one called "Dangerous Twins," that one is old now since they make almost a million movies in one year. I thought the directing and video effect in that movie was great … They even had the Eddie Murphy Thing where one actor acted two parts and spoke to himself that was cool.

From the above it can be inferred that the speed-to-market is a contributory factor to the bootstrapping business model that characterises Nollywood and constrains its optimal investment in, and deployment of, digital technology.[7] While on a media tour to promote his latest

---

[7] The UK film industry is a valuable part of the British economy, contributing £4.6 billion toward the UK's GDP in 2011 (British Film Institute, 2014). Tax relief schemes have played a major role in driving economic growth by incentivising international investment. This has attracted the six major Hollywood studios (Paramount, Sony, Walt Disney, 20th Century Fox, Universal, and Warner Bros) to invest heavily in the UK.

Hollywood film, *Pacific Rim Uprising*, John Boyega[8] made a stopover in Nigeria in April 2018. Speaking about his ₦8 billion (about US$20–25 million) planned investment in a Nollywood movie, he pointed out:

> It's a chance for me to develop these stories, merge Hollywood with Nollywood, to bring the genuine and most important stories to light but captured in a very important and professional way. (Augoye 2018)

He also reportedly pointed out (see Augoye 2018), "I grew up on Nollywood. The first Nollywood film I ever watched was Blood Sisters with Genevieve Nnaji."

Ultimately, it is worth reiterating that the development of a viable and sustainable indigenous film industry in Nigeria has been trialled with only minimal success, irrespective of the duality of forces at play—digitalisation and globalisation. Key constraints still bedevil the sector—from the cost of shooting on celluloid and editing, to the lack of government support, limited investment in the production of films, competition from foreign films, and the aversion to exhibiting locally produced films in Nigerian cinemas.

---

[8] A British-Nigerian actor, John Boyega, has hinted that he is ready to invest in Nollywood by shooting a low-budget Nigerian movie with about US$20–25 million (N8 billion). Best known for his role in the *Star Wars* sequel trilogy, Boyega states, "We're developing a few Nigerian stories and choosing one which makes sense budget-wise. We're probably looking at an indie budget of 20–25 million dollars … I'm very interested in original Nigerian stories". Twenty-five million dollars may seem like a "low budget" compared with his latest *flick*, Pacific Rim Uprising, which has a budget of US$150 million. But in Nollywood, where budgets are a tiny fraction of that, a movie budget of N8 billion is no doubt a record-breaker. He recently held talks with Marvel bosses about a potential role in the Marvel Cinematic Universe and added that the funds he hopes to inject into the project is an opportunity to tell Nigerian stories in a professional way. See also: YouTube (5 April 2018), "John Boyega Plans on Producing Nigerian Stories for The Big Screen" | Pulse TV. Retrieved from: https://youtu.be/jJiM5bJqtBo.

5.7 Conclusions

The main focus of this chapter has been to highlight the place of Nollywood as a film industry in the context of technological and digital advancements. The chapter is unique in several ways. Firstly, the authors approach the subject through different lenses—practitioner versus academic. Secondly, and from an academic standpoint, the chapter builds upon a paper published almost a decade ago in 2010 where some of the key challenges facing the emergent movie industry were outlined. Thirdly, the chapter builds on the aforementioned study by acknowledging how technological advancements have impacted upon every sphere of the Nigerian economy with a particular emphasis on the creative industry, which has been one of the key sectors propelling the country back to the number one spot in a rebased GDP exercise. Overall, the main contribution of this chapter is its coverage of the entire movie value chain from the production, distribution, and marketing of the movies, to the internationalisation of the cultural product. Consequently, the chapter is split into three broad groups—notably digital production, digital distribution, and digital marketing of Nigerian movies to both the domestic and international (including the Nigerian diaspora) audiences.

References

Adibe, J. (2014). MINT, Re-based GDP and Poverty: A Commentary on the Identity Crisis in Africa's Largest Economy. *African Journal of Business and Economic Research, 9*(1), 119–134.

Akoh, B. (2014). The Cost of Deploying a Successful Video Broadband Business in Africa and the Cost of Not Deploying: Domestic and Transborder Implications and Applications. In *Broadband as a Video Platform* (pp. 51–65). Cham: Springer.

Arthur, T. (2016a). *The Reimagined Paradise: African Immigrants in the United States, Nollywood Film, and the Digital Remediation of 'Home'.* Doctoral dissertation, Bowling Green State University.

Arthur, T. (2016b). Nollywood Afrogeeks: Nigerian Cinema, Digital Diasporas, and African Immigrants in the United States. *International Journal of E-Politics, 7*(3), 49–64.

Augoye, J. (2018, April 4). Hollywood Actor John Boyega Plans N8 Billion Nollywood Movie. *Premium Times*. Retrieved April 15, 2018, from https://www.premiumtimesng.com/entertainment/nollywood/264041-hollywood-actor-john-boyega-plans-n8-billion-nollywood-movie.html.

Bamgbose, T. (2015). *For Every Copy Sold, Nine are Fake. Can Nollywood Beat Piracy?* [Online]. Retrieved March 13, 2017, from https://www.trueAfrica.com.

Barnard, H., & Tuomi, K. (2008). How Demand Sophistication (De-)limits Economic Upgrading: Comparing the Film Industries of South Africa and Nigeria (Nollywood). *Industry and Innovation, 15*(6), 647–668. https://doi.org/10.1080/13662710802568986.

Bisschoff, L. (2015). *From Nollywood to New Nollywood: The Story of Nigeria's Runaway Success* [Online]. Retrieved March 13, 2017, from http://theconversation.com.

Bloore, P. (2009). Re-defining the Independent Film Value Chain. *UK Film Council*. Retrieved from http://www.bfi.org.uk/sites/bfi.org.uk/files/downloads/redefining-the-independent-film-value-chain.pdf.

British Film Institute. (2014, April 24). UK Film's Contribution to UK GDP over £4.6b. Retrieved from https://www.bfi.org.uk/news/uk-film-s-contribution-uk-gdp-over-46b.

Chapain, C., & Stachowiak, K. (2017). Innovation Dynamic in the Film Industry: The Case of the Soho Cluster in London. In *Creative Industries in Europe* (pp. 65–94). Cham: Springer.

Crissey, J. (2010). Any Value in the Chain. *Unpublished Working Paper*. Retrieved from https://www.academia.edu/637947/Any_value_in_the_chain

Darbi, W. P. K., & Hall, C. M. (2014). Elite Interviews: Critical Practice and Tourism. *Current Issues in Tourism, 17*(9), 832–848.

Ferrer-Roca, N. (2014). Business Innovation in the Film Industry: A New Zealand Case Study. In R. DeFillippi & P. Wikström (Eds.), *International Perspectives on Business Innovation and Disruption in the Creative Industries: Film, Video, and Photography* (pp. 18–36). Cheltenham, UK: Edward Elgar Publishing.

Finney, A. (2010, June). Value Chain Restructuring in the Global Film Industry. In *4th Annual Conference on "Cultural Production in a Global Context: The Worldwide Film Industries"*. Grenoble, France: Grenoble Ecole de Management.

Goldstein, K. (2002). Getting in the Door: Sampling and Completing Elite Interviews. *PS: Political Science & Politics, 35*(4), 669–672.

Grichnik, D., Brinckmann, J., Singh, L., & Manigart, S. (2014). Beyond Environmental Scarcity: Human and Social Capital as Driving Forces of Bootstrapping Activities. *Journal of Business Venturing, 29*(2), 310–326.
Gubbins, M. (2012). Digital Revolution: Active Audiences and Fragmented Consumption. In *Digital Disruption: Cinema Moves On-line* (pp. 67–100). St Andrews: St Andrews Film Studies.
Harvey, W. S. (2011). Strategies for Conducting Elite Interviews. *Qualitative Research, 11*(4), 431–441.
Hayes, A. (2015). *20 Industries Threatened by Tech Disruption* [Online]. Retrieved March 12, 2017, from http://www.investopedia.com/article/investing/020615/20-industries-threatened-tech-disruption.asp#ixzz4awiTOxli.
Haynes, J. (2016). *Nollywood: The Creation of Nigerian Film Genres*. Chicago: University of Chicago Press.
Horst, S. O., Murschetz, P. C., Brennan, D. N., & Friedrichsen, M. (2018). TV Film Financing in the Era of "Connected TV": How Do "Legacy" Broadcasters Respond to Market Changes? In *Handbook of State Aid for Film* (pp. 615–633). Cham: Springer.
Igwe, C. (2015). *Nollywood: Second Largest Film Industry* [Online]. Retrieved March 12, 2017, from https://www.britishcouncil.org/voices-magazine/nollywood-second-largest-film-industry.
Jedlowski, A. (2016). Studying Media "From" the South: African Media Studies and Global Perspectives. *Black Camera: An International Film Journal, 7*(2), 174–193.
Jonsson, S., & Lindbergh, J. (2013). The Development of Social Capital and Financing of Entrepreneurial Firms: From Financial Bootstrapping to Bank Funding. *Entrepreneurship Theory and Practice, 37*(4), 661–686.
Kehoe, K., & Mateer, J. (2015). The Impact of Digital Technology on the Distribution Value Chain Model of Independent Feature Films in the UK. *International Journal on Media Management, 17*(2), 93–108. https://doi.org/10.1080/14241277.2015.1055533.
Lam, W. (2010). Funding Gap, What Funding Gap? Financial Bootstrapping: Supply, Demand and Creation of Entrepreneurial Finance. *International Journal of Entrepreneurial Behavior & Research, 16*(4), 268–295.
Madichie, N. (2010). The Nigerian Movie Industry "Nollywood"—A Nearly Perfect Marketing Case Study. *Marketing Intelligence & Planning, 28*(5), 625–649.
Madichie, N. (2013). An Interview with Chidi Mokeme—Chief Executive Officer of Renegade Group, Chidi Mokeme Foundation & The GQ

Wearhouse. Executive Opinion. *African Journal of Business and Economic Research, 8*(1), 163–167.
Madichie, N. (2015). A Commentary on African Business & Economic Environment in 2015. *African Journal of Business and Economic Research, 10*(1), 5–24.
Madichie, N., & Madichie, C. (2018). *Changing Dynamics of Migrant Entrepreneurial Activities: Implications for the African Diaspora and the UN SDGs*. Paper presented at the Migration, Inter-Connectivity and Regional Development (MICaRD) Symposium. Regional Studies Association, University of Lincoln, April 26. SSRN. Retrieved from https://papers.ssrn.com/sol3/papers.cfm?abstract_id=3170064.
Mikecz, R. (2012). Interviewing Elites: Addressing Methodological Issues. *Qualitative Inquiry, 18*(6), 482–493.
Omanufeme, S. (2016). *Runaway Success—Finance & Development* [Online]. Vol. 53, No. 2. Retrieved March 12, 2017, from http://www.imf.org/external/pubs/ft/fandd/2016/06/omanufeme.htm.
Onookome, O., & Matthias, K. (2013). *Global Nollywood: The Transnational Dimensions of an African Video Film Industry*. Bloomington, IN: Indiana University Press.
Pardo, A. (2015). From the Big Screen to the Small Ones: How Digitization is Transforming the Distribution, Exhibition and Consumption of Movies. In *Besides the Screen* (pp. 23–45). London: Palgrave Macmillan.
Parsons, A., Zeisser, M., & Waitman, R. (1998). Organizing Today for the Digital Marketing of Tomorrow. *Journal of Interactive Marketing, 12*(1), 31–46.
Richards, D. (1996). Elite Interviewing: Approaches and Pitfalls. *Politics, 16*(3), 199–204.
Rutherford, M. W., Pollack, J. M., Mazzei, M. J., & Sanchez-Ruiz, P. (2017). Bootstrapping: Reviewing the Literature, Clarifying the Construct, and Charting a New Path Forward. *Group & Organization Management, 42*(5), 657–706.
Soroczynski, V. (2012, November 12). *Nollywood 2.0: How Tech is Making Africa's Movie Industry a Global Leader*. Retrieved from http://ventureburn.com/2012/11/nollywood-2-0-how-tech-is-making-africas-movie-industry-a-global-leader/.
Stoller, T., & Wray, E. (2017). 1984 and All That: The Impact of Political Change on Independent Radio in the UK. *Communication Journal of New Zealand, 11*(1), 22–36.

UK Film Council. (2004). *UK Film Council Statistical Yearbook: Annual Review 2003/4*. Retrieved from http://www.bfi.org.uk/sites/bfi.org.uk/files/downloads/uk-film-council-statistical-yearbook-annual-review-2003-2004.pdf.

Ulin, J. (2010). *The Business of Media Distribution: Monetizing Film, TV, and Video Content in an Online World*. Burlington, MA: Focal Press.

Uzo, U., & Mair, J. (2014). Source and Patterns of Organizational Defiance of Formal Institutions: Insights from Nollywood, the Nigerian Movie Industry. *Strategic Entrepreneurship Journal, 8*(1), 56–74.

YouTube. (2018, April 5). John Boyega Plans on Producing Nigerian Stories For The Big Screen | Pulse TV. Retrieved from https://youtu.be/jJiM5bJqtBo.

Zoe, F. (2016). *How Technology Revolutionising Africa Entertainment Industry, Film Industry* [Online]. Retrieved March 08, 2017, from https://www.theguardian.com/world/2016/aug/06/how-technology-revolutionising-africa-entertainment-industry-film-tv.

Part IV

Animation and Games: Unlimited Opportunities for Exploration

6

Shifting Cultural Capital: Kenyan Arts in Digital Spaces

Paula Callus

6.1 Shifting Cultural Capital: Kenyan Arts in Digital Spaces

The discourse on African arts has, in the past, been framed by a dialectic between earlier traditions and practices (Kasfir 1999) and contemporary modes that face the problematic question of 'authenticity' (Oguibe and Enwezor 1999). More recently, scholars such as Bischoff (2017) and Bristow (2017) have recognized the emergence of so-called African digital arts, in a context where 'Africa has certainly embraced new technologies, as is prevalent in the rising statistics of mobile phone, smartphone and Internet usage in many parts of the continent' (Bischoff 2017, p. 261).

Alongside this, a growing discussion of the impact of digital tools and technology in the arts and culture in general has moved beyond earlier ontological concerns to socio-political aspects of how these are

P. Callus (✉)
Bournemouth University, Bournemouth, UK
e-mail: PCallus@bournemouth.ac.uk

N. D. Taura et al. (eds.), *Digital Entrepreneurship in Sub-Saharan Africa*, Palgrave Studies of Entrepreneurship in Africa, https://doi.org/10.1007/978-3-030-04924-9_6

'dramatically transforming traditional curatorial practice and by extension archival practice, so that we are moving from a gatekeeping model to an open model steeped in digital relationships across global networks and the Internet' (Giannini and Bowen 2016, p. 237).

This chapter focuses on how digital technology impacts further on this discourse by challenging the cultural capital that is typically associated with curatorial practice, the gallery, and the marketplace (Bourdieu 1986) and how digital art practices can challenge notions of authenticity in the discourse on African art. Through a range of cases of Kenyan multi-media artists that operate virtually and physically, and stakeholders such as bloggers, the chapter seeks to identify whether a shift in cultural capital is emerging from popular and subcultural online spaces and the interactions that these bring about.

6.2 Technological Geographies

In the context of the African continent, digital technologies have impacted on many facets of social, economic, and political life including creative and cultural spaces. The impact of the computer and ICT in various sub-Saharan countries, in particular South Africa, Kenya, Nigeria, Ghana, Zimbabwe, and Rwanda, can be seen at face value by the rising presence of users in the digital communications virtual space (The World Bank 2013, p. 8) and an overall rise in Internet usage, from 0% in 1990 to 14.8% in 2012, among the population of the sub-Saharan region.

While it is easy be optimistic about the developmental potential associated with ICTs, it is also important to identify at this stage that access to these technologies is still limited to proportionally few. Even with a measurable growth in access to mobile phones, many people are still disadvantaged and consider access to Facebook a luxury (Wyche et al. 2013). In addition, there remains an ongoing digital divide between the West and various African countries. In the year 2000, for instance, it was noted that 'out of the estimated 300 million computers in the world, only one per cent of them are in Africa' (Mbogo 2000, p. 128). The extent of this digital divide was captured more recently in 2018 in the photograph that paradoxically went viral on social media, of Richard Appiah Akoto, a

Ghanaian teacher, using a blackboard to teach software as he faced a 'discouraging dilemma. His students need to pass a national exam that includes questions on information and communication technology (ICT)—but the school hasn't had a computer since 2011' (Mezzofiore 2018).

The digital divide remains closely linked to social, political, and economic factors (Guillén and Suárez 2005), and consequently positions the West as central and developing countries as peripheral, such as in 'dependency and world-system' types of research. In the discussion of any activity that is connected to digital technology, optimism can be misplaced, if one considers for example that in Kenya, outside of the major cities such as Nairobi, Kisumu, and Mombasa, the infrastructure necessary to support the growth in interaction with these technologies is lacking.

In 2013, while over 70% of the Kenyan population had subscribed to mobile phones, only 7.9% of households had access to a computer and only 20% of Kenyans had access to electricity (Nyabuga and Booker 2013). That said, as Bristow identifies, urban spaces across different African countries are becoming sites of innovation in communication technologies as their economies undergo rapid changes (Bristow 2014, p. 333). In Nairobi, for example, the introduction of M-Pesa, the mobile banking system, the appearance of technology hubs such as iHub, and online content providers such as BuniTV and SlumTV, are all examples of a shift in the engagement with technology from a production and reception perspective.

Kenya performs particularly well in terms of technology hubs: in 2016 it was in the top five countries in Africa, with the total number of hubs amounting to 27 (GSMA 2016). In Mombasa, the hub SwahiliBox was set up in 2015 for 'socio-economic technology empowerment' and, like other spaces of this kind, acts as a knowledge-building space, 'training members on how to code, set up websites, or effectively use social media to promote their work' (Dahir 2017). For the purpose of this discussion, many of the Kenyan artists discussed here work within these urban spaces, tend to be technologically dexterous, and have access to the infrastructure that enables them to work within a digital context.

One of the contributing factors to this change in the technological landscape is the investment in mobile phone infrastructure and access to the Internet. In 2011, the Ford Foundation report on the impact of digital communications on media and human rights in Africa, *A New Frontier, An Old Landscape*, highlighted an important change in access to the Internet. In six of seven African countries it examined, mobile broadband subscriptions notably surpassed fixed broadband subscriptions, and correlated to the economic status of different groups within the population. These specific technologies have impacted on media practices across a range of fields including community radio, journalism, and broadcasting.

For example, in 2007, capitalizing on mobile phones and GPS (Global Positioning System), the Ushahidi software (developed by Kenyan entrepreneurs Juliana Rotich, Eric Hersman, Ory Okolloh, and David Kobia) allowed ordinary citizens to use their devices to map and record areas of trouble during post-election violence.[1]

Following this watershed moment, civil society activists took to digital spaces to blog, report, and campaign on local socio-political issues. In the entertainment and creative industries, this widespread adoption of mobile phones and related access to the Web in Kenya has lent itself to the cross-fertilization of digital artists, designers, computer animators, and programmers, namely those working in the app development industry. Companies such as Leti Arts, Avandu, and Black Division Games are producing a range of creative content including comics, animations, and mobile phone games (Callus and Potter 2017).

Occasionally these games also have socio-political resonances, such as *The Election Thief* (2013) by University of Games, designed as a multi-level platform 2D game, developed for mobile phone platforms as an Android app. The game features Omu, an ordinary citizen whose goal is to catch the 'election thief' who has stolen votes during an election. Conversely, independent contemporary artists such as Michael Soi from the GoDown Arts Centre (whose work tends to be mostly political painting) also capitalize on these technologies and the access they give to a

[1] The use of these technologies does not always result in positive social activism, as Nyabuga and Booker mention in the report *Mapping Digital Media Kenya* (2013): some of the 'violence was blamed on the use of mobile telephony to mobilize tribal vigilante groups' (2013, p. 10).

range of digital networked spaces to promote their work, announce exhibitions, or sell designer handbags.

Most of these 'prod-users' (Bruns 2007) pursue dynamic online activities that run alongside their own practice, where they deploy other content such as illustrations, drawings, or photographs on Instagram, animations and videos on YouTube, and multi-media content on social networking groups. These creative interjections are not usually seen to be aligned with the body of work called 'art'. They belong to spaces of popular culture and challenge the official paradigms.

6.3 But Is It 'Authentic'?

The discussion of art from Africa has often been framed by paradigms of 'craft/art, functional/aesthetic, traditional/contemporary, rural/urban' but as John Picton (1999, p. 122) has argued, these structures are in fact untenable as they foreground invented categories and are based on preconceptions about so-called African art. The legacy of these stereotypes is still felt, as to talk of technology and art from Africa still flies in the face of most people's preconceptions. As Hamilton has argued, tendencies to disqualify Africa from claims of technological invention and innovation dominate in favour of a discourse of tradition; additionally, 'this tendency has more to do with the validity and prosperity of art markets as they traffic in authenticity and tradition (almost fetishizing the possibility) and the stubborn persistence of imposing a chronologically driven canon upon African art' (Hamilton 2017, p. 18).

Questions of cultural authenticity and appropriation are compounded in digital contexts where fixed geographies of North/South collapse and images, sounds, and text move fluidly and with ease across great distances for those who have access to these technologies. Who determines what is considered 'authentic'? How does curatorial practice determine what is collected and displayed? Which bits and bytes of data become collectively valued and on whose terms? The conventional presumption is that curators and experts carry the cultural and social capital that empowers them to perform as gatekeepers, legitimizing artists' work and framing it as valuable (Bourdieu 1986), but what happens when technology intervenes in institutionalized knowledge?

In 2015, when the *Making Africa: A Continent of Contemporary Design* exhibition was launched at the Vitra Design Museum, it set out to specifically address and challenge the tropes of recycling, 'traditional' crafts, and humanitarian design, and included creative outputs that engaged with digital media in all its formats. Its focus upon the digital was notable:

> The exhibition focuses on a new generation of entrepreneurs, thinkers and designers from and within Africa, who—as "digital natives"—address a global audience and provide the world with a new vantage point on their continent. (Making Africa 2018)

Included among the artists and designers presented at this exhibition were Kenyan artists Jim Chuchu from The Nest and previously a member of Just a Band; Wangechi Mutu with her video piece *The End of Eating Everything* (2010); filmmaker/writer Wanuri Kahiu and the science fiction film *Pumzi* (2009); Sam Hopkins, co-founder of Slum TV; digital artist Jepchumba's website/archive *AfricanDigitalArt*; and game designer Wesley Kirinya from Leti Arts games. This exhibition was interesting in that it collected and combined objects of art and design in the same space. The type of real or virtual objects included in this collection challenged curatorial practice and suggested a change in the engagement with technology and media and the arts in Kenya.

Two years later, The Nest published a book titled *Not African Enough*. This publication is a response that seeks to speak back, in image and text, to the 'derogatory comment of 'Not African Enough' that is frequently put to African designers. It illustrates the ongoing challenges that many African artists face as they create work that cannot be neatly be categorized into according to the typical so-called African tropes, or clearly differentiated from other forms of contemporary art. In a video interview for the *Making Africa* exhibition, Chuchu from The Nest states, 'the idea of un-African things is very interesting, because it supposes the idea of what is African is set in stone somewhere' (Chuchu 2015).

Chuchu identifies that there is a persistent expectation of exoticized notions of the 'African' aesthetic that continues to plague artists from different African countries. Since 2008, as a member of Just a Band and later as co-founder of The Nest, Chuchu has engaged in a range of work that sits in liminal spaces, straddling popular culture and fine art, merging filmmaking with fashion and design, photography and digital painting. This portfolio of work illustrates an ongoing conversation that Chuchu and other Kenyan artists have with framing identities, futures, and reimagined pasts.

The photographer Osborne Macharia, for example, challenges stereotypes of Africa by playing with fantasy to create new fictions in his photographs. He frequently reimagines casts of characters: Kenyans with dwarfism as fighters that could have found themselves in a *Mad Max* (2015, 1985, 1980, 1979) setting, as in the *Mengo* series; old men as trendy hipsters from a 1980s hip-hop group in the *Kabango* series; or the old women from Kenya's League of Extravagant Grannies who were once corporate and government leaders in the 1970s but are now retired in *Nyane* (Macharia 2018b). He also challenges the establishment, as his pictures take on the aesthetic of fashion photography and feel like they belong inside a magazine. The photographs are also a clear engagement with digital technologies and related practices as they often deploy aesthetics such as HRDI (High Dynamic Range Imaging).[2] Like Chuchu, Osborne Macharia is a digital native, and his work is visible on his own studio website, Instagram account, Facebook, and Twitter account. Additionally, he is also visible in front of the camera in a number of Vimeo interviews and making-of videos that profile his work.

In the work of Kenyan animators and game designers, we find technology surfacing within science fiction settings with the likes of Andrew Kaggia's political animation *Waguezi 2012* (2011), with Kenya's political figureheads as robotic transformers engaged in battle, and *Nairobi X* (2015), a 3D computer game set in Nairobi where the player is a soldier

[2] High Dynamic Range Imaging is a digital photography technique that improves the range of colour and luminosity in an image by capturing a range of exposures within a single image. This process is only possible using digital cameras.

defending the city from an alien invasion. Similarly, illustrators and designers at Avandu created a platform game (for mobile phones) called *Operation Mlinzi* (2015), referencing 'old-school space invaders aesthetics' where the player is a member of the Kenyan Air Force defending the city, and Salim Busuru (from Avandu) has an ArtStation online profile (Busuru 2018) with a collection of illustrations that recast African superheroes, such as the young Jedi from the Congo. These examples straddle a range of cultural spaces, on the one hand referencing American franchises such as Transformers, Star Wars or Space Invaders, and at the same time locating the image firmly as Kenyan. They illustrate the issues around transnational aesthetics; whether one would speak of these as 'authentic' or as 'art' for that matter, alludes to the ontological difficulties that still connect to the discourse on new media and art (Fig. 6.1).

Conventional classifications of media formats are increasingly difficult to differentiate in a digital context, and for this reason they also compound previously separate cultural and artistic spaces. As we have seen in the earlier examples, the range of aesthetic influences attest to the connected and networked environment within which these artists operate and the challenges they face as they respond to 'Not African Enough'.

Digital art practice necessitates convergences: photography, video, sound, painting, drawing, text, graphic design, and even coding and programming become part of the digital artist's skill set. The Nest offer an example of this dexterity: as self-described 'multi-disciplinary artists' their works include film projects, fashion and visual arts projects, music projects, and literature projects. In some of these cases their short films begin life online, such as the surreal fashion film *To Catch a Dream* (2014), a collaboration between The Nest and fashion designer Chico Leco. This short film is free to view on Vimeo as is other content, such as the online series *Tuko Macho* (2016), a neorealist portrayal of Kenya's crime and vigilante justice, and *We Need Prayers* (2017), a parody series that was produced for online viewing.

In an episode on contemporary African art from the series *We Need Prayers* (2017), The Nest goes about critically engaging and confronting us with the problems that arise from discrete classifications in the arts (see

Fig. 6.1 Young Jedi from the Congo, by Salim Busuru (2018)

Fig. 6.2). The Nest revisits the discourse of authenticity as it critiques and illustrates the politics of contemporary international art and its connections to global currency through parody and humour. In this version, the discourse is no longer that of 'traditional/ contemporary' or 'art/craft', but a discourse of 'Afro-futurism' that is deployed to speak of current trends in contemporary African art. In *We Need Prayers: This One Went to Market* (2018) we meet a fictional character, Kui Ngirachu, a young Kenyan artist who is trying to make it as an international artist. The film begins with a behind-the-scenes take of her in conversation with a photographer as she poses for her so-called Afro-futurist piece. She references the Western fascination with this term while ridiculing it as she deploys the expert's'

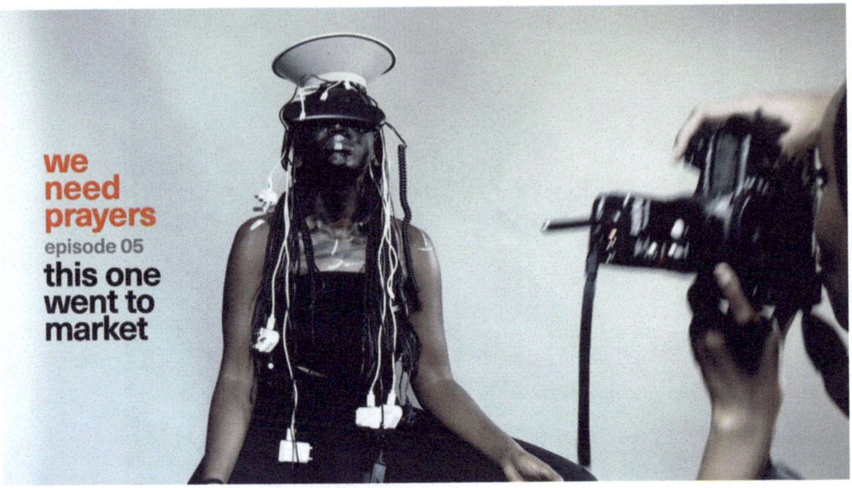

Fig. 6.2 Poster for *We Need Prayers* (2018) by The Nest. Reprinted with permission from The Nest Collective

language. This same language is used to validate her work, which in the film leads her to eventual success. The witty video was uploaded on Vimeo, YouTube, and Facebook with a description that read:

> WE NEED PRAYERS 05—How far are you willing to go for your hustle? In this week's episode, a young Kenyan visual artist comes up with a sly plan to take over the art world abroad. Will it work? #Afrofuturism #Hustle #MakeItOrMakeIt. (The Nest Collective 2018a)

This One Went to Market (2018) is particularly successful in the presentation of a mockumentary format that is uncomfortably close to the real discourse on contemporary African arts and digital technology.[3] Additionally, it brings to light the ongoing discussion in Kenya about the use and adoption of terms such as 'Afrofuturism' as a borrowed term with

[3] For a discussion of this episode and the politics of the word "Afrofuturism" by Sheba Hirst, Patricia Kihoro, and Njoki Ngumi from The Nest, see *We Need Prayers: Patricia and Sheba in Conversation (Part 01)* on The Nest Facebook page at https://www.facebook.com/NestCollective/videos/1001068396711518/.

a mutable meaning. The viewer comments on this video demonstrate this as multiple users engage in discussion about these definitions, and about the politics of contemporary art. One response from The Nest illustrates the tensions that may arise in these interfaces between artists, curators, and audiences:

> We've noticed the number of artists who have created work that has been labelled Afrofuturist, despite the artists themselves disavowing themselves of the label (this has happened to us as well—with the term being used to describe our *Stories of Our Lives* film as well as our 2015 short—*To Catch A Dream*—and in both instances we were not entirely convinced). Is it kosher to label a work using a term that the creator of the work doesn't necessarily ascribe to? Probably not. (The Nest Collective, Facebook Comment Feb. 2018)

6.4 Curating the Virtual

Curatorial practice has often been discussed as a creative activity whereby the selection and display of objects has the purpose of making meaning and offering context (Rugg and Sedgwick 2007). Additionally, as Bourdieu has argued, the role of the curator is critical not only in the production of meaning but also in the production of value (Bourdieu 1993, p. 37). The curator offers a frame, motif, or theme that can connect the work to others, and more importantly the curator can endorse and promote this work through her/his own social networks. The 'field of cultural production is a site of struggles', and as Bourdieu identified, the curator, specialist, and art historian enter this hierarchy with the power to impose their own definitions, 'to say with authority, who are authorized to call themselves [artists]' (Bourdieu 1993, p. 42). As discussed earlier, the notion of power as it plays out in the discourse of 'authenticity' in African arts is not new, especially as it sits within a wider post-colonial discourse on the control that the West has had in determining value and meaning (on their own terms) in an international marketplace, or as John Picton puts it, 'selectivity may not be wrong in itself: it depends on who is making the selection' (Picton 1999, p. 125).

So-called new media can pose a challenge to conventional curatorial practices, as it encourages a move from a centralized model to a distributed network model of curation (Krysa 2006, p. 16). The digital object is able to occupy and circulate through virtual spaces that are not necessarily tied to geographic locations with their centres and peripheries. It can escape the grasp of the institutions that inhabit these spaces with their legitimized hierarchies of knowledge (Foucault 1980). Furthermore, the digital origins of this material can prove theoretically problematic as it appears ephemeral and intangible, as it presents ontological questions about the nature of the image, text, or sound, as it is stored as numerical data sets. However, every digital trace that is created is, as Giannini and Bowen (2016) state, 'waiting to be curated'.

Images, videos, and text can be uploaded and saved anywhere, and who decides what is valuable or not shifts from a handful of experts to potentially millions of users on the Web. The separation between art and popular culture becomes obfuscated and curation can become a collective endeavour. YouTube, Vimeo, Instagram, and Facebook become galleries and exhibition spaces, and online bloggers become the new curators of this work. In a sense, the Internet can be framed as a living archive that inhabits a virtual space, offering evidence of the creation and circulation of ephemeral information.

The combination of the speed of the technology that informs the Internet and the immediacy of the use of social networking sites calls for a 'microtemporal' quality to the information that users provide (Ernst 2013). That is to say, the pictures and text are presented in such a way that they are short-lived, and are replaced by new images, information, text, and so on. The Internet is a living virtual space and the community that informs the Internet as archive adds, retrieves, and alters the content and data as an ongoing process. As Ernst suggests, the Internet offers a dynamic archive, 'the essence of which is permanent updating' (Ernst 2013, p. 84).

This dynamic quality radically alters how meaning and value are created and how culture is understood or remembered. For this reason, projects such as Kenyan digital artist Jepchumba's website *AfricanDigitalArt* are critical as they set out to extend the life of these digital traces by collecting and storing them in one virtual space. *AfricanDigitalArt* began its life as a blog in 2008 written by Jepchumba, who set out to explore cultures of technology in Africa as expressed through their intersections with the arts (Jepchumba 2018). As a blogger, the author reposted links to African digital artists' work, or articles about their work, or simply embedded an image or video with a reference to the author of the piece. Now the site includes options to select and view interviews with these artists, and to search over 1000 entries that are sorted regionally and by country, and by type such as animation, character design, contemporary art, gaming, interactive, fashion, illustration, graphic design, photography, film, and others.

These classifications are important as they function as tag words that are informed by the folksonomies created on the web.[4] Communities of African digital artists are not only producing and disseminating work that straddles real and digital spaces, but they can also act as curators of digital content in their own right. The conventional gatekeepers that possess the perceived cultural capital to endorse an artist's work, whether as a non-governmental organization or a curator, for example, have limited control over what is likely to gain popularity and how. In these digital spaces, artists such as Just a Band create music videos such as *Ha-He* (2010) that they post on YouTube, and create heroic characters such as Makmende. Once online, these creations take on a life of their own: Makmende became 'Kenya's first Internet meme', and moved from being an iconic image printed on T-Shirts, artwork, and posters to a 'collective reimagining' through productive consumption of this reappropriated Blaxploitation hero (Ekdale and Tully 2013). Unlike traditional archives that present their own limitations on processes of selection and preservation, the Internet is less stringent. It encourages participatory behaviour that circumvents traditional institutional barriers.

Within this space one can discover alternative accounts or narratives that may be positioned subversively, as in the case of Kenyan political animation in the context of the post-election violence (Callus 2018). The

[4] Seth Hooland's (2006, 2011) papers on metadata, user-generated content, and the archive can shed some light on the changing perceptions on the retrieval of 'visual cultural heritage' on the Internet and uses of user comments (and other metadata). Unlike traditional methods of indexing and cataloguing, there is no control over the description or content that is created by metadata from users.

so-called authors of these narratives or accounts, on occasion, play with the openness that this space allows, presenting different identities. Just a Band, for example, is a collective of artists/musicians with a variety of online identities and a presence that presents the group on the one hand as young musicians, and on the other hand as video/digital artists exhibiting at the Goethe Institute, and at the same time as cartoonists, political activists, and educationalists. While this openness can result in an overwhelming amount of data, it also draws attention to the agency that is afforded to the subject (within the archive), made possible through the participatory nature of Web 2.0.[5]

6.5 Digital Visibility and Invisibility

Digital technologies afford a degree of simultaneous visibility and invisibility that artists are able to exploit. On the one hand, Kenyan digital artists use these technologies to make visible their work by actively contributing to the creation of digital still, animated, and interactive content. By tactical alignments with online networks, artists can gain traction and an online following. Whether we look at emergent digital artist Magati Maosa's Instagram page (Maosa 2018), for example, with its 3599 followers and posts that include some of his own photographs, designs, and animated illustrations as well as images and photos from other Kenyan artists' work, or Michael Soi's page with its 12,800 followers, it is possible to identify networks and communities of Kenyan prod-users interacting with this work. In a sense it is possible to view a detailed version of life-logging through blogs, social media, online newspapers and magazines, YouTube channels, and so on. This cacophony of data can be collected

[5] Discussions have moved away from the benefits of a democratized distribution of user-creative content that was heralded at the start of Web 2.0, and have since been replaced by a concern with the data that these users provide, and that large companies such as Google can use for economic gain. While this is true for all users of the Web, in the context of African artists, the political emphasis changes. Data mongering, while still present for African users, does not outweigh the benefits of being offered a platform to create, promote, and distribute their work and surrounding ideas or views.

and considered when looking at the artists and their work to arrive at some sort of understanding of value and meaning in local terms.

However, it is also true that the rate of growth of data across the Internet risks drowning out these voices, and 'today's memorializing occurs in a climate of rapid obsolescence' (Haskins 2007). With search algorithms predetermining the results that are made visible to users, stumbling across these artists can become harder. If these digital moving and still images are embedded among a much larger collection of other videos or images on sites such as YouTube, it makes it harder to search for and select the content one wishes to view. Furthermore, the embedded migration of this content and its multi-sited appearance can compound the attribution of 'prod-user' to specific users and authorship can be hard to determine. However, it is worth considering that this invisibility can be an important aspect of the creative production of socially engaged work, especially in the case of politically subversive work. Here invisibility can be capitalized upon, allowing artists to smuggle subversive work into public spaces that can circulate below official institutional radar. The paradox in these cases is that once a piece of work gains online traction, its distribution cannot be controlled as well by the artist or author.

6.6 Flowing from the Immaterial to the Physical

As discussed previously, digitally born artefacts suffer from a dematerialized condition. Having no fixed physical state, a digital image, film, sound, or text becomes harder to commodify and problematic in conventional curatorial spaces. Online digital spaces, however, can accommodate this fluid, sometimes hybrid, quality. As Giannini and Bowen observe, the expansion of the world of art is exponential, 'especially on the Web where gatekeepers no longer hold sway … Digital life and culture now flow through human activity via networks, platforms and digital devices as laptops, tablets, phones and wrist-watches, to devices embedded in our daily activities and environment from the home, to cars, trains, planes, streets, subways, elevators, escalators ...' (Giannini and Bowen 2016, p. 238).

As if to mirror this flow, digital artists in Kenya also move with ease between commercial spaces in design, advertising, popular culture, entertainment, and 'art' and their work tends to straddle these indiscriminately. As a result, it is possible to speak of a shift in cultural capital, emerging from digital social networks and moving into real curated galleries. Artists such as Osborne Macharia and Jacque Njeri (aka FruitJunkie) offer cases of Kenyan digital artists whose popularity online was a key driving factor in their flow from an individual or commercial virtual context of production and exhibition towards a so-called real gallery context.

Many of Macharia's digital photographic series have been shown as large prints across galleries in Amsterdam, Milan, Dubai, and Bahrain (K63 Studio 2018a). Similarly, Jacque Njeri's *Maa-sci* (2017), a digital photomontage series of a reimagining of Maasai characters in a science fiction space, led to her exhibiting work at the *Other Futures* exhibition in Amsterdam, with international press coverage ensuring continued visibility online (Mukthar 2017) and at the *Other Futures* website (2018). These flows are indicative of a significant shift in the terrain of a discourse on African arts and may offer new paradigms of value and authenticity in the arts. Finally, as this chapter has demonstrated, while access to these technologies in Kenya is not widespread, digital entrepreneurship in its different guises (in this case to create, exhibit, and disseminate art on a range of platforms, to share knowledge, skills, and networks, etc.) is a valuable skill that can result in the generation of new cultural capital and is a key component in the visibility and invisibility of this work.

References

Bischoff, L. (2017). The Future is Digital: An Introduction to African Digital Arts. *Critical African Studies, 9*(3), 261–267.

Bourdieu, P. (1986). The Forms of Capital. In J. Richardson (Ed.), *Handbook of Theory and Research for the Sociology of Education* (pp. 241–258). Westport, CT: Greenwood.

Bourdieu, P. (1993). *The Field of Cultural Production*. Columbia: Columbia University Press.

Bristow, T. (2014). Cultures of Technology: Digital Technology and New Aesthetics in African Digital Art. *Critical Interventions, 8*(3), 331–341.

Bristow, T. (2017). Post African Futures: Positioning the Globalized Digital within Contemporary African Cultural and Decolonizing Practices. *Critical African Studies, 9*(3), 281–301.

Bruns, A. (2007). Produsage: Towards a Broader Framework for User-Led Content Creation. In *Proceedings Creativity & Cognition*, Vol. 6, Washington, DC.

Busuru, S. (2018). *Artstation Artist Page*. Retrieved June 25, 2018, from https://www.artstation.com/salim_busuru.

Callus, P. (2018). The Rise of Kenyan Political Animation: Tactics of Subversion. In O. Tejumola & P. Limb (Eds.), *Taking African Cartoon Art Seriously: Satire, Politics and Culture*. East Lansing, MI: Michigan State University Press.

Callus, P., & Potter, C. (2017). Michezo Video: Nairobi's Gamers and the Developers Who are Promoting Local Content. *Critical African Studies, 9*(3), 302–326.

Chuchu, J. (2015). *Making Africa* Interview Video. Retrieved June 12, 2018, from http://makingafrica.net/2015/07/interview-videosunny-dolat-and-jim-chuchu/.

Dahir, Abdi (2017, August 23). Kenya's Newest Tech Hubs are Sprouting Outside Its "Silicon Savannah" in Nairobi. *Quartz Africa*. Retrieved March 20, 2018, from https://qz.com/1059305/kenyas-newest-tech-hubs-are-sprouting-outside-its-silicon-savannah-in-nairobi/.

Ekdale, B., & Tully, M. (2013). Makmende Amerudi: Kenya's Collective Reimaging as a Meme of Aspiration. *Critical Studies in Media Communication., 31*(4), 283–298.

Ernst, W. (2013). *Digital Memory and the Archive*. Minnesota: University of Minnesota Press.

Foucault, M. (1980). *Power/Knowledge: Selected Interviews and Other Writings, 1972–1977*. New York: Pantheon.

Giannini, T., & Bowen, J. (2016). Curating Digital Life and Culture: Art and Information. In *Proceedings of the Conference on Electronic Visualisation and the Arts* (pp. 237–244), July 12–14, London, UK.

GSMA. (2016). The Mobile Economy. *GSMA Intelligence*. Retrieved December 26, 2018, from www.gsmaintelligence.com.

Guillén, M., & Suárez, S. (2005). Explaining the Global Digital Divide: Economic, Political and Sociological Drivers of Cross-National Internet Use. *Social Forces, 84*(2), 681–708.

Hamilton, E. (2017). Afrofuturism and the Technologies of Survival. *African Arts, 50*(4), 18–23.

Haskins, E. (2007). Between Archive and Participation: Public Memory in a Digital Age. *Rhetoric Society Quarterly, 37*, 401–422.

Hooland, S. (2006). Spectator Becomes Annotator: Possibilities Offered by User-Generated Metadata for Image Databases. In *Immaculate Catalogues: Taxonomy, Metadata and Resource Discovery in the 21st Century. Proceedings of CILIP Conference*. Norwich: University of East Anglia.

Hooland, S., Mendez Rodriguez, E. Boydens, I. (2011), 'Between Commodification and Engagement: On the Double-Edged Impact of User-Generated Metadata within the Cultural Heritage Sector', in Library Trends, Vol. 59, No. 4. ("Involving Users in the Co-Construction of Digital Knowledge in Libraries, Archives, and Museums," edited by Paul F. Marty and Michelle M. Kazmer, pp. 707–720).

Jepchumba. (2018). *African Digital Art*. Retrieved June 30, 2018, from http://africandigitalart.com/.

Kasfir, S. (1999). *Contemporary African Art*. London: Thames & Hudson.

Krysa, J. (2006). *Curating Immateriality: The Work of the Curator in the Age of Network Systems (Data Browser)*. Brooklyn: Autonomedia Publishing.

Macharia, O. (2018a). *K63 Studio* website Exhibition Page. Retrieved July 1, 2018, from https://k63.studio/exhibitions/.

Macharia, O. (2018b). *K63 Studio* Nyanye Page. Retrieved June 30, 2018, from https://k63.studio/#/nyanye/.

Magati Maosa, J. (2018). *Instagram Page Magatimaosa*. Retrieved July 1, 2018, from https://www.instagram.com/magatimaosa/?hl=en.

Making Africa. (2018). *Making Africa: A Continent of Contemporary Design* exhibition webpage. Retrieved June 14, 2018, from http://makingafrica.net/exhibition/.

Mbogo, S. (2000). Can Africa Exploit the Internet. *Review of African Political Economy, 27*(83), 127–129.

Mezzofiore, Gianluca (2018, March 1). New Word Order: Ghanaian Teacher Uses Blackboard to Explain Software. *CNN World*. Retrieved May 10, 2018, from https://edition.cnn.com/2018/03/01/africa/ghana-teacher-blackboard-intl/index.html.

Mukthar, I. (2017, August 28). The Kenyan Artist Who is Taking the Maasai to Space. Retrieved October 10, 2018, from https://edition.cnn.com/2017/08/28/africa/jacque-njeri-maasai-space/index.html.

Nyabuga, G., & Booker, N. (2013, March). *Mapping Digital Media: Kenya*. A report by the Open Society Foundations. Retrieved June 2, 2018, from https://www.opensocietyfoundations.org/reports/mapping-digital-media-kenya.

Oguibe, O., & Enwezor, O. (Eds.). (1999). *Reading the Contemporary: African Art from Theory to the Marketplace*. London: Iniva.

Other Futures. (2018, February). *Jacque Njeri Artist Profile Other Futures*. Retrieved July 1, 2018, from https://otherfutures.nl/en/artist/jacque-njeri.

Picton, J. (1999). In Vogue, or the Flavour of the Month: The New Way to Wear Black. In O. Oguibe & O. Enwezor (Eds.), *Reading the Contemporary: African Art from Theory to the Marketplace* (pp. 114–127). London: Iniva.

Rugg, J., & Sedgwick, M. (2007). *Issues in Curating Contemporary Art and Performance*. Bristol: Intellect Publishing.

The Nest Collective. (2018a, February 28). *We Need Prayers 05 Video Post, Facebook Comment Reply/ Page*. Retrieved June 1, 2018, from https://www.facebook.com/NestCollective/videos/997944340357257/?comment_id=998174527000905&reply_comment_id=998692756949082&comment_tracking=%7B%22tn%22%3A%22R9%22%7D.

The Nest Collective. (2018b, February 9). *We Need Prayers: Patricia and Sheba in Conversation (Part 01)*. Retrieved June 12, 2018, from https://www.facebook.com/NestCollective/videos/1001068396711518/.

The World Bank. (2013). *Insight Report: The Africa Competitiveness Report*. Geneva: World Economic Forum.

Wyche, S., Schoenebeck, S., & Forte, A. (2013). Facebook is a Luxury: An Exploratory Study of Social Media Use in Rural Kenya. In *Into the Petridish: Culture and Collaboration* (pp. 33–43), February 23–27, San Antonio, TX.

Part V

Inclusive-tech: Gender Inequality, Poverty, and Digital Ecosystems

7

Technopreneurship: A Discursive Analysis of the Impact of Technology on the Success of Women Entrepreneurs in South Africa

B. N. O. Irene

7.1 Introduction

There has been a steady increase in the number of women-owned businesses in South Africa since 2008. Research has shown that women-owned businesses tend to be concentrated in service-oriented sectors such as healthcare and social assistance, information and cultural industries, arts, entertainment, recreation, and retail. Despite the increased number of women engaged in entrepreneurial activities, most women owner-managers still struggle to access and use the technology, networks, and knowledge they need to start and to grow their business. According to Mumba (2014), this can be attributed to the fact that most governments in Africa have failed to provide the necessary support for the growth of women's entrepreneurship due to their lack of understanding of the impact of women's entrepreneurship on the GDP of the country. Numerous declarations and conventions aimed at improving women's economic status and bridging the gender gap have been ratified by many African govern-

B. N. O. Irene (✉)
Universidad de Las Américas Puebla, Cape Town, South Africa

N. D. Taura et al. (eds.), *Digital Entrepreneurship in Sub-Saharan Africa*, Palgrave Studies of Entrepreneurship in Africa, https://doi.org/10.1007/978-3-030-04924-9_7

ments; nevertheless, very little has been done to comprehensively address the actual problems faced by women entrepreneurs. To this end, Mayoux (2001) posits that gender bias persists in the social and economic environment in which women operate, and women are faced with different socio-cultural, educational, and technological challenges from their male counterparts in relation to business start-ups and business growth.

The adoption of technology by women entrepreneurs is not so much related to the ICT infrastructure,[1] but rather to understanding the type of technology the business requires and the tools for integrating social media into the core business processes, which is buoyed by a clear digital strategy. According to Saifuddin (2015), women entrepreneurs would benefit from personalized assistance provided by a knowledgeable adviser on both their business needs and the technical requirements of the business.

This research examines the current state of women's entrepreneurship and the technological requirements for ensuring business growth and sustainability in the digital generation. From a review of published literature and subsequent interviews with organizations that support women's enterprises, the study examines the digital gender divide in sub-Saharan Africa (particularly South Africa) with a view to establishing an understanding of the types of opportunities and challenges that technology presents to women Small, Medium, and Micro Enterprises and the process of integrating social media tools into core business processes that is supported by a clear digital strategy.

7.2 Women's Entrepreneurship in South Africa

Since 2008, there has been increased academic interest in women entrepreneurs, inspired not only by the economic implications but also by gender equality. Given that entrepreneurship is considered vital to eco-

[1] ICT, or information and communications technology (or technologies), is the infrastructure and components that enable modern computing.

nomic growth, employment, and innovation, women can therefore be considered a valuable resource that can be employed by countries at different stages on the path to national economic emancipation and the development of its citizens. Verheul et al. (2005) suggest that there is a positive correlation between the female share in entrepreneurship and economic performance at country and regional levels.

A twofold relationship exists between female entrepreneurs and the aggregate economic activity, making it difficult to determine the causal link between the two variables: (a) the level of per capita GDP in a country determines the level and type of female entrepreneurial activities regardless of the entrepreneurial motivation, whether it be "necessity" or "opportunity"; and (b) the level of well-being in a country is greatly impacted by the level and types of female entrepreneurial activity, thereby creating a "virtuous circle" (Minniti et al. 2006). According to the Global Entrepreneurship Monitor (GEM) (2009) report for South Africa, female entrepreneurship could be the key to unlocking South African economic growth if more effort is made by the government to support female entrepreneurs in a targeted way. The report maintains that an important way to develop the South African economy is to encourage and improve female self-employment as well as to pursue intervention programmes that are aimed at increasing female participation in business. According to the study, female entrepreneurs are easier and less risky to finance than their male counterparts; female-owned businesses could have a lower business failure rate and create more jobs compared with those of their male counterparts. Despite this, male entrepreneurs are 1.7 times more likely to be involved in early-stage entrepreneurship or to become developed business managers than women (which is higher than the global average of 1.6 times). The 2012 TEA rate for men was 8.1%, while women accounted for 4.9%.[2] This difference could be attributed to the fact that men are more "opportunity" entrepreneurs than "necessity" entrepreneurs. The overall TEA rate of South Africa is lower than the other BRICS (Brazil, Russia, India, China, and South Africa) countries, which can be attributed

[2] The main indicator used is called TEA (total early-stage entrepreneurial activity), which assesses the percentage of the working-age population that is about to start an entrepreneurial activity, and those that have started one in the past three and a half years.

Table 7.1 Involvement in entrepreneurial activity by gender in South Africa

Entrepreneurial activity	Male (%)	Female (%)
Business start-up (TEA)	62	38
Business start-up (TEA): Opportunity entrepreneurs	67	33
Business start-up (TEA): Necessity entrepreneurs	46	54
Established business owner/manager	65	35

Source: Own compilation as adapted from author's PhD thesis

to the fact that many South Africans (male and female) do not believe they have the skills required for venture start-up (GEM 2004). The report also concludes that South Africa has the lowest rate of new and established firms, thereby suggesting that the contribution of the entrepreneurial sector is below the norm for other developing countries. This can be improved considerably by developing the female entrepreneurial market (Table 7.1).

7.3 ICT Infrastructure for Businesses in South Africa

According to the 2015 UN Secretary-General's High-Level Panel (HLP) report on Women's Economic Empowerment, the ability to eliminate gender disparities in work and in society will depend on effectively eliminating disparities in access to key assets such as digital, financial, and property assets. The report also suggests that around 2.3 billion women worldwide do not have internet access, more than 1.7 billion do not own a mobile phone, and about 200 million fewer women have online access or mobile phones in comparison with their male counterparts. Accordingly, the panel proposes that women's access to technology needs to be improved significantly as mobile phones and digital platforms are already proving to be beneficial to female entrepreneurs, connecting them to markets, providing multilingual training, and facilitating their collective action. To this end, organizations such as the Business Women's Association (BWA) in South Africa, the Leading Women Association (LWA), also in South Africa, as well as other organizations interested in the economic development of women in South Africa are advocating for and supporting women's networking and access to market information on digital platforms such as their mobile phones, email, and social media tools. These technologies and platforms have great potential that is further advanced by the 5 billion-dollar Sustainable Development Goal target aimed at increasing the use of enabling technologies to promote women's economic empowerment. However, 1.7 billion women in low- and middle-income countries such as South Africa do not own mobile phones, and women in the poorer regions of developing countries are 50% less likely to have internet access than their male counterparts (according to the panel report).

The effectiveness of technology and social business tools is dependent on the ICT infrastructure of a country. According to the World Bank and the International Telecommunication Union's (2015) ICT infrastructure indicators, South Africa's ICT infrastructure is developing well. South Africa's average household internet access and fixed broadband subscription remains lower than the high-income countries average subscriptions as presented in Table 7.2. This is also consistent with the ranking of the Networked Readiness Index, where South Africa is ranked 75th in the global ranking of 143 countries and third among African countries. Although South Africa's ICT infrastructure was ranked third among the top ten digital nations in sub-Saharan Africa, it ranked 92nd in the overall usage with mobile broadband penetration, well below other countries in the high-income group. Overall, mobile broadband penetration was found to be weak due to affordability issues, and the survey found that internet access via mobile phone is common among business decision-makers. According to the report, South African companies also have a tendency to imitate the digital strategies of large industrial nations, which prevents them from contextualizing digital strategies to their own industrial reality; as a result, they often fail to customize their offerings to meet rapidly changing customer expectations. The report concludes by suggesting that South African companies need to generate the improvements that will enable them to leapfrog to digital leadership, reinvent their operating models completely, and rethink production and value chains.

Table 7.2 ICT report on sub-Saharan Africa

	2005	2014
Economic and social context		
Population (millions)	762.0	973.0
Urban population (% of total)	33.0	37.0
GNI per capita, World Bank Atlas method ($)	785.0	1699.0
GDP growth, 2000–05 and 2005–14 (avg. annual %)	5.3	4.5
Adult literacy rate (% ages 15 and older)	57.0	60.0
Gross primary, secondary, tertiary school enrolment (%)	52.0	59.0
Sector structure		
Separate telecommunications/ICT regulator		
Status of main fixed-line telephone operator		
Level of competition (competition, partial competition, monopoly)		
International gateway(s)		
Mobile telephone service		
Internet service		
Foreign ownership (not allowed, restricted, allowed)		
Reg. treatment of VoIP (banned, closed, no framework, allowed)		
Sector efficiency and capacity		
Telecommunications revenue (% of GDP)	4.5	3.1
Telecommunications investment (% of revenue)	–	26.4
Sector performance		
Access		
Fixed-telephone subscriptions (per 100 people)	1.5	1.2
Mobile-cellular telephone subscriptions (per 100 people)	12.0	71.1
Fixed-broadband subscriptions (per 100 people)	0.0	0.4
Households with a computer (%)	3.6	9.4
Households with internet access at home (%)	1.1	9.8
Usage		
Int'l. voice traffic, total (minutes/subscription/month)	–	5.1
Domestic mobile traffic (minutes/subscription/month)	–	60.0
Individuals using the internet (%)	2.1	19.2
Quality		
Population covered by a mobile-cellular network (%)	51.0	82.0
International internet bandwidth (bit/s per internet user)	230.0	26,549.0
Affordability		
Fixed-telephone sub-basket ($/month)	–	10.5
Mobile-cellular sub-basket ($/month)	–	13.0
Fixed-broadband sub-basket ($/month)	–	40.6
Trade		
ICT goods exports (% of total goods exports)	0.6	0.5
ICT goods imports (% of total goods imports)	7.6	5.6

(continued)

Table 7.2 (continued)

	2005	2014
ICT service exports (% of total service exports)	12.5	17.3
Applications		
Online service index (0–1, 1 = highest presence)	0.3	0.2
Secure internet servers (per million people)	2.0	8.6

7.4 The Digital Gender Divide

Digital technologies provide the immense advantage of improving the productivity and performance of work and social life. Nearly half of the global population is connected to ICT networks, an increase of 4% from 1995. ICT provides the platform for new and emerging businesses to thrive and helps improve firm performance, by ensuring a better flow of communication and information (OECD 2017). However, this extraordinary growth in connectivity has not been equally enjoyed by everyone, especially in sub-Saharan Africa. Differences in resources and in the ability to access and effectively utilise ICT within and between countries, regions, sectors, and socio-economic groups have led to a digital gender divide, relegating women-owned businesses to a disadvantaged position (UN Women 2005). There are around 250 million fewer women online globally than men (ITU 2016). This is concerning, especially as the gender gap in terms of penetration has been on the increase since 2013. Furthermore, according to Groupe Spéciale Mobile Association (GSMA) (2015), 200 million fewer women own a mobile phone compared with men (see Fig. 7.1), and even those who own one tend to use it for less complicated tasks than men (Demirguc-Kunt et al. 2015). While the majority of women who lack access to digital technologies are in developing countries—the gender gap in mobile broadband access is 45% in sub-Saharan Africa, and up to 50% in some parts of rural Asia—gaps in usage, for example, are also observed in developing countries: internet usage among women is below that of men in countries such as Turkey (−16%), Italy (−6%), and Germany (−3%). Because gender differences in internet uptake are more marked for older generations, a projected narrowing of the gender gap can be expected in the future, as the technology continues to reduce the cost of online access and today's "digital natives" become adults (OECD 2017).

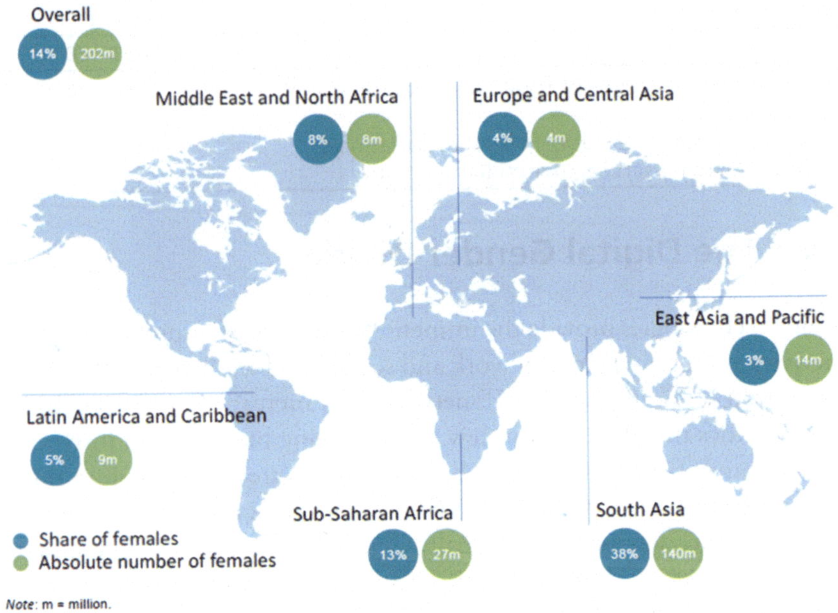

Fig. 7.1 The gender gap in mobile phone ownership, by region. Source: OECD (2017)

A major reason for the global digital gender divide is lack of relevant knowledge and skills in using digital tools. This is highlighted among other reasons, such as affordability of the technology and access to ICT infrastructure. In addition to the reasons mentioned above, socio-cultural perceptions are often reported as among the top barriers for women in owning and using mobile phones, especially in rural zones of developing countries. In South Africa, for instance, around 12% of women in the townships would not use the internet because of negative social perceptions, and 8% of women in India don't use it due to the lack of acceptance by family members (Intel and Dalberg 2012). Socio-cultural perceptions and stereotypes may also play a role in determining a different facet of the gender divide—the under-representation of women in senior roles within digital companies and in ICT fields, both in emerging and advanced economies alike. In the mobile communications industry, for instance, women worldwide are 20% less likely to hold a senior leadership position (GSMA and ATKearny 2015), while only 8% of the investing partners at the top 100 venture capital (VC) firms are women. Furthermore, in the ICT industry, the quit rate seems to be more than twice as high for women (41%) than it is for men (17%) (National Center for Women & Information Technology 2016).

According to research by WomeninTechZA 2017, out of 236,000 ICT (tech) roles, women occupy 56,000 (only 23%) of tech jobs in South Africa. They advocate for the need to hire women to improve diversity in the workplace (and it has been proven that higher diversity equals higher productivity and profit) as well as the need for more women technopreneurs. However, the reality is that South African women with the required skills are not readily available, and tech-savvy women entrepreneurs are even more difficult to find in South Africa. To this end, WomeninTechZA provides a platform where technology companies can find women to hire, and to start changing the image of the tech sector by showing the world the diverse faces of ICT and also provide a training platform for businesswomen seeking to integrate ICT into their businesses.

7.5 The Gender Gap in Business Activities

Innovative entrepreneurship is vital for developing economies. So far, notwithstanding the proven role of entrepreneurship as an engine of social inclusion (OECD and European Commission 2014), the gender gap in entrepreneurship remains strikingly conspicuous, with men being nearly twice as likely as women to engage in entrepreneurial activities (OECD and European Union 2017), and three times more likely than women to be business owners and employers of labour across OECD countries (Piacentini 2013).

Globalization and digitalization have created great opportunities for businesses, but women entrepreneurs appear not to be the beneficiaries, as women-owned businesses are less likely to go into exportation, and less likely to engage in international business-to-business (B2B) transactions (OECD 2017b). The reason for this could be attributed to perceptions, as only 37% of women in OECD countries believe they have the skills for venture creation, compared with 51% of men. Furthermore, new female entrepreneurs are expected to create at least 19% of jobs over a five-year period (half as likely as their male counterparts) (OECD and European Union 2017). The gender gap is even more obvious among innovative start-ups looking for VC investments: only 11% of VC start-up founders are female. This share varies significantly across countries and business sectors; however, in a best case scenario, women entrepreneurs make up 33% of all start-up founders as against 77% of male entrepreneurs (see Fig. 7.2a and b). There is, therefore, a need to unleash the full potential of female entrepreneurial talents in order to allow women entrepreneurs to thrive.

Pitching in the VC market can be a very difficult process, and not all start-ups look for investors in the VC market to help get their businesses off the ground.[3] According to the findings from a recent analysis of the OECD based on Crunchbase data, female-owned businesses have more difficulty raising capital (Breschi et al. 2018). The research, which surveyed 25,000 start-ups operating across different countries and business sectors, revealed that female-owned businesses (i.e., start-ups with at least one female founder) are notably less likely to be funded than male-owned businesses. The report also revealed that among those with funding, women-owned businesses received on average 23% less funding than their male counterparts, regardless of how much control they had over the location and nature of the business, as well as the educational level and professional background of the women entrepreneurs (Fig. 7.3). Female-owned start-ups are reported to be 30% less likely to have a positive exit, i.e. be acquired or to issue an initial public offering; and in other start-up hot-spots, this is a well-known anecdote in various reporting and "a particularly toxic atmosphere for women in Silicon Valley" (Burleigh 2015).

[3] Start-up or growth equity capital or loan capital provided by private investors (the venture capitalists) or specialised financial institutions (development finance houses or venture capital firms). Also called risk capital. Venture capital is a type of funding for a new or growing business.

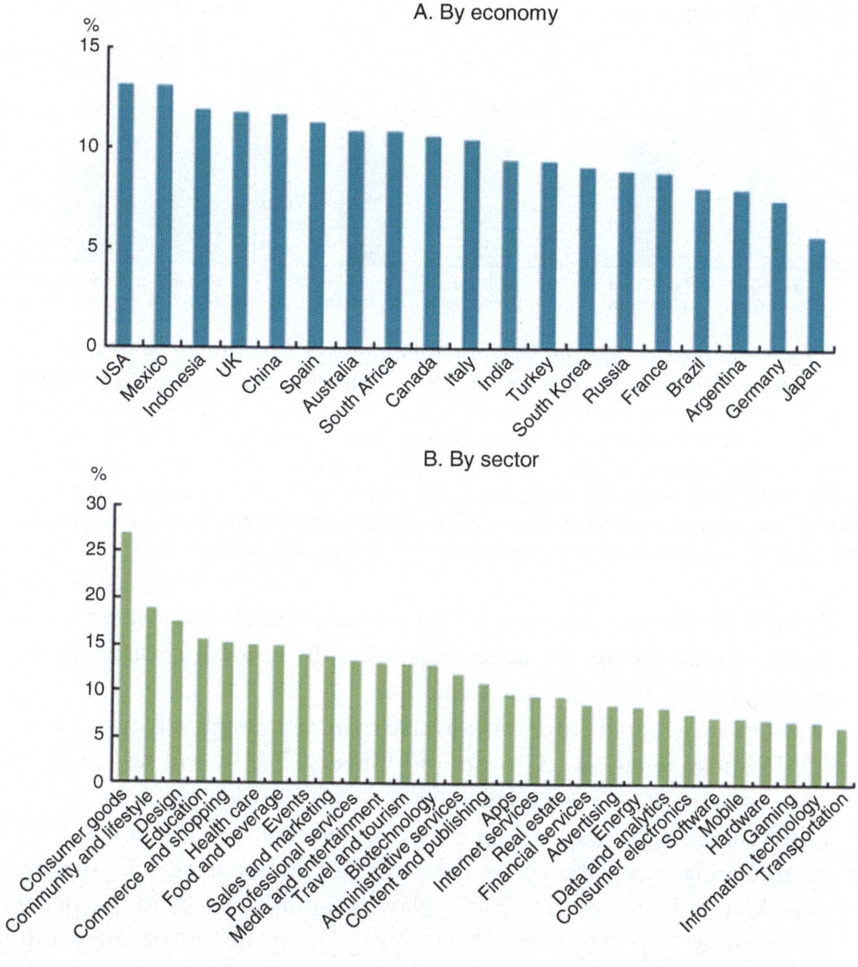

Fig. 7.2 (a and b) The share of females among start-up founders. Source: OECD (2017). Note: Percentage of females in the sample of founders of companies less than ten years old and for whom gender is known

The gender gap in entrepreneurship can be attributed to several factors that also determine the gap in start-up activity and VC investment (Johnstone et al. forthcoming). These factors include:

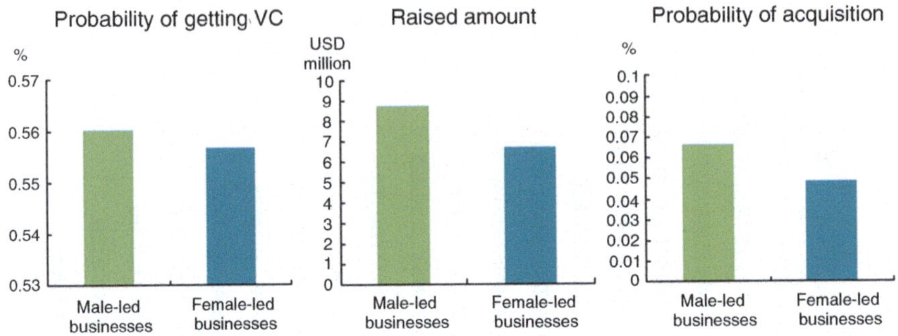

Fig. 7.3 The gender gap in start-up funding and acquisition. Source: OECD (2017). Note: The graphs show results from Ordinary Least Squares (OLS) regressions of the three outcomes variables on a set of founders and firms characteristics, and country and sector fixed effects. Bars show the average predicted probability of receiving VC, the amount of funding conditional on getting VC, and the probability of acquisition for male- and female-led businesses. The advantage of this way of representing the data is that it gets rid of potential confounding effects such as education or prior experience of start-up founders

- A wide gender gap exists in STEM studies,[4] which is considered particularly relevant for the acquisition of skills needed to thrive in the world of innovative entrepreneurship.
- Women are generally more risk-averse than men, especially when making financial decisions (Croson and Gneezy 2009), and less likely to start a new venture after a failed one.
- Differences in the way entrepreneurs network across the genders and in the social network space that can aid in securing VC funding (Stephan and El-Ganainy 2007) plays a significant role in the persistent gender gap. Similarly, "homophily" may be impacting equity financing, as investors—who are disproportionately male—are more likely to finance other men.

According to the 2017 Crunchbase News, when one considers that the share of women taking on "partner" positions in VC firms has been

[4] STEM is a curriculum based on the idea of educating students in four specific disciplines—science, technology, engineering, and mathematics—through an interdisciplinary and applied approach.

increasing in recent years at an extremely slow pace, the glass may seem half empty, as the number of female partners at the top one hundred venture companies only increased by 1% in 18 months (i.e., 64 female partners out of 752 partners at the top 100 VC firms). However, when taking into consideration that even a small increase in the number of female partners in venture firms could mean that women-owned businesses would receive more favourable outcomes in the VC market, the same glass may look half full. The findings from the 2014 Diana Project research shows that VC firms with a female partner are more than twice as likely to invest in a female-managed business (34% vs 13%), and three times more likely to invest in female CEOs (58% vs 15%). Therefore, promoting an increase in the number of women active in the financial markets will be a step in the right direction. While many G20 countries are increasing their support for female entrepreneurs, a lot more still needs to be done. This is important because women entrepreneurs have huge potential for making greater contributions to economic growth, job creation, innovation, and social inclusion, with some recent estimates suggesting that global GDP could rise by as much as 2% annually should the gender gap in entrepreneurship be eliminated (Blomquist et al. 2014).

7.6 Women Entrepreneurs in the Digital Era: The myth of high returns

The nature and content of jobs are changing rapidly as the digital revolution unfolds. Consequently, skills requirements for job or role performance are also changing. Women are required to have solid cognitive skills, juxtaposed with problem-solving abilities. Therefore, in order to adapt to the scale, speed, and scope of digital transformation, women need to have the ability to learn and think creatively. A recent study based on the frequency of tasks performed at work revealed that, on average, people working in industries that are digitally intensive displayed a greater aptitude in all types of skills (OECD 2017c). This claim is valid for cognitive, non-cognitive, and social skills, and more so for ICT abilities, STEM-quantitative, and personal organization skills. Basically, all of these skills are of utmost importance for women entrepreneurs to successfully navigate the current global digital transformation, and more so in sub-Saharan Africa.

A review of the skill levels of male and female workers across 31 developed and developing countries showed that female workers (and entrepreneurs) generally appear to have developed skills in the areas of literacy, basic ICT, marketing, and accounting, while male workers appear to display greater endowments of numeracy and STEM-quantitative skills, and better problem-solving and personal organization skills (Fig. 7.4). While this skills disparity might be explained to some extent by women's relatively lower propensity to undertake STEM-related studies (as shown in various research), it must be stated that there is a strong positive correlation between these skills and labour market returns (OECD 2017c, based on Grundke et al. forthcoming). This is even true for employees in

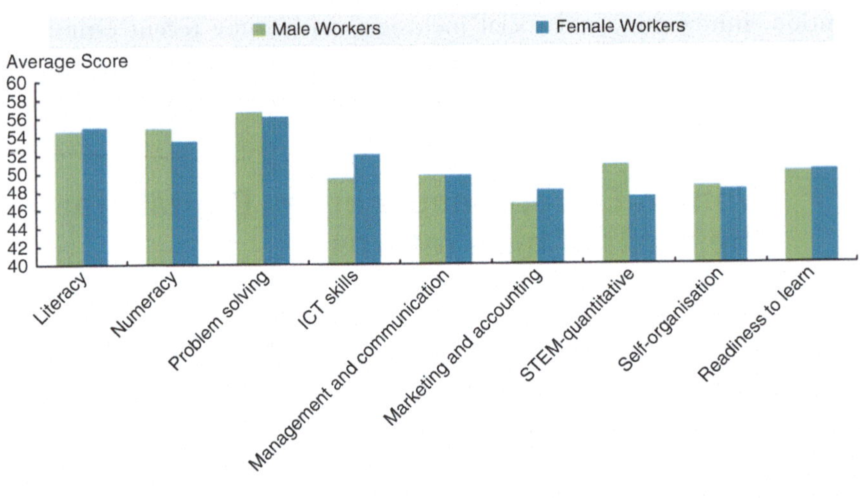

Fig. 7.4 Average skill levels for male and female workers, 31 OECD countries and partner economies, 2012 or 2015. Source: OECD (2017). Notes: ICT = information and communication technology; STEM = science, technology, engineering, and mathematics. All skill indicators are rescaled to the interval 0–100. Averages across 31 OECD countries and partner economies are computed giving the same weight to each country. All differences in skill means between male and female workers are significant at the 5% level, except for Management and communication and Readiness to learn

digitally intensive industries, and one plausible reason for the persistent gender wage gap across countries could be men's current greater aptitude for numeracy and STEM-quantitative skills.

There are certain skills that are vital in this age of digital transformation, and their relative importance is highlighted when looking at the various ways that labour markets reward different skills and the differences that exist between the genders in this regard. The 2017 OECD report shows that while men have higher returns based on management and communication skills, based on ICT skills and readiness to learn, women were ranked higher in this category (Fig. 7.5). These results hold also when differences among individuals in age, education, country, industry, or occupation are taken into account. Various reports show a 4% increase in earnings of female employees with ICT skills in Denmark

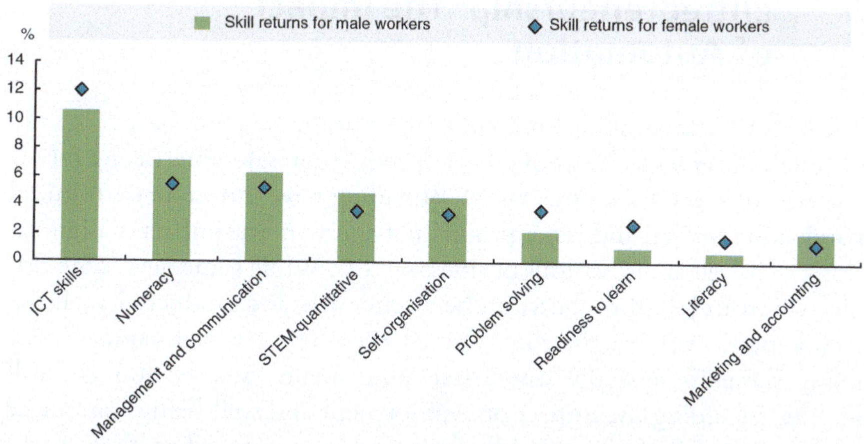

Fig. 7.5 Labour market returns to skills by gender across 31 OECD countries and partner economies, 2012 or 2015. Source: OECD (2017). Notes: ICT = information and communication technology; STEM = science, technology, engineering, and mathematics. Labour market returns to skills are based on Ordinary Least Square (OLS) wage regressions (Mincer equations) using data from the *OECD Survey of Adult Skills (PIAAC)* (OECD 2017h) for 31 OECD countries and partner economies. The estimates by gender are obtained through including an interaction term of the skill variable and the gender variable. The figure shows the percentage changes in wages determined by an increase in skills by one standard deviation, holding other correlates of individual wages constant. Shaded diamonds indicate that the difference between men and women is not significant at the 5% level

and a 19% increase in South Korea, as well as an average increase of 12% on other observable characteristics of the individual constant. The implication is that the digital world could offer better rewards for women with demonstrable ICT skills. It is anticipated that by providing opportunities for women to develop ICT skills, the gender wage gap in the short term can be breached before an influx of ICT skilled workers into the labour market. It may also require policies aimed at equipping female workers with better numeracy, STEM-quantitative, and ICT skills to narrow the gender wage gap, starting with encouraging them to take up STEM-related studies and supporting the ever-increasing need for systematic updating and enhancement of employee skill sets.

7.7 The Future of Women's Entrepreneurship: The Impact of Automation

The contributions of technological innovations cannot be overstated. Through the enhancement of greener production, safer jobs (using robots to perform some hazardous tasks), providing new and more customized goods and services, and faster productivity growth, the impact of digitization can be felt across various business sectors. While some new technologies will create jobs through a number of channels, and productivity-raising technologies will benefit the national economy, the consequences on many domains and the associated adjustments that technology will require, including the impact on employment and well-being, cannot be oversimplified (OECD 2017d). One such resultant effect that sparks much debate is automation. There is a general fear that automation may cause significant loss of jobs, especially when robots are used to carry out tasks usually performed by humans (OECD 2017a). According to Graetz and Michaels (2015) and Acemoglu and Restrepo (2016, 2017), the impact of robots on employment and wages remains ambiguous, even though robots have been proven to improve productivity. Alongside the effect of increasing automation, labour market polarization and the share of high-skilled jobs (and some low-skilled jobs) has increased since

1998 in most OECD countries, while the share of employment in middle-skilled jobs has decreased (Autor et al. 2006; Marcolin et al. 2016; OECD 2017f). The difficulty, however, lies in estimating the extent to which technological advances in artificial intelligence, ICT, and robotics will lead to further automation, as estimates vary significantly. Recent reports suggest that jobs could be at a high risk of being displaced by automation with over 70% of jobs becoming automated (i.e. not requiring humans to undertake them e.g. automated tellers and automated checkout cashiers) in the next 15 to 20 years in the range 9% (OECD 2016a) to 14%, for OECD countries (Quintini 2018) per annum. It is also predicted that another 30% or so of jobs could be at risk of changing significantly as a result of automation (Fig. 7.6).

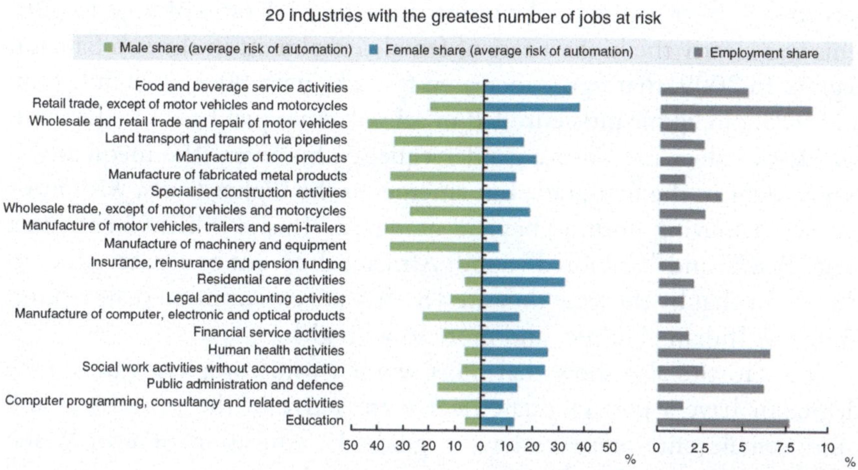

Fig. 7.6 The average risk of automation, by industry and by gender. Notes: The chart shows the 20 industries with the greatest number of jobs at risk (measured as the average risk of automation weighted by the employment share of the industry), in descending order of overall risk of automation (left panel). The width of each bar in the left panel represents the average share of jobs at risk in each industry. The placement of each bar relative to the centre line depicts how that risk is shared between men (light blue) and women (grey). Values in the right panel represent the share of total employment held by each industry. Risk of automation values are based on likelihoods calculated in Arntz et al. (2016). Countries covered in this analysis include the 29 OECD countries that participated in the first and second rounds of the *OECD Survey of Adult Skills (PIAAC)* (OECD 2017h)

All of these have serious implications for women entrepreneurs in sub-Saharan Africa, and especially in South Africa, which ranks third in the list of ICT-ready countries in the African continent. Training and education play a vital role in ICT readiness, as the application of ICT requires certain skill sets. In South Africa, the enrolment figures for schools for girls are high, as is the discrimination against them. There are gender-based differences in learning that have not yet been addressed due to the fact that they are not fully understood. For example, the dropout rate in schools for adolescents is higher for boys than for girls (CREATE–Consortium for Educational Access, Transitions and Equity 2007).

South African government statistics show that the gender gap in literacy is small or non-existent. According to a 2008 United Nations Development Programme (UNDP) report on Africa, South Africa recorded 77% overall school enrolment, with a 1:1 ratio of boys to girls. This was clearly the highest rate of female enrolment in the sub-Saharan region. In 2009, that figure increased to 91%, with 90% of eligible boys and 92% of eligible girls enrolled in school. An equal level of education on its own does not ensure gender equality, however. The inequality is not evident in the first grade but emerges at the higher levels, with most women achieving nothing beyond grade 12. This is evident in the fact that "Black" and "Coloured" South Africans drop out or repeat grades to the extent that by the time they are 18, they are two or more years behind White or Indian children, and more so with girls.

The statistics also show that most women who complete a university degree or have a post-graduate degree are active in the workforce, and more female entrepreneurs have a grade 12 education or less. When women with grade 12 education or less embark on their entrepreneurial journeys, they have little or no entrepreneurial knowledge or training. Not only are they ill-equipped for entrepreneurship financially, they are also ill-equipped educationally, especially in relation to ICT. Considering the fact that most of them are "pushed" into entrepreneurship by their circumstances, they therefore have no preparation by way of education, skills, and finances for venture start-up, growth, and sustenance. This could also explain the reluctance of lenders to grant loans, as they have little or no knowledge of the workings of the business environment, especially on budgets and business performance. Women also lack self-confidence, compounded by low levels of education. According to Irene (2016), African women have less access to resources than men in terms of land, loans, education, and training. Although education is not a prerequisite for venture creation, the skills, contacts, and opportunities it provides are vital to business success (Botha 2006). Irene (2016) posits that entrepreneurial education raises awareness in the early stages of entrepreneurial intention, as this serves to provide skills that will be required to practically run and scale a business as the environment dictates.

7.8 Bridging the Digital Divide

It is believed that a more digitally inclusive world can be created by improving access to digital technologies, by empowering people with the skills needed to cope with and thrive in the age of digital transformation, and by fostering employment, entrepreneurship, financing, and leadership in the digital era. However, this can only be achieved by formulating the right policies. In April 2017, the G20 ministers in charge of the Digital Economy in Düsseldorf unanimously voted to promote and support the equal participation of women in the digital economy, recognizing both the opportunities that digitalization provides for empowering women economically and the challenges of ensuring an equitable share of benefits of the digital transformation for all. To this end, the G20 members agreed to "share national practices on efforts to bridge the digital gender divide" (Action 11 in G20 [2017]) as an initial phase in their actions to help increase the economic empowerment of women in the digital economy. Consequently, many G20 countries, including South Africa, now have a national strategy, policy, or plan that includes efforts to reduce the digital gender divide (Table 7.3). South Africa now has laws or regulations which include gender-related provisions when developing digital economy policies, and has set time-bound targets for women's participation in STEM, in entrepreneurship activities, and in the workforce of the ICT sector. In a recent workshop titled "Mechanism to Strengthen Gender Equality", South African Communications Minister Mmamoloko Kubayi-Ngubane said that women's participation in the

Table 7.3 Examples of countries' efforts to reduce the digital gender divide

Examples of countries' efforts to reduce the digital gender divide
A number of countries have taken measures to engage women and girls in STEM across education systems, for example: • The Australian Government is investing AUD 13 million over five years from 2016/17 in initiatives focused on women's participation in STEM. The National Innovation and Science Agenda is contributing to ongoing efforts across the Australian Government to encourage more girls and women to study STEM and pursue STEM-based and entrepreneurial careers. • Meninas Digitais in Brazil aims to promote technology and STEM subjects by motivating female high school students and by developing their skills with short computing courses. • South Korea is supporting a research fund for female student research teams in architecture, materials, and machinery, as well as computers. They are also promoting female talent in science and engineering fields by providing field experience programmes. • The Japanese Government is carrying out the Riko Challenge to inspire women to choose careers in STEM and increase the number of female science and engineering professionals. • The OECD Mexico initiative, NiñaSTEM PUEDEN, launched in early 2017, invites Mexican women who have prominent careers in science and mathematics to act as mentors to encourage girls to choose STEM subjects. Codigo X in Mexico is a programme to orientate women to disciplines related to STEM and to promote the inclusion of girls and women in ICT sectors. • Germany launched in 2008 the National Pact for Women in MINT (STEM) Careers to increase women's interest in scientific and technical studies. The initiative brings together politics, business, science, and the media to improve the image of STEM-related professions in society. • In the United States, the Department of Education's programme Race to the Top, launched in 2009, prioritises increasing the share of STEM in the grants it awards to states; the Investing in Innovation programme seeks to increase the number of STEM teachers from groups traditionally under-represented in STEM; and the National Science Foundation awards grants to support the ADVANCE programme, which aims at increasing the participation and advancement of women in academic science and engineering careers.
Alongside the G20 German Presidency's eskills4Girls initiative, endorsed by the G20 leaders in 2017, there are a range of national programmes that aim to support girls and women in improving their digital literacy and boosting female employment rates in the digital economy:

(*continued*)

Table 7.3 (continued)

Examples of countries' efforts to reduce the digital gender divide
• South Africa's initiative, including South Africa's Women's Net, provides tailor-made training on basic digital skills, advocacy, and lobbying online. • Argentina's Ellas Hacen (They Do) programme, in conjunction with the National Plan for Digital Inclusion and the Digital Educators Network of Argentina, aims to increase digital literacy among unemployed women and provide the most vulnerable sectors of the population with the necessary skills, motivation, and confidence to use new technologies for their own benefit, through courses for the creation of basic internet use capabilities. • Russia's Love2Code course teaches the creation of mobile applications. Furthermore, G20 countries have programmes in place supporting efforts in other countries, particularly developing ones, for example: • Canada has four different initiatives, including increasing access to education and training in selected Commonwealth countries with a high prevalence of child marriage, and improving the skills and employability of girls and women in Haiti and African countries. • Germany has initiatives and public–private partnerships to address the need for improving gender equality in the workplace by raising the digital skill levels of women in South East Asia.

ICT sector was woefully low, and more so in the sub-Saharan region. According to her,

> It is important to encourage young women to consider careers in areas such as science and ICT sectors. Studies show that women still have limited access to education and therefore fewer women are able to enter the ICT sector.

Notwithstanding the notable efforts of the G20 countries, more work still needs to be done in order to close the gender gap in entrepreneurship. Some areas of work have been highlighted by the OECD (2018):

- The basic frameworks to boost ICT access in developing countries need to be reinforced (in particular through enhancing competition that contributes to lower cost, which disproportionately benefits women).

- A framework needs to be developed for providing life-long learning opportunities for women to deal with changing skills and job profiles in the digital economy.
- A supportive environment needs to be provided for workplace flexibility in both emerging and developed countries (i.e., adjusting social systems for the digital reality and ensuring their appropriateness for women).

Furthermore, it is believed that efforts at the G20 level can play a key role in fostering digital gender inclusion. This can be done by helping countries identify appropriate interventions to prioritise as well as promoting better evidence-based gender-disaggregated ICT statistics, in order to facilitate the design of targeted policy interventions. Moreover, digital tools could be part of the solution as they can be instrumental in enhancing policy design, implementation, monitoring, evaluation, and enforcement.

7.9 Conclusion and Recommendations

As indicated above, the majority of women-owned businesses are not in the tech sector or industry but rather in service-oriented sectors. Technology, therefore, is not the core of their businesses; rather, it is a tool to enhance their businesses and make them more effective. The kind of technology that will be most effective for many women entrepreneurs is difficult to assess and considered to be time-consuming. Many women entrepreneurs are now adopting the use of ICT in their businesses, with younger women entrepreneurs naturally feeling more comfortable using social media platforms. However, adoption of social media platforms is only one of the technology needs of entrepreneurs. To be effective, technology needs to be linked with the strategic metrics for goals and outcomes for the enterprise. Although technology is customized to impact business performance, women entrepreneurs are not obtaining full value or benefit from it. Many women entrepreneurs are occupied with daily activities in relation to juggling business and family responsibilities, such that they have not set aside time to lay out their strategic goals and desired outcomes in terms of income and return on investment (ROI). In addition, while there are a variety of available innovative devices and ICT tools and platforms, some women entrepreneurs do not have the knowledge of all that is available and how to determine and assess what is best for their organization given the money they have to spend and the requisite skills needed to integrate the systems into their businesses.

Additionally, entrepreneurs seldom find technology experts that understand their business needs, and when they do find and hire an expert, the advice may not be beneficial in enhancing their understanding of the most effective technology and the best way of integrating ICT into their businesses to enhance performance. Technological solutions for entrepreneurs are not one-size-fits-all or cookie-cutter, but rather should be specific to each business and its particular needs. New digital tools are empowering and can help to meet complex global challenges, as well as become a new source of inclusive global economic growth. However, to make the most of this opportunity it is vital that no one, and especially no woman, is hindered in trying to achieve their aspirations. The future of women's entrepreneurship in sub-Saharan Africa will depend largely on policies that are formulated today: the time to step up efforts and take advantage of the digital transformation to ensure that it represents a leapfrogging opportunity for women and a chance to build a more inclusive digital world is NOW. The efforts of the G20 countries are an important and timely first step towards better policies to close the digital gender gap so that everyone can benefit from the global digital transformation.

References

Acemoglu, D., & Restrepo, P. (2016). *The Race between Machine and Man: Implications of Technology for Growth, Factor Shares and Employment* (NBER Working Papers 22252). Cambridge, MA: National Bureau of Economic Research, Inc.

Acemoglu, D., & Restrepo, P. (2017). *Robots and Jobs: Evidence from US Labour Markets* (NBER Working Papers 23285). Cambridge, MA: National Bureau of Economic Research, Inc.

Arntz, M., Gregory, T., & Zierahn, U.. (2016). The Risk of Automation for Jobs in OECD Countries: A Comparative Analysis. *OECD Social, Employment and Migration Working Papers, No. 189*. Paris: OECD Publishing. https://doi.org/10.1787/5jlz9h56dvq7-en

Autor, D., Katz, L., & Kearney, M. (2006). The Polarization of the US Labour Market. *The American Economic Review, 96*(2), 189–194.

Blomquist, M., Chastain, E., Thickett, B., Unnikrishnan, S., & Woods, W. (2014). *Bridging the Entrepreneurship Gender Gap: The Power of Networks*. Boston: Boston Consulting Group.

Botha, M. (2006). *Measuring the Effectiveness of the Women's Entrepreneurship Programme, as a Training Intervention, on Potential, Start-up and Established Women Entrepreneurs in South Africa*. PhD thesis, University of Pretoria.

Breschi, S., Lassébie, J., & Menon, C. (2018). A Portrait of Innovative Start-ups Across Countries. *OECD Science, Technology, and Industry Working Papers*. Paris: OECD Publishing. Retrieved March 21, 2018, from https://doi.org/10.1787/f9ff02f4-en

Burleigh, N. (2015, January 28). What Silicon Valley Thinks of Women. *Newsweek*. Retrieved January 22, 2018, from www.newsweek.com/2015/02/06/what-silicon-valley-thinks-women-302821.html

CREATE (Consortium for Educational Access, Transitions and Equity). Improving Access, Equity and Transitions in Education: Creating a Research Agenda 2007. Retrieved from http://sro.sussex.ac.uk/1828/1/PTA1.pdf

Croson, R., & Gneezy, U. (2009). Gender Differences in Preferences. *Journal of Economic Literature, 47*(2), 448–474.

Demirguc-Kunt, A., Klapper, L., Singer, D., & Van Oudheusden, P. (2015). *The Global Findex Database 2014: Measuring Financial Inclusion around the World* (Policy Research Working Paper 7255). Washington, DC: World Bank. Retrieved from http://documents.worldbank.org/curated/en/187761468179367706/pdf/WPS7255.pdf

G20. (2017). A Roadmap for Digitalisation: Policies for a Digital Future. Düsseldorf: G20. Retrieved from www.bmwi.de/Redaktion/DE/Downloads/P-R/roadmap-for-dgitalisation.pdf

Graetz, G., & G. Michaels. (2015, March). Robots at Work. *CEPR Discussion Paper 10477*. Retrieved from www.cepr.org/active/publications/discussion_papers/dp.php?dpno=10477.

Grundke, R., et al. (Forthcoming). Which Skills for the Digital Era? A Returns to Skills Analysis. *OECD Science, Technology and Industry Working Papers*. Paris: OECD Publishing.

GSMA. (2015). Connected Women, Bridging the Gender Gap: Mobile Access and Usage in Low- and Middle-Income Countries. Retrieved January 15, 2018, from https://www.gsma.com/mobilefordevelopment/programmes/connected-women/bridging-gender-gap

GSMA and ATKearny. (2015). Accelerating the Digital Economy: Gender Diversity in the Telecommunications Sector. Retrieved from https://www.atkearney.com/documents/10192/5580445/Connected+Women+2015-WDReport.pdf/d3c08b0a-fab6-431c-80c0-0d332b9e882d

Intel and Dalberg. (2012). Women and the Web. Bridging the Internet and Creating New Global Opportunities in Low and Middle-Income Countries. Intel Corporation and Dalberg Global Development Advisors. Retrieved from https://www.intel.com/content/dam/www/public/us/en/documents/pdf/women-and-theweb.pdf

Irene, B. (2016). *Gender and Entrepreneurial Success: A Cross Cultural Study of Competencies of Female SMEs Operators in South Africa*. PhD thesis, Cardiff Metropolitan University.

ITU. (2016). ICT Facts and Figures 2016. Retrieved February 3, 2018, from https://www.itu.int/en/ITU-D/Statistics/Documents/facts/ICTFactsFigures2016.pdf

Johnstone, N., Managi, S., Rodríguez, M. C., Haščič, I., Fujii, H., & Souchier, M. (forthcoming). The Gender Gap in the Venture Capital Market. *OECD Science, Technology and Industry Working Paper*. Paris: OECD Publishing.

Maas, G., & Herrington, M. (2009). *Global Entrepreneurship Monitor—South Africa Report*. The UCT Center for Innovation and Entrepreneurship, University of Cape Town, South Africa.

Marcolin, L., Miroudot, S., & Squicciarini, M.. (2016). Routine Jobs, Employment and Technological Innovation in Global Value Chains. *OECD Science, Technology and Industry Working Papers, No. 2016/01*. OECD Publishing.

Mayoux, L. (2001). *Jobs, Gender and Small Enterprises: Getting the Policy Environment Right*. Geneva: ILO.

Minniti, M., Bygrave, W., & Autio, E. (2006). *2005 Global Entrepreneurship Monitor Executive Report*. London: Global Entrepreneurship Monitor.

Mumba, Daniel. (2014). *Empowering Women Entrepreneurs in Africa: Investigating Information Access and Use of Information and Communication Technologies by Women-Owned Enterprises in Zambia*. Electronic thesis and Dissertation Repository. 2502. Retrieved from https://ir.lib.uwo.ca/etd/2502

National Center for Women & Information Technology. (2016). Women in Tech: The Facts (2016 Update). Retrieved from https://www.ncwit.org/sites/default/files/resources/womenintech_facts_fullreport_05132016.pdf.

OECD. (2016a). Automation and Independent Work in a Digital Economy. *OECD Policy Briefs on the Future of Work*. Paris: OECD. Retrieved February 18, 2018, from www.oecd.org/employment/emp/Policy%20brief%20-%20Automation%20and%20Independent%20Work%20in%20a%20Digital%20Economy.pdf

OECD. (2017a). *OECD Science, Technology and Industry Scoreboard 2017: The Digital Transformation*. Paris: OECD Publishing. Retrieved February 2, 2018, from https://doi.org/10.1787/9789264268821-en

OECD. (2017b). *Entrepreneurship at a Glance 2017*. Paris: OECD Publishing. Retrieved February 2, 2018, from https://doi.org/10.1787/entrepreneur_aag-2017-en

OECD. (2017c). *Global Economic Outlook* (Chap. 2, vol. 2017/1). Paris: OECD Publishing.

OECD. (2017d). *The Next Production Revolution: Implications for Governments and Business*. Paris: OECD Publishing. Retrieved from https://doi.org/10.1787/9789264271036-en

OECD. (2017f). How Technology and Globalisation are Transforming the Labour Market. In *OECD Employment Outlook 2017* (Chapter 3). Paris: OECD Publishing. Retrieved from https://doi.org/10.1787/empl_outlook-2017-7-en

OECD. (2017h). *Survey of Adult Skills (PIAAC), Database*. Paris: OECD Publishing. Retrieved November, 2017, from www.oecd.org/skills/piaac/

OECD. (2018). *STI Micro-data Lab: Intellectual Property, Database*. Paris: OECD. Retrieved February, 2018, from http://oe.cd/ipstats

OECD and European Union. (2014). *The Missing Entrepreneurs 2014: Policies for Inclusive Entrepreneurship in Europe*. Paris: OECD Publishing. Retrieved February 22, from https://doi.org/10.1787/9789264213593-en

OECD and European Union. (2017). *Missing Entrepreneurs 2017*. Paris: OECD Publishing. Retrieved January 5, 2018, from https://doi.org/10.1787/9789264283602-en

Orford, J., Herrington, M., & Wood, E. (2004). *Global Entrepreneurship Monitor (GEM): South African Report*. University of Cape Town, South Africa.

Piacentini, M. (2013). Women Entrepreneurs in the OECD: Key Evidence and Policy Challenges. *OECD Social, Employment and Migration Working Papers, No. 147*. Paris: OECD Publishing. https://doi.org/10.1787/5k43bvtkmb8v-en

Quintini, G. (2018). Automation, Skills Use and Training. *OECD Social, Employment and Migration Working Papers, No. 202*. Paris: OECD Publishing. https://doi.org/10.1787/2e2f4eea-en.

Saifuddin, S. M. (2015). *Women Entrepreneurs' Adoption and Use of Technology*. Special report prepared for Cisco Systems by Centre for Women in Politics and Public Leadership Carleton University.

Stephan, P. E., & El-Ganainy, A. (2007). The Entrepreneurial Puzzle: Explaining the Gender Gap. *The Journal of Technology Transfer, 32*(5), 475–487.

UNDP. (2008). Breaking Barriers the Potential of Free and Open Source Software for Sustainable Human Development. Asia-Pacific Development Information Programme (UNDP-APDIP).

UN Women. (2005). Gender Equality and Empowerment of Women through ICT. UN Division for the Advancement of Women, Department of Economic and Social Affairs of the United Nations Secretariat, New York. Retrieved from www.un.org/womenwatch/daw/public/w2000-09.05-ict-e.pdf.

Verheul, I., Uhlaner, L., & Thurik, R. (2005). Business Accomplishments, Gender and Entrepreneurial Self-image. *Journal of Business Venturing, 20*(4), 483–518.

World Bank and the International Telecommunication Union. (2015). *The Little Data Book on Information and Telecommunication Technology*. Retrieved from http://data.worldbank.org/products/data-books/little-data-book

due to the fact that cocoa is the largest commercial crop that facilitates 21% of the country's international trade activities.

Aside from cocoa production, which is the largest crop grown in the country, other major staple crops include cereals (mainly rice and maize) and starchy staples such as yams, cocoyams, cassava, and plantains (Asiedu and Sartie 2010). Likewise, when it comes to agriculture in Ghana, livestock production is also evident. In the Ghanaian economy, livestock production includes but is not limited to the rearing of cattle, goats, poultry, pigs, and many others and this is normally done on a subsistence and commercial basis.

The agriculture sector is expected to lead economic growth in the country. This is confirmed by Lanz et al. (2017)'s study which found out that the growth and development of developing countries is dependent on agriculture. In Ghana, government development objectives hinge on a demand-driven national agricultural strategy whose goals are development, productivity, and competitiveness (Asuming-Brempong 1991). According to Bogetic et al. (2007), agriculture initiatives reduced Ghana's poverty rate from a whopping 51.7% in 1991–92 to 39.5% in 1998–99, and further to 28.5% in 2005–06. Interestingly, in 2011, FAO found that as agricultural growth decreased by 2.2%, the poverty level rose by 6.9%.

To enhance productivity in food production, technical efficiency measurements are crucial in providing the opportunity to increase agricultural productivity without necessarily increasing the resource base of the country. Squires and Tabor (1991) define technical efficiency as a farmer's ability to produce the maximum output possible from a given set of inputs and production technology.

This concept is relative since each farm's production performance is compared with the best practice input–output relationship or frontier. The best practices are established by the practices of the most efficient farmers. The deviation of the individual farm from the frontier measures technical inefficiency. From an aggregate and time series perspective, the best practice frontier is the potential output for the best practice year. Thus, the technical inefficiency in that case is the gap between the actual output for any particular year and the potential output of the best practice year.

Agricultural Entrepreneurship

The agriculture sector plays a strategic and dominant role in the growth and development of most developing countries, and in this Ghana is no exception. Most prominently, the role of the sector as a source of employment cannot be overemphasised. Statistics from sub-Saharan Africa, Asia, and the Pacific show that over 60% of the population is agriculture-dependent, while in Latin America and high-income economies the proportions are estimated to be around 18% and 4% respectively (Osumanu et al. 2017).

This therefore shows that the agriculture sector is very important when it comes to economic growth and development, overcoming poverty, and enhancing food security. As mentioned in a 2008 World Development report, the aforementioned potentials of agriculture can only be achieved through continuous increases in productivity among farmers. Thus, boosting agricultural productivity has been an issue of paramount importance to development institutions across the globe (Acheampong et al. 2017; Maertens and Barrett 2013).

Innovations in agricultural activities through the adoption of digital technology also play a significant role in fighting poverty, lowering per unit costs of production (Kassie et al. 2011), boosting rural incomes, and reducing hunger (Maertens and Barrett 2013).

However, many farmers continue to face economic pressures (Van Coppenolle 2017). In addition, the recent reforms, or "greening", of agricultural policies require farmers to meet environmental targets, which may also have a negative impact on farm productivity (Boere and van Kooten 2015). There are growing concerns regarding the increasing divide between urban and rural economies, with further concerns about the digital divide between urban and rural locations. In response to these challenges, agriculture requires an entrepreneurial stance and the exploitation of efficiency and value-added strategies.

This implies that agriculture needs to increase innovation and technology adoption, an area where agriculture has traditionally been laggardly (i.e. Barrett and Tinelli 2018). In Ghana, there is growing interest among scholars and practitioners regarding the concept of agricultural entrepreneurship. Scholars such as Acheampong et al. (2017),

Acheampong (2018), and Acheampong and Hinson (2018) have made interesting contributions to the agricultural entrepreneurship discourse.

Entrepreneurship plays an important role in farm management, although it is often overlooked for several reasons that will be discussed. Firstly, the definition of entrepreneurship needs to be clarified. Here, the link with opportunity again becomes important. York and Venkataraman define "the act of entrepreneurship as one of discovering and evaluating opportunity" as well as the creation of new opportunities (York and Venkataraman 2010, p. 451).

Morgan and Gergel (2010) define entrepreneurship as being associated with "innovation, re-organisation and creative action and in (re-) ordering resources to take advantage of, or to create, opportunities for realising value" (Morgan and Gergel 2010, p. 119). In this context, entrepreneurship is "inherently concerned with solving problems of uncertainty, innovation and resource allocation" (York and Venkataraman 2010, p. 452). Block et al. (2017) identified entrepreneurship as a key creative force, where disruption of the old was necessary to usher in the new—coining the term "creative destruction" (Schut et al. 2016).

The problem is that the existence of entrepreneurs in the farming community is often overlooked and there has been little research devoted to the subject (Richards and Bulkley 2007). The exception are authors such as Kilelu et al. (2017), who describe farmers as agricultural entrepreneurs and highlight that the constraints experienced by agricultural entrepreneurs are similar to those experienced by non-agricultural small to medium enterprises (SMEs)—as both types of enterprise display similar characteristics.

Resistance to considering farmers as entrepreneurs partly flows from a traditional view of farms and farmers as being separate from "normal market logic", where a farmer's identity is primarily that of producer rather than business person (Morgan and Gergel 2010, p. 119).

Entrepreneurship is also usually described as a neoliberal value, alongside competition and efficiency (Lockie et al. 2002). The result is that by perceiving farms primarily as businesses and farmers as entrepreneurs (similar to other industrial sectors), the reflex is to assume that they are agents of the agro-industrial paradigm (Morgan and Gergel 2010). For example, Dibden et al. suggest that the neoliberal emphasis on sound business practices and "resulting construction of farmers as self-reliant entrepreneurs sits uneasily with the narrative of farmers as altruistic land stewards" (Fielke and Wilson 2017, p. 1063).

Though having potentially different objectives, there is an interesting consistency between the emphasis in innovation literature on entrepreneurialism and that of neoliberalism. In this thesis, it is not assumed that entrepreneurship precludes environmental stewardship. Rather, it is argued that looking at entrepreneurial behaviour can provide insights on innovation and actions taken to create opportunities for realising value (Morgan and Gergel 2010).

Indeed, there is a growing literature on the potential for entrepreneurship (outside agriculture) to solve environmental problems. While environmental problems can arise from market failure, so too can environmental solutions, with entrepreneurship being the means to capitalise on what is essentially a gap in the market (Shepherd and Patzelt 2017; York and Venkataraman 2010).

However, the ability to realise an opportunity (as opposed to perceiving it) can also be constrained by context (e.g., climate, market, regulations) and resources (e.g., labour, capital, assets). The challenge is that for profit-seeking entrepreneurs, the market benefits of agricultural sustainability are few. Yet if governments intervene to create new markets, the opportunity that was in itself a function of market failure may disappear. In other words, the window for entrepreneurs may be too short-lived. In agriculture, this is a particular challenge, not only due to the lack of environmental markets, but because of the lack of profitability for farmers within commodity markets and the sector at large. The second challenge distinct to agriculture is that farms are often long-lived businesses, potentially over a period of generations. In other industries, environmental innovations are considered more likely to emerge from new firms that can do what incumbent firms cannot (York and Venkataraman 2010).

Agricultural Technology

Success stories emanating from the Green Revolution in Asia have often noted that efforts to increase agricultural productivity in Africa have been directed towards the adoption of improved agricultural technology, which could inspire the changeover from the current low-productivity, peasant, and subsistence farming to commercial farming. Improved agricultural technology adoption has the potential to deepen the market share of agricultural output through which farmers' resource use and output diversification decisions could be guided increasingly by their objective of profit maximisation.

For some time now, scholars and researchers have been attempting to undertake a holistic assessment of the introduction and adoption of technologies among poor rural farming communities using a variety of different approaches and models (Odoom et al. 2017; Acheampong et al. 2014; Maertens and Barrett 2012). These models generally range from normative decision-making and accounting techniques, such as benefit–cost ratios (BCR), internal rate of returns (IRR), and the net present value (NPV), to econometric models, such as multi-market models and supply response models, continuous production functions and efficiency measures, farm household models (FHMs), economic surplus models, general equilibrium models (GCE), policy analysis matrix (PAM) procedures, farming system research (FSR) procedures, and statistical simulation models such as mathematical programming, linear programming, or measures of welfare dominance (Ruben et al. 1998; Ruben and van Ruijven 2001).

Extant empirical literature has also examined the adoption of technology among rural farmers. A study by Olwande et al. (2009) used panel data to examine determinants of technology adoption and intensity of use. Using a double-hurdle model, they found that age and education of the farmer, access to credit, presence of a cash crop, distance to fertiliser market, and agro-ecological potential influence the probability of adoption. Gender of the farmer, dependency ratio, credit access, presence of cash crop, distance to extension services, and agro-ecological potential were found to influence intensity of technology use.

Another empirical study shows that household demographic, location, and socio-economic and institutional factors are important determinants of farm technology adoption and equilibrium level of use (Ogada et al. 2014; Mengistu et al. 2016; Mwangi and Kariuki 2015). However, their effects may not be universal. A factor is universal if it promotes or impedes technology adoption irrespective of location and type of technology.

Wainaina et al. (2016) and Rubas (2004) tested the universality of age, education, outreach, and farm size in influencing adoption of agricultural technologies.

Using ordinary least squares (OLS) and minimum absolute deviation (MAD) approaches, the study found that education and farm size were positive universal (encouraging adoption of all types of technology irrespective of location), while outreach was not universal. Age was not universal by OLS, and negative universal (discouraging adoption of all types of technology irrespective of location) by MAD. The study further noted that universality of age, education, and farm size was weak. This indicates that farm households in different locations may not respond to different technologies in the same way.

Other studies followed the path of the seminal paper by Griliches (1957) on adoption of new agricultural technologies. Griliches examined heterogeneity of local conditions and how it affected adoption of hybrid corn in the mid-western United States. The study noted the role of economic factors such as expected profits in influencing the variation in farm technology spread rates.

Further, the study noted that speed of adoption across geographical locations depended on the suppliers of the technology and suitability of the seed to local conditions. It is indeed from the work of Griliches that the economic literature on agricultural technology adoption developed. Some of the factors that may explain the rate of adoption and the long-run equilibrium level of use of new agricultural technology as identified in the economic literature include: credit constraints, risk aversion, the farmer's landholding size, land tenure system, human capital endowment, quality and quantity of farm equipment, and supply of complementary inputs (Feder et al. 1985).

Lio and Liu (2006) find a positive relationship exists between ICT adoption and agricultural productivity through increased market information and knowledge of new production inputs and methods. These can improve the efficiency of transactions between rural areas and core markets. The benefits of ICT adoption extend further than agriculture alone, where rural livelihoods can also be improved. Richardson (2005, p. 1) comments:

> Any ICT intervention that improves the livelihoods of poor rural families will likely have significant direct and indirect impacts on enhancing agricultural production, marketing and post-harvest activities—which in turn can further contribute to poverty reduction.

While this research is in the context of developing countries, we find that the same could be true in parts of the developed world. Galloway and Mochrie (2005) find that the delays in ICT adoption in rural areas are caused by both supply regarding poor technological infrastructure and demand issues due to the perceived lack of need.

8.3 Methodology

The nature of digital corporate agricultural entrepreneurship is relatively nascent and under-researched in emerging markets. To assess the nature of digital corporate entrepreneurship within the Ghanaian context, website analysis and interviews were used. Qualitative content analysis has been extensively used by scholars (Sweetser and Lariscy 2008; Hinson et al. 2014). This technique was chosen because of its flexibility in analysing text data (Cavanagh 2015). Such an approach has been shown to be suitable for improving knowledge (Bruton et al. 2015).

For this study, a sample of three corporate agricultural entrepreneurs in the Ghanaian market, namely Farmable, Farmerline, and Esoko, were utilised. Regarding the procedure of analysis, the home pages on the websites of the corporate agricultural entrepreneurs included in the study were chosen as the unit of analysis.

A content analysis of the websites was performed. A checklist was developed to ascertain the content of the three digital corporate agricultural entrepreneurs' websites included in the study. Features regarding the content of the websites needed to achieve the objectives of the study were grouped under three subheadings: how the corporate agricultural entrepreneurs improve agriculture productivity in Ghana through technology; how the corporate agricultural entrepreneurs use technology to nurture an entrepreneurial spirit among farmers; and the challenges faced by corporate agricultural entrepreneurs when deploying technology in the improvement of farmers' productivity.

8.4 Findings and Discussions

Profile of Corporate Agricultural Entrepreneurship in Ghana

Three corporate agricultural entrepreneurs in Ghana were interviewed for this study. These entrepreneurs comprised Farmerline (Case 1), Esoko (Case 2), and Farmable (Case 3). The profiles of these corporate agricultural entrepreneurs are shown below.

Case 1 is a Ghanaian software company with a social enterprise slant. Located in Kumasi and Accra with a current staff of 23, it builds mobile technologies that put information, financial services, and supply chains in the hands of small-scale rural farmers, as many small-scale farmers in Ghana lack information about farming techniques and market prices. Case 1 tackles this challenge by bridging this information gap through the use of mobile technology. The company provides three service lines.

The first is their outbound messaging service, which provides personalised voice alerts that communicate critical information related to price, weather, and farming techniques. Secondly, the company provides a mobile surveys service which allows farmer-based organisations (FBOs) to conduct surveys to capture the impact of their interventions. Lastly, the company provides a support line, which gives farmers direct access to expert advice. All of the company's services are offered via SMS and Android as well as a voice-based messaging service to help reach farmers with low literacy levels. Furthermore, all content is provided in local languages.

By offering these mobile-based services, Case 1 provides critical market information to Ghana's small-scale farmers, which helps them increase their yields by adopting improved farming practices. The company's customers, many of whom are women, ultimately benefit from increased income.

Founded in 2004, Case 2 is an information and communication service provider for the agricultural markets in Africa. It was formed in response to the explosive growth of cellular services across the continent. The company provides advice to farmers (market prices, weather forecasts, and growing tips) to help them increase yields and profits, as well as solutions to businesses (marketing products, monitoring activities, and sourcing goods) to help them connect with farmers. The technology platform itself includes automatic and personalised SMS alerts, buy and sell offers, built messaging, SMS polling, Android (operating system) surveys, and more.

A private initiative based in Accra, Ghana, Case 2 was built and is supported by a team of local developers and consulting staff. In addition to the technology, Case 2 provides extensive deployment support, strategic planning, and field training to clients.

Case 3 is a crowdfunding platform for small cattle farmers. This corporate agricultural entrepreneur equips farmers with the necessary tools and resources to fight hunger. It also raises awareness of the challenges facing farmers and helps make them independent in their various businesses. The vision of Case 3 is to help fight hunger in Ghana and reduce the intake of external aid by helping small-scale farmers to be self-sustainable. The business line of Case 3 was taken from the idea of the "Innoboa" concept. "Innoboa" is an Akan word which means communal help.

With this, all members within the Innoboa club help each other on their farms and this helps them share farming ideas, cultures, and practices that help in large farm yields. Over the next five years, this agricultural corporate entrepreneur seeks to partner with 250 smallholder farmers; increase farmer herd size by up to 25%; increase average profits of smallholder partners by 10%; crowdfarm over 7,500 cattle from smallholder farmers on the Farmable CFP; and sell 5000 cattle and build a database of 100,000 paying subscribers on the Farmable CFP.

Objective One: Improvement of Agricultural Activities Through Technology

The first objective of this study was to find out what kind of platforms and initiatives these corporate agricultural entrepreneurs have created using technology to improve the activities of farmers in Ghana. In line with this objective, results were obtained from a critical analysis of the content of the websites of the three cases included in the study.

From the analysis of the content of the website of Case 1, the researchers found out that:

> The company has in place an information-service platform known as the 399 information service, which provides real-time agriculture education via farmers' mobile phones.
>
> Also, [Case 1] has outbound messaging services which provide personalised voice alerts that communicate critical information related to price, weather, and farming techniques to farmers.
>
> Additionally, [Case 1] provides a mobile survey service which allows farmer-based organizations (FBOs) to conduct surveys to capture the impact of their interventions.
>
> The company also provides a support line which gives farmers direct access to expert advice. Additionally, all of the company's services are offered via SMS, and Android as well as voice-based messaging services, to help reach farmers with low literacy levels.
>
> The services of [Case 1] have made it possible for farmers to compete in the global market with their local farm products, connect to global markets, enable them to improve sustainability practices, increase productivity, and learn and apply global certification.

In line with the same objective, the website analysis of Case 2 also provided some valuable and insightful information regarding the platforms and activities they have employed in using technology to improve agriculture. Their website states that:

> The Voice Helpline and SMS-based Information Dissemination platforms are doing a wonderful job in improving agricultural activities among farmers.

When we probed further to find out how these platforms operate and boost agriculture in Ghana, results from the content analysis of Case 2's website showed that,

> through partnerships with agricultural research institutions both within and outside Ghana, [Case 2] is constantly recommending sophisticated technology to local farmers in Ghana.

> with the voice helpline, farmers can call in to figure out how to work new agricultural technology—sharpen their skill set.

Additionally, the content analysis of the website of Case 2 revealed that,

> the SMS platform attempts to enhance and augment farmers' and agricultural stakeholders' skill levels.
>
> Again, through the platforms of [Case 2], farmers are provided with information such as crop calendars. These calendars take weather patterns into consideration and inform farmers about the appropriate time to carry out certain farming activities like sourcing of crop inputs, preparing soil for cultivation, removal of weed, inspection of crops, application of pesticide, crop harvesting, sale of crops, and many more activities.

With regard to the same objectives, the website content analysis of Case 3 showed that,

> the company has in place a crowdfunding platform for small-cattle farmers.
>
> [Case 3] has also developed an innovative on-line funding model (crowdFarming), in which social investors (cowbackers) can purchase a "share" in a real cow in Ghana (a cowShare) in return for exclusive rewards.

Additionally, through continuous innovation in their technology, [Case 3] is able to provide training for farmers and also equip them to come up with innovative ideas for improving their productivity.

The findings from the study above indicate that technology is providing greater opportunity for enhancing agricultural activities in Ghana. These findings confirm the results of Emerick et al. (2016) and Madsen et al. (2016).

Objective Two: Nurturing Entrepreneurship Through Technology

The second objective of the study was to explore how technology is helping to nurture entrepreneurs within the agricultural sector in Ghana.

Interesting results were obtained from the digital corporate entrepreneurs included in the study.

Through in-depth, face-to-face interviews with key experts and heads of IT departments of the cases included in the study, the researchers elicited responses pertaining to how technology is used to nurture entrepreneurship intent among farmers.

> The heads of IT of Case 1 had this to say: "With our platforms, farmers are given easy access to information regarding agricultural prices on the market and get quick and easy access to the ready market for agricultural products, equipping them to partake in business ventures and making profit from their produce using technology".
>
> Key experts of Case 2 had this to say: "Through our platforms, we have enabled most farmers who were just catering for their family to be entrepreneurial active. With the use of our platform farmers have a direct relationship with various agricultural stakeholders, combine best practises to maximise success, and gain knowledge and save time in the performance of business activities".

Results from the in-depth interviews with key experts and heads of the IT department showed that with the introduction of these technological platforms, entrepreneurship intent was boosted as farmers gained easy access to information regarding agricultural prices, got quick and easy access to the ready market for agricultural products, had a direct relationship with various agricultural stakeholders, combined best practises to maximise success, and gained knowledge and saved time in the performance of business activities. The findings of this study are in line with those of Klerkx et al. (2010), who found out that the adoption of technology among agriculture adopters promoted innovation and boosted entrepreneurship intent.

Objective Three: Challenges Faced by Digital Corporate Agricultural Entrepreneurs in Ghana

The third objective of the study was to explore the challenges facing digital corporate agriculture entrepreneurs in Ghana. Information from interviews with key experts and the heads of the IT department of all the three cases regarding the challenges faced when utilising technology to boost agriculture in Ghana are shown below.

> The head of IT mentioned that: "Lack of electricity in remote communities remains a primary challenge to successful data collection using smart devices". (Case 1)
>
> The key experts said that: "Lack of mobile connectivity and bandwidth is another major obstacle to deploying data collection technology in remote communities". (Case 2)
>
> According to the head of IT of [Case 2], "most mobile network organizations (MNOs) do not yet provide high-speed connectivity in rural areas, although they can support several valuable synchronous and low-bandwidth applications".
>
> The head of IT of [Case 3] mentioned that: "Internet connectivity, bundle width, power issues, and many other problems have made it difficult for most companies including [Case 3] to successfully perform their duty towards providing timely information to farmers to boost productivity on time".

8.5 Conclusion and Future Studies

This study sought to explore the nature of digital corporate agricultural entrepreneurship in Ghana. The objectives of the study were to examine how agriculture has improved through technology; identify how technology nurtures entrepreneurship among farmers; and finally to find out what challenges corporate agricultural entrepreneurs face when utilising technology to improve productivity among farmers.

The corporate agricultural entrepreneurs are seen to be improving farmers' productivity through technology in ways such as providing farmers with pricing data, crop inputs, soil preparation and cultivation training, inspection of crops services, application of pesticides, crop harvesting techniques, sale of crops, and so on, as well as through voice helplines, SMS platforms, crowdfunding, and training for farmers through technology and mobile phones.

Additionally, corporate agricultural entrepreneurs were seen to be using technology to build entrepreneurial intent among farmers. Through technology, buyers and sellers were brought together, offering better opportunities for trade. Farmers who were just fending for their family saw the opportunity to utilise their platforms to become entrepreneurs carrying out business activities with potential buyers. Additionally, through these technological platforms, farmers are educated about how to start a business and make a profit using software developed by digital corporate agricultural entrepreneurs.

Finally, the study revealed that power fluctuations and mobile connectivity were the major challenges that hindered the timely and successful activities of corporate agricultural entrepreneurs in Ghana in using technology to improve the performance of farmers. This study makes a significant contribution to the discourse of digital corporate agricultural entrepreneurship in Ghana, which is arguably sparse in the literature. Further studies should focus on exploring a cross-sector study to identify the nature of digital corporate entrepreneurship in other sectors in Ghana besides the agriculture sector. It is, however, highly recommended that corporate entrepreneurs aim at creating in-depth discussions on how ICT could be integrated into agriculture to modernise the sector for sustainable national development.

References

Acheampong, G., Braimah, M., Quaye, D. M., & Buame, S. K. (2014). Impact of Demographic Factors on Technological Orientations of BOP Entrepreneurs in Ghana. *International Journal of Innovation and Technology Management, 11*(6), 1450037.

Acheampong, G., & Hinson, R. E. (2018). Benefitting from Alter Resources: Network Diffusion and SME Survival. *Journal of Small Business & Entrepreneurship, 30*(1), 1–18.

Acheampong, G., Narteh, B., & Rand, J. (2017). Network Ties and Survival: A Study of Small Commercial Poultry Farms in Ghana. *The International Journal of Entrepreneurship and Innovation, 18*(1), 14–24.

Amankwah, E., & Ocloo, T. O. (2012). Contribution of Small Scale Irrigated Agriculture to Food Security in the Upper West Region of Ghana. *Journal of Developments in Sustainable Agriculture, 7*(2), 115–121.

Asiedu, R., & Sartie, A. (2010). Crops that Feed the World 1. Yams. *Food Security, 2*(4), 305–315.

Asuming-Brempong, S. (1991). Yam for Foreign Exchange: Potentials and Prospects in Ghana. *In Symposium on Tropical Root Crops in a Developing Economy, 380*(1), 382–387.

Barrett, C., & Tinelli, C. (2018). Satisfiability Modulo Theories. In *Handbook of Model Checking* (pp. 305–343). Cham: Springer.

Benitez, J., Chen, Y., Teo, T. S., & Ajamieh, A. (2018). Evolution of the Impact of e-Business Technology on Operational Competence and Firm Profitability: A Panel Data Investigation. *Information & Management, 55*(1), 120–130.

Block, J. H., Fisch, C. O., & Van Praag, M. (2017). The Schumpeterian Entrepreneur: A Review of the Empirical Evidence on the Antecedents, Behaviour and Consequences of Innovative Entrepreneurship. *Industry and Innovation, 24*(1), 61–95.

Boere, E., & van Kooten, G. C. (2015). Reforming the Common Agricultural Policy: Decoupling Agricultural Payments from Production and Promoting the Environment. *Working Paper No. 2015-01*. REPA Research Group, Department of Economics University of Victoria, Wellington.

Bogetic, Y., Bussolo, M., Ye, X., Medvedev, D., Wodon, Q., & Boakye, D. (2007). Ghana's Growth Story: How to Accelerate Growth and Achieve MDGs. *Background Paper for Ghana CEM*.

Bruton, G. D., Ahlstrom, D., & Si, S. (2015). Entrepreneurship, Poverty, and Asia: Moving Beyond Subsistence Entrepreneurship. *Asia Pacific Journal of Management, 32*(1), 1–22.

Butt, T. M., Qijie, G., Hassan, M. Z. Y., Luqman, M., Khan, M., Tian, X., & Mehmood, K. (2017). An Exploration of Information Communication Technology (ICTs) in Agricultural Development: The Experiences of Rural Punjab-Pakistan. *Transylvanian Review, 25*(16), 2–9.

Cavanagh, K. (2015, January). The Shape of Things to Come: Inspiration in the Organizational Sciences. In *Academy of Management Proceedings* (Vol. 2015, No. 1, p. 15485). Briarcliff Manor, NY: Academy of Management.

Corbett, A., Covin, J. G., O'Connor, G. C., & Tucci, C. L. (2013). Corporate Entrepreneurship: State-of-the-Art Research and a Future Research Agenda. *Journal of Product Innovation Management, 30*(5), 812–820.

Davidson, E., & Vaast, E. (2010, January). Digital Entrepreneurship and Its Sociomaterial Enactment. In *2010 43rd Hawaii International Conference on System Sciences (HICSS)* (pp. 1–10). IEEE.

Deichmann, U., Goyal, A., & Mishra, D. (2016). *Will Digital Technologies Transform Agriculture in Developing Countries?* Washington, DC: The World Bank.

Emerick, K., de Janvry, A., Sadoulet, E., & Dar, M. H. (2016). Technological Innovations, Downside Risk, and the Modernization of Agriculture. *American Economic Review, 106*(6), 1537–1561.

FAO. (2010). Food and Agriculture Organization of the United Nations. Retrieved from http://www.fao.org/docrep/006/y5143e/y5143e12.htm

Feder, G., Just, R. E., & Zilberman, D. (1985). Adoption of Agricultural Innovations in Developing Countries: A Survey. *Economic Development and Cultural Change, 33*(2), 255–298.

Fielke, S. J., & Wilson, G. A. (2017). Multifunctional Intervention and Market Rationality in Agricultural Governance: A Comparative Study of England and South Australia. *GeoJournal, 82*(5), 1067–1083.

Galloway, L., & Mochrie, R. (2005). The Use of ICT in Rural Firms: A Policy-Orientated Literature Review. *Info, 7*(3), 33–46.

Goldin, C., & Katz, L. F. (2018). The Race between Education and Technology. In *Inequality in the 21st Century* (pp. 49–54). Abingdon: Routledge.

Griliches, Z. (1957). Hybrid Corn: An Exploration in the Economics of Technological Change. *Econometrica, Journal of the Econometric Society, 25*(4), 501–522.

GSS. (2012). *2010 Population and Housing Census, Summary of Final Results.* Accra: GSS.

Gunasekaran, A., Subramanian, N., & Papadopoulos, T. (2017). Information Technology for Competitive Advantage within Logistics and Supply Chains: A Review. *Transportation Research Part E: Logistics and Transportation Review, 99*, 14–33.

Hair, J. F., Sarstedt, M., Pieper, T. M., & Ringle, C. M. (2012a). The Use of Partial Least Squares Structural Equation Modeling in Strategic Management Research: A Review of Past Practices and Recommendations for Future Applications. *Long Range Planning, 45*(5–6), 320–340.

Hair, J. F., Sarstedt, M., Ringle, C. M., & Mena, J. A. (2012b). An Assessment of the Use of Partial Least Squares Structural Equation Modeling in Marketing Research. *Journal of the Academy of Marketing Science, 40*(3), 414–433.

Hinson, R. E., van Zyl, H., & Agbleze, S. (2014). An Interrogation of the Dialogic Potential of Insurance Firm Websites in Ghana. *Information Development, 30*(1), 59–69.

Jancenelle, V. E., Storrud-Barnes, S., & Javalgi, R. R. G. (2017). Corporate Entrepreneurship and Market Performance: A Content Analysis of Earnings Conference Calls. *Management Research Review, 40*(3), 352–367.

Javalgi, R. R. G., Todd, P. R., Johnston, W. J., & Granot, E. (2012). Entrepreneurship, Muddling through, and Indian Internet-Enabled SMEs. *Journal of Business Research, 65*(6), 740–744.

Kassie, M., Shiferaw, B., & Muricho, G. (2011). Agricultural Technology, Crop Income, and Poverty Alleviation in Uganda. *World Development, 39*(10), 1784–1795.

Kilelu, C. W., Klerkx, L., & Leeuwis, C. (2017). Supporting Smallholder Commercialisation by Enhancing Integrated Coordination in Agrifood Value Chains: Experiences with Dairy Hubs in Kenya. *Experimental Agriculture, 53*(2), 269–287.

Klerkx, L., Aarts, N., & Leeuwis, C. (2010). Adaptive Management in Agricultural Innovation Systems: The Interactions between Innovation Networks and Their Environment. *Agricultural Systems, 103*(6), 390–400.

Kuratko, D. F., & Morris, M. H. (2018). Corporate Entrepreneurship: A Critical Challenge for Educators and Researchers. *Entrepreneurship Education and Pedagogy, 1*(1), 42–60.

Kwarteng, J. A., & Towler, M. J. (1994). *West African Agriculture: A Textbook for Schools and Colleges*. London: Macmillan.

Lackéus, M., & Middleton, K. W. (2018). Assessing Experiential Entrepreneurship Education: Key Insights from Five Methods in Use at a Venture Creation Programme. In *Experiential Learning for Entrepreneurship* (pp. 19–49). Cham: Palgrave Macmillan.

Lanz, B., Dietz, S., & Swanson, T. (2017). Global Economic Growth and Agricultural Land Conversion under Uncertain Productivity Improvements in Agriculture. *American Journal of Agricultural Economics, 100*(2), 545–569.

Lio, M., & Liu, M. C. (2006). ICT and Agricultural Productivity: Evidence from Cross-country Data. *Agricultural Economics, 34*(3), 221–228.

Lockie, S., Lyons, K., Lawrence, G., & Mummery, K. (2002). Eating Green: Motivations behind Organic Food Consumption in Australia. *Sociologia Ruralis, 42*(1), 23–40.

Madsen, M. D., Davies, K. W., Boyd, C. S., Kerby, J. D., & Svejcar, T. J. (2016). Emerging Seed Enhancement Technologies for Overcoming Barriers to Restoration. *Restoration Ecology, 24*, S77–S84.

Maertens, A., & Barrett, C. B. (2012). Measuring Social Networks' Effects on Agricultural Technology Adoption. *American Journal of Agricultural Economics, 95*(2), 353–359.

Maertens, A., & Barrett, C. B. (2013). Measuring Social Networks' Effects on Agricultural Technology Adoption. *American Journal of Agricultural Economics, 95*(2), 353–359.

Maredia, K. M., Whalon, M. E., Gage, S. H., & Kaeb, M. J. (2018). Observations of First Occurrence and Severity of Potato Leafhopper, Empoasca Fabae (Harris), (Homoptera: Cicadellidae) in the North Central and Eastern United States. *The Great Lakes Entomologist, 31*(1), 8–12.

Martín-Rojas, R., Fernández-Pérez, V., & García-Sánchez, E. (2017). Encouraging Organizational Performance through the Influence of Technological Distinctive Competencies on Components of Corporate Entrepreneurship. *International Entrepreneurship and Management Journal, 13*(2), 397–426.

Mengistu, M. G., Simane, B., Eshete, G., & Workneh, T. S. (2016). Factors Affecting Households' Decisions in Biogas Technology Adoption, the Case of Ofla and Mecha Districts, Northern Ethiopia. *Renewable Energy, 93*, 215–227.

Morgan, J. L., & Gergel, S. E. (2010). Quantifying Historic Landscape Heterogeneity from Aerial Photographs Using Object-based Analysis. *Landscape Ecology, 25*, 985–998.

Mwangi, M., & Kariuki, S. (2015). Factors Determining Adoption of New Agricultural Technology by Smallholder Farmers in Developing Countries. *Journal of Economics and Sustainable Development, 6*(5), 208–216.

Odoom, R., Anning-Dorson, T., & Acheampong, G. (2017). Antecedents of Social Media Usage and Performance Benefits in Small- and Medium-Sized Enterprises (SMEs). *Journal of Enterprise Information Management, 30*(3), 383–399.

Ogada, M. J., Mwabu, G., & Muchai, D. (2014). Farm Technology Adoption in Kenya: A Simultaneous Estimation of Inorganic Fertilizer and Improved Maize Variety Adoption Decisions. *Agricultural and Food Economics, 2*(1), 12.

Olaniyan, O. F. (2017). Adapting Gambian Women Livestock Farmers' Roles in Food Production to Climate Change. *Future of Food: Journal on Food, Agriculture and Society, 5*(2), 56–66.

Olwande, J., Sikei, G., & Mathenge, M. (2009). *Agricultural Technology Adoption: A Panel Analysis of Smallholder Farmers' Fertilizer Use in Kenya.* Berkeley: eScholarship, University of California.

Onetti, A., Zucchella, A., Jones, M. V., & McDougall-Covin, P. P. (2012). Internationalization, Innovation and Entrepreneurship: Business Models for New Technology-based Firms. *Journal of Management & Governance, 16*(3), 337–368.

Osumanu, I. K., Aniah, P., & Yelfaanibe, A. (2017). Determinants of Adaptive Capacity to Climate Change among Smallholder Rural Households in the

Bongo District, Ghana. *Ghana Journal of Development Studies, 14*(2), 142–162.
Reed, J., van Vianen, J., Foli, S., Clendenning, J., Yang, K., MacDonald, M., et al. (2017). Trees for Life: The Ecosystem Service Contribution of Trees to Food Production and Livelihoods in the Tropics. *Forest Policy and Economics, 84*, 62–71.
Richards, S. T., & Bulkley, S. (2007). Agricultural Entrepreneur: The First and the Forgotten? *Hudson Institute Research Paper, 7*(1), 1–34.
Richardson, D. (2005). How Can Agricultural Extension Best Harness ICTs to Improve Rural Livelihoods in Developing Countries? In *ICT in Agriculture: Perspectives of Technological Innovation* (Vol. 6, pp. 1–8). Jerusalem: EFITA.
Rubas, D. J. (2004). *Technology Adoption: Who is Likely to Adopt and How Does the Timing Affect the Benefits?* Doctoral dissertation, Texas A&M University.
Ruben, R., Moll, H., & Kuyvenhoven, A. (1998). Integrating Agricultural Research and Policy Analysis: Analytical Framework and Policy Applications for Bio-economic Modelling. *Agricultural Systems, 58*(3), 331–349.
Ruben, R., & van Ruijven, A. (2001). Technical Coefficients for Bio-economic Farm Household Models: A Meta-Modelling Approach with Applications for Southern Mali. *Ecological Economics, 36*(3), 427–441.
Schmitt, A., Raisch, S., & Volberda, H. W. (2018). Strategic Renewal: Past Research, Theoretical Tensions and Future Challenges. *International Journal of Management Reviews, 20*(1), 81–98.
Schut, M., Klerkx, L., Sartas, M., Lamers, D., Mc Campbell, M., Ogbonna, I., et al. (2016). Innovation Platforms: Experiences with Their Institutional Embedding in Agricultural Research for Development. *Experimental Agriculture, 52*(4), 537–561.
Shepherd, D. A., & Patzelt, H. (2017). Researching Entrepreneurships' Role in Sustainable Development. In *Trailblazing in Entrepreneurship* (pp. 149–179). Cham: Palgrave Macmillan.
Sheth, J. N. (2011). Impact of Emerging Markets on Marketing: Rethinking Existing Perspectives and Practices. *Journal of Marketing, 75*(4), 166–182.
Squires, D., & Tabor, S. (1991). Technical Efficiency and Future Production Gains in Indonesian Agriculture. *The Developing Economies, 29*, 258–270.
Sumberg, J., Yeboah, T., Flynn, J., & Anyidoho, N. A. (2017). Young People's Perspectives on Farming in Ghana: A Q Study. *Food Security, 9*(1), 151–161.
Sweetser, K. D., & Lariscy, R. W. (2008). Candidates Make Good Friends: An Analysis of Candidates' Uses of Facebook. *International Journal of Strategic Communication, 2*(3), 175–198.

Van Coppenolle, B. (2017). Political Dynasties in the UK House of Commons: The Null Effect of Narrow Electoral Selection. *Legislative Studies Quarterly, 42*(3), 449–475.

Vasilchenko, E., & Morrish, S. (2011). The Role of Entrepreneurial Networks in the Exploration and Exploitation of Internationalization Opportunities by Information and Communication Technology Firms. *Journal of International Marketing, 19*(4), 88–105.

Vasquez, C., Chia, E., Escobar, M., Kuper, M., & Henriquez, D. (2017). Creating Small Farm Entrepreneurs or Doing away with Peasants? State-Driven Implementation of Drip Irrigation in Chile. In *Drip Irrigation for Agriculture* (pp. 122–133). Abingdon: Routledge.

Wainaina, P., Tongruksawattana, S., & Qaim, M. (2016). Tradeoffs and Complementarities in the Adoption of Improved Seeds, Fertilizer, and Natural Resource Management Technologies in Kenya. *Agricultural Economics, 47*(3), 351–362.

York, J. G., & Venkataraman, S. (2010). The Entrepreneur–Environment Nexus: Uncertainty, Innovation, and Allocation. *Journal of Business Venturing, 25*, 449–463.

Yunis, M., El-Kassar, A. N., & Tarhini, A. (2017). Impact of ICT-based Innovations on Organizational Performance: The Role of Corporate Entrepreneurship. *Journal of Enterprise Information Management, 30*(1), 122–141.

9

Agri-tech Opportunities at the Bottom of the Pyramid: How Big Is the Opportunity and How Little Has Been Exploited? Some Selected Cases in Nigeria

Ali Muhammad Garba

9.1 Introduction

The application of digital technology in Nigeria to boost farm production has been minimal and has developed painfully slowly, and where it is used (in large firms), it relies heavily on foreign technology unavailable to local entrepreneurs. Perhaps, for all the years of farming in Nigeria, the most revolutionary attempt at using technology in agriculture involves so-called mechanised farming, which was given fresh impetus with the introduction of the Green Revolution Policy in the early 1980s by Nigeria's central government.[1]

[1] President Shehu Shagari (1979–83) introduced the Green Revolution. The policy aimed to encourage commercial farming through mechanised agriculture to boost employment and productivity and create linkages with industry.

A. M. Garba (✉)
Dangote Business School, Bayero University, Kano, Nigeria

N. D. Taura et al. (eds.), *Digital Entrepreneurship in Sub-Saharan Africa*, Palgrave Studies of Entrepreneurship in Africa, https://doi.org/10.1007/978-3-030-04924-9_9

The main feature of the policy was the use of mechanical farm tools, such as tractors and its associated tools, to replace oxen and human labour, which had been used for centuries. Little else has happened in the application of technology to boost farming output and productivity since then.

Government agricultural policy has remained unfocused and unenthusiastic. In recent years, however, there have been new developments in the application of information and communication technology (ICT) to supply input, such as fertilisers, seeds/seedlings, and insecticides, to farmers. A more exciting development is the use of ICT to support farmers in farm management and, therewith, improve farm yields and overall farming output. It may be many years, however, before this development becomes widely accepted and used.[2]

The domestic development and adoption of technology in agriculture in Nigeria has also been painfully slow. Aided by the availability of cheap foreign exchange, weak infrastructure, and unstable agricultural policy, the government has relied on importing tractors and leasing them out to farmers, reselling them to large farmers, or simply distributing them as patronage to party stalwarts and government officials.

There is a renewed effort in this direction, with many state governors in recent years visiting China to buy tractors and other farm equipment (Katsina State Agriculture Restoration Project 2016). Some state governors have indicated that agreements have been signed with foreign companies to begin assembling tractors in their states.

Overall, there is no significant private sector initiative in the drive to develop, domesticate, or adopt and apply digital or other forms of technology in agriculture in Nigeria. Large agricultural firms are mostly foreign-owned and import much of the technology they require from overseas. There are, however, indications that things might be changing.

[2] One of the most celebrated ICT ventures is Verdant Enterprises, founded by Nasir Yammama (a multiple award winner, including the British Council and Virgin Atlantic's Enterprise Challenge in 2015). Verdant is a social enterprise whose main aim is to democratise agricultural information for farmers via low-cost mobile phones to access weather information, managerial skills, and financial services. In collaboration with Oxfam and GIZ, Verdant is now supporting over 25,000 local Nigerian farmers through its mobile platform.

The central government's 'accidental' policy on rice production, which involves a ban on rice importation and provision of credit, and the recent currency crisis may have provided the needed incentive for the private sector to develop innovative ways to exploit the vast new opportunities in rice production and its associated value chain.

This chapter discusses how this initiative is shaping up and providing a platform for the development of digital technology in the rice value chain. The chapter makes a brief statement on the rice policy and describes the stages involved in rice processing. It then presents a case study of two companies (Prime Wave and Al-Wabel) involved in the innovative processes that are changing rice processing. The chapter concludes with implications and recommendations for future research and policy to sustain this development.

9.2 The Rice Production Policy

In 2015, a new government was sworn into power in Nigeria—Africa's largest country and economy. The new government inherited an economy in recession and was quick to implement certain initiatives, such as economic diversification, removal of fuel subsidy, and putting a technical ban on the importation of rice to improve food security, and other measures to reduce the cost of governance.

The immediate impact of these economic stabilisation initiatives was a high cost of food items including rice, which is arguably the main staple food in Nigeria. The domestic market price for imported rice from neighbouring countries went up by almost 50%, increasing from about ₦12,000 (US$24) to about ₦18,000 (US$36) per 50 kilograms in the first six months of 2018 (Global Agricultural Information Network (GAIN) Report 2017). There was a mild currency crisis and unemployment was rising to an alarming level.

To check the effect of these, the administration experimented with a number of policy initiatives. One such policy initiative is food security, and in this the government focused on rice production, issuing loans to rice farmers in states such as Kebbi with comparative advantages in rice production. The loan facility, under the Presidential Anchor Borrower

Scheme,[3] provided incentives to farmers that produced record quantities of rice paddy.[4]

According to the ECOWAS Rice Factbook (2018), demand for rice in Nigeria is estimated to be 6300 metric tons per annum while production is put at 2300 metric tons. Per capita rice consumption is estimated to be 27 kg per annum. Nigeria imports 2000 metric tons annually. The processing capacity of rice plants in Nigeria is less than one million metric tons per annum.

This means the opportunity for investment in processing is large, it is expanding, and it looks set to last in the long term, making rice processing an excellent opportunity for investors and for government efforts to reduce unemployment and poverty.

9.3 Rice Processing in Nigeria

Rice processing has been practised in Nigeria for decades at two distinct levels. The first level consists of micro or small processors—mostly women using 'local' techniques involving manual cleaning of the paddy, which is then steamed using large cooking pots. The steamed rice is then dried in open spaces at home or, more often, on public tarred roads. The rice husk is then milled through a 'beating' process using a mortar.

Small milling machines were later introduced by micro/small farmers for milling purposes. In many cases, the millers are separate 'businesses' offering milling services to the women, who could not ordinarily afford to buy the milling machines. There is a concentration of these micro/small processors around the sources of raw materials—around farms and areas producing rice paddy. The per capita quantity of processed rice at

[3] A total of ₦55 billion has been disbursed by the Central Bank of Nigeria to over 250,000 farmers under the scheme. *Punch Newspaper*, 15 February 2018.

[4] Between 2015 and 2016 the production of rice increased by over 100%, from 751,000 metric tons (MT) to 1,805,000 MT. Shehu and Lolo (2017) Promoting Rice Productivity in Kebbi State: Linking Data and Policy, State Policy Note 2, June 2017, Innovation Lab for Food Security Policy Nigeria Agricultural Policy Project *FEED the FUTURE (The US Government's Global and Food Security Initiatives.*

this level is usually very small. The processed rice is usually of poor quality in terms of appearance, taste, and yield when cooked. The grains, when cooked, are 'gummed' to each other. It is also never free from impurities, requiring a tedious process of de-stoning by the user. This rice is identified by the generic name 'local rice'. The end product is usually targeted at low-income buyers.

The second level of processors consists of large firms that use costly modern technology, which is mostly imported from Asia (usually India or China). Average investment in these firms runs at more than US$1 million (billions of naira in the local currency equivalent).

All processes (cleaning, soaking, steaming, milling, and bagging) are automated using appropriate digital technology. The movement of paddy from warehouse to factory is done using conveyor belts and elevators. As expected, the finished product is of higher quality—the rice looks 'foreign', it tastes better, and it has higher yield when cooked. The cooked grain is also not 'gummed' together as is the case with the local rice. This level has established brands of 'parboiled' rice that compete effectively with imported rice from Thailand and other Asian countries (Interview with Prime Wave).

Rice processing, at whatever level (micro, small, medium, and large operations), involves a 'combination of several operations to convert paddy rice into well milled silky-white rice, which has superior cooking quality attributes' (WAAPP-Nigeria, Rice Production, Processing, Utilisation and Marketing in Nigeria, Extension Bulletin No. 230, p. 26). Most consumers of rice prefer the rice that is well milled with little bran observable on the grain. The objectives of rice processing include: (1) to produce a maximum quantity of unbroken grains with standardised bran layers, desired colours, and lustre; (2) to maximise factory throughput and capacity as well as human resources; and (3) to minimise consumption of energy and consumable parts (ibid.). There are essentially two stages in rice processing. The first stage is the pre-treatment stage, which involves:

- Cleaning the rice paddy of impurities, removing of foreign particles, and de-stoning the paddy. This process uses simple mechanical devices that are cheap to obtain and poses little threat. However, most of the technology is imported from China or India;

- Parboiling (which means partial boiling, to boil halfway). This involves:

  - Soaking the rice paddy in hot water to achieve complete gelatinisation of starch, steaming the paddy at temperatures ranging from 80–90 Celsius depending on the variety of rice paddy. This process allows the processor to upgrade the rice variety, mend rice breakages, reduce breaks during milling, and ensure that the nutrients in the husk and bran are absorbed by the endosperm of the paddy canal;
  - Drying of the rice paddy, which involves reducing the moisture content of the steamed rice paddy, which could be up to 40%. The drying process brings down the moisture content to 11–12%, which is the required level before milling.

The second stage is milling, which involves cleaning, de-husking, and polishing the rice paddy, grading and sorting, and finally packaging. Milling, both for rice and for other grains, has never been a challenge in Nigeria—micro mills are multipurpose mills and have been available for use for different milling purposes. Clusters can use a single milling machine, as is observed in several locations of rice milling activities.

9.4 Case Studies: Prime Wave Limited and Al-Wabel Star Trading Company Limited

To identify the new innovations in rice processing, a qualitative case study design was used for the research, in line with the suggestions of Van Maanen (1988) that this type of research 'should be empirical enough to be credible and analytical enough to be interesting'. An extensive interview was conducted with the owners and the Chief Executive Officers of Prime Wave Limited and Al-Wabel Trading Company Limited.

The CEO of Prime Wave, along with his father, was previously involved in the importation of machines and equipment for various types of manufacturers. In 2015, following the currency crisis that devalued the naira, it became impossible to thrive in the import business. With an engineering background, he decided to go into the fabrication of equipment for the emerging rice processing business. Since then, he has supplied rice processing equipment to more than 25 firms across Nigeria. The CEO of Al-Wabel Trading Company, on the other hand, started as an importer of children's clothing. Having established a strong position in the business with an excellent brand, he diversified into other fields including drinking water, solar energy, and construction materials before trying his hand in rice processing. Questions and responses from the two companies are discussed below.

Prime Wave Limited

Prime Wave is an engineering company that fabricates soaking tanks, elevators, and heating and steaming equipment for the mid-level rice processing market. So far, Prime Wave is the only company of its type in Nigeria supplying equipment to the mid-level market. Al-Wabel Trading Company is one of Prime Wave's largest customers. An interview script was prepared comprising basic, open-ended questions. Table 9.1 presents the questions asked of the CEO of Prime Wave.

Al-Wabel Trading Company Limited

Al-Wabel Trading Company is one of the largest rice processing mills in Kano. It started business in 2017 and currently has operating capacity to process 100 tons of rice paddies per day. It is one of two companies in Kano admitted into the prestigious Rice Processors Association of Nigeria (RIPAN)—an organisation resembling a 'rice cartel' because of its growing influence in the market. The interview with the CEO of Al-Wabel was designed to confirm some of the answers provided by the CEO of Prime Wave. Table 9.2 presents the questions asked of the CEO of Al-Wabel.

Table 9.1 Prime Wave Limited—questions and responses

S/N	Questions	Responses
1	What pushed you to start this business?	The economic environment, particularly the loss of value of the local currency was a major threat to the family business. The prospects were bleak. However, it also represented an opportunity, if one was prepared to take the risk and be proactive. The rice processing market provided such an opportunity and with a background in engineering, I decided to take the risk. We went into both the rice processing business as well as the manufacturing of equipment business.
2	What goods do you supply?	Decided to focus on the pre-treatment stage. That is the area of greatest need for mid-level start-ups in rice processing. Milling is not a problem—very little complain in that area. But treatment, especially parboiling aspect is a major challenge. Initial investment to import the required goods from overseas was a major challenge for most investors especially since the local currency is weak against the dollar. This is an area I feel I have the greatest competence to do this given my background in engineering.
3	How did you enter the market?	The first thing we did was to conduct research in the pre-treatment stage. So we observed the processes followed by local women in the pre-treatment stage. We observed the processes and noted the challenges the processors faced. It looked simple and straightforward. And we decided that it should be possible to fabricate simple mechanical tools to perform the functions cheaper, better, faster, and more effectively for the users. Our challenge then was to find businessmen that could trust us enough to try our goods. We had several meetings with several investors. The most forthcoming of them all was Al-Wabel. He took a major risk despite the fact that some investors tried to discourage him claiming that our goods do not work/function properly.

(continued)

Table 9.1 (continued)

S/N	Questions	Responses
4	What are the key factors for success in this business?	It is important that you deliver on your promise—the goods supplied worked. Relationships are very important—we visit our clients' factories to reassure them. We observe the goods as they work and are always available to provide quick repairs, advice, and other support—mostly free. Experimentation is key to success. Many of our goods are tested on factory sites as pilots. We observe what happens and develop them to perfection.
5	What are the main competitive and other challenges you face?	There are currently no competitors in the market. We are the first and, so far, the only supplier of goods in our chosen market in Nigeria. However, we feel the threat of a possible change in government policy. If the government at some point soon removes the ban on importation of rice our business will suffer. We still need to import the iron and steel we use to make our products. Any worsening situation of the naira will affect us. Lack of government support—to underwrite our risks in research and development—will also slow us down. Capital requirement for expansion is also a challenge.
6	What value do you add to your customers?	We believe that we support our customers to improve their bottom line. We also believe we offer a better alternative in the level of market we operate. Initial investment is much cheaper compared to importing the same goods. We also believe the performance of our products in terms of the basic functions for which they are designed is comparable to any imported good from anywhere in the world. They are simple to operate and easy to maintain by the operators. This saves our customer the high expense of inviting an expert from overseas to fix any breakdown.

The interview with Prime Wave took two hours to complete, while that with Al-Wabel took one hour and 30 minutes to complete. Responses were recorded (typed as they were given) and clarifications sought and given. The typed responses were read out and confirmed by the two respondents.

Table 9.2 Al-Wabel Trading Company Limited—questions and responses

S/N	Questions	Responses
11	What goods do you buy from Prime Wave?	We buy goods such as delivery machines (from pre-cleaning before pouring into tanks), soaking tanks, steaming tanks, elevators to deliver grains to reserve tanks/holding bins—all equipment in the pre-treatment stage of rice processing.
22	What value do these goods add to your business?	Prime Wave helps us on a number of fronts, such as: (1) improve on quality and achieve some of the advantages of large producers but at a smaller cost (Prime Wave helps us to advance to industrial level); (2) source of energy from the by-product—husk used to heat boiler; (3) helps us to do a pilot study as a start-up to avoid costly mistakes; (4) minimise rate of rice breakages as a result of improved soaking system; (5) develop simple drying system that uses firewood; (6) availability of spare parts, which are cheap; and, (7) overall cost of operations is much cheaper. In fact, since I started business I have never been in a business with such high turnover and profitability. My customers pay in cash and sometimes wait on me to finish.
33	What problems or challenges do you face using the goods supplied by Prime Wave?	Perhaps it is too early to say—we have been in operation for about a year. But so far, we have not had any problem with any of the equipment supplied by Prime Wave.
44	How has Prime Wave helped you with future expansion and/or other plans?	We are currently experimenting [with] a new heating system for drying. We currently use firewood for this process and it takes an average of ten hours to achieve a circle. We hope the new heating system would help reduce this by about 50%.

9.5 Analysis and Findings

Data analysis for this study followed the process outlined by Miles and Huberman (1994). The process includes: (1) preparing respondent's summary sheet to record the main points and issues identified (see Tables 9.1 and 9.2), (2) creating a theme list—a list of 'common' topics/issues/interests on which the respondents appear to converge, (3) narrative analysis—preparing a report that 'tells a story' of what happened, which follows below, and (4) validity check—a copy of the respondent's summary and themes was given back to each respondent for validation. Analysis of these responses indicates that the new government policy on rice (provision of credit to farmers and rice import ban) and the currency crisis led to the emergence of a mid-level rice process in between the micro/small and large rice processors.

The mid-level processors could not afford the large capital requirement to support the investment in imported technology. In response to a question, the CEO of Prime Wave stated that:

> [We] decided to focus on the pre-treatment stage. That is the area of greatest need for start-ups in rice processing. Initial investment to import the required goods from overseas was a major challenge for most investors especially since the local currency is weak against the dollar.

The response of Al-Wabel echoes this belief:

> [We] achieve some of the advantages of large producers but at a smaller cost (Prime Wave helps us to advance to industrial level). We buy equipment in the pre-treatment stage of rice processing. Overall cost of operation is much cheaper.

This finding indicates that circumstances provide compelling incentives for the two companies to emerge and take action. This view is generally supported by the literature, which argues that factors within the industry environment, operating environment, and remote environment affect firm performance (Porter 1980; Pearce and Robinson 2011).

That the two firms decided to take action indicates the role of the personal dispositions and mindsets of the CEOs in firm performance. Both have shown capacity for investing in ventures with uncertain outcomes, both have been proactive and have shown capacity to try innovative ideas. The two CEOs believe they are creating necessary and much-needed solutions. Both CEOs exhibit the characteristics of Entrepreneurial Orientation (EO) (innovativeness, proactiveness, risk-taking, fantasy frame, and missionary outlook) as defined by Miller (1983), Covin and Slevin (1991), Covin and Lumpkin (2011), and Garba et al. (2018). The literature on EO generally indicates that EO is related to firm performance (see, e.g., Gudmundsson and Lechner 2014; Gupta and Gupta 2015; Pratono 2016).

Responses from the two companies affirm this view. The response of Prime Wave on what value they give to their customers and how the company entered the market affirms these:

> [There is] an opportunity, if one was prepared to take the risk and be proactive. We believe that we support our customers to improve their bottom-line. We also believe we offer a better alternative in the level of market we operate. We also believe the performance of our products in terms of the basic functions for which they are designed is comparable to any imported good from anywhere in the world. This is an area I feel I have the greatest competence to do this given my background in Engineering. There are currently no competitors in the market. We are the first and, so far, the only supplier of goods in our chosen market in Nigeria. The most forthcoming of them all was Al-Wabel. He took a major risk despite the fact that some investors tried to discourage him, claiming that our goods do not work/function properly.

All these are indications of missionary outlook, risk-taking, and proactiveness—action and value-driven behaviours of an entrepreneur (Garba et al. 2018).

An interesting finding of this chapter is that collaboration is as important as competition for business success. This finding is supported by the view of Hamel (2007), who argued that future managers should pay attention to collaboration as much as they now do to competition. Prime Wave is not only in the business of the production of equipment, it is also involved in rice processing and, therefore, is in direct competition with its customers, such as Al-Wabel. The rice processing market is large enough and growing faster than available capacity. Competitive rivalry between firms in the industry is almost nil. Prime Wave learns management and marketing skills from Al-Wabel to improve the performance of its rice processing business, while Al-Wabel learns how to improve operations, reduce cost, and boost overall performance.

This study also found that both companies have a targeted focus—they are not aiming 'to be everything to every person'. Instead the companies have chosen a specific market with specific needs. Prime Wave is focused on medium-level processors (not the micro, small, or large processors). The company is only interested in, and therefore focused on, the pre-treatment stage of rice processing and not on the milling stage, which it feels is not a problem, and that other firms are better than it in that stage. Al-Wabel is focused on the middle-income consumer that wants clean, high-quality rice with a 'foreign look' at an affordable price.

The ability to do this gives Al-Wabel the satisfaction of being an industrial-level processor with all the advantages of large-scale processors. Responses from the two CEOs affirm this. According to the CEO of Prime Wave:

> We decided to focus on the pre-treatment stage. That is the area of greatest need for start-ups in rice processing. Milling is not a problem—very little complain in that area. But treatment, especially parboiling aspect is a major challenge for processors. Initial investment to import the required goods from overseas was a major challenge for most investors especially since the local currency is weak against the dollar.

The CEO of Al-Wabel said:

> Prime Wave helps us to (1) minimise rate of rice breakages as a result of improved soaking system; (2) develop simple drying system that uses firewood; (3) [make available] spare parts, which are cheap. Overall cost of operations is much cheaper. In fact, since I started business I have never been in a business with such high turnover and profitability. My customers pay in cash and sometimes wait on me to finish.

The literature affirms the role of a targeted focus (also called focus differentiation and customer intimacy) on firm performance (i.e. Porter 1980; Wiersema 1996; Ridderstrale and Nordstrom 2007).

The role of piloting—the practice of experimentation, developing, and testing equipment before full operational use—is an important finding of this study. A study of excellent American companies by Peters and Waterman (1982) confirms the role of experimentation in firm performance. Several other studies affirm this (i.e. Thomke 2003; Collins and Hansen 2011).

At the stage of research, equipment for drying rice (an important stage in rice processing) was sited at its development stage on the premises of Prime Wave. The same equipment was seen being installed at the Al-Wabel factory for testing. Prime Wave's CEO stated:

> We decided that it should be possible to fabricate simple mechanical tools to perform the functions [of rice processing at the pre-treatment stage] better, faster and more effectively. Our challenge then was to find businessmen that could trust us enough to try our goods.

The response of Al-Wabel's CEO affirms this:

> [Prime Wave] helps us to do a pilot study as a start-up to avoid costly mistakes. We are currently experimenting [with] a new heating system for drying. We currently use firewood for this process and it takes an average of ten hours to achieve a circle. We hope the new heating system would help reduce this by about 50%.

These symbiotic relationships create a win–win situation for all stakeholders involved in rice processing—the prospects of a sale for Prime Wave are improved, Al-Wabel benefits from improved efficiency leading to lower cost and higher profitability, and the rice consumer benefits from a rice of improved quality.

This study found elements of disruptive innovation in the efforts of Prime Wave. The company exhibits a knack for understanding the customer dimension of value and uses this knowledge to disrupt the market. According to Christensen and Raynor (2003), 'customers have a problem and they hire a product to solve it'.

To solve this problem, a supplier targets specific dimensions that the supplier believes will best solve the customer's problem. These dimensions, according to Christensen and Raynor (2003), are: product functions, product quality, product features, and product aesthetics. Large companies tend to focus on sustaining innovation (improvements in all the dimensions) in order to remain competitive. However, such improvements reach a point where the customer is no longer interested in paying for 'gimmicks'. The customer is usually made aware of these gimmicks by new entrants into the market, which are, however, usually ignored by the powerful incumbents until it is too late (Christensen 1997).

Prime Wave, and its entry strategy into the market, resembles such a new entrant. Firstly, its disruptive innovation is redefining the concept of *value in use* of the sophisticated and polished equipment and gadgets supplied by foreign firms relative to the function of process and prices charged for performing the function. In so doing, Prime Wave has disrupted the market—finding potential customers for the function who could not afford the prices currently charged by incumbent suppliers.

The incumbents are not interested in these users nor in the activities of Prime Wave. By focusing on the function, Prime Wave is able to supply this market. Evidence of this is in the response of the CEO of Prime Wave:

> The first thing we did was to conduct research in the pre-treatment stage. We observed the processes followed by local women in the pre-treatment stage. We observed the processes and noted the challenges the processors faced. It looked simple and straightforward, and we decided that it should be possible to fabricate simple mechanical tools to perform the functions cheaper, better, faster, and more effectively for the users.

Finally, this chapter found that challenges for deeper and wide acceptance of Prime Wave's products are still evident. There are also challenges of future development and growth. The pace of growth in rice processing is still very slow compared with the rising demand. In a speech during a meeting with 'key' stakeholders in the rice value chain on 13 March 2018, the President said that in 2015 there were 13 rice mills in the country.

The President further noted that eight new mills had been established since 2016.[5] But this is largely attributable to the poor risk culture of the investment community, which is sceptical of government policy stability. Such investors prefer to 'wait and see' how things play out. With little government support for research and development and innovation in particular, development in terms of sustaining innovation—improvement in processes, such as automation of key activities (on and off switching of steaming machines, filling and draining of soaking tanks, etc.)—will be very slow.

The response from Prime Wave attests to this:

> We feel the threat of a possible change in government policy. If the government at some point soon removes the ban on importation of rice our business will suffer. We still need to import the iron and steel we use to make our products. Any worsening situation of the naira will affect us. Lack of government support—to underwrite our risks in research and development—will also slow us down. Capital requirement for expansion is also a challenge.

9.6 Conclusions

From the above analysis and findings, it would seem that Prime Wave and Al-Wabel are leveraging environmental factors and their capabilities to benefit from the evolving rice processing market. The two companies have applied strategic management and entrepreneurial orientation principles and practices to create valuable relationships that help them lock in key benefits. In the process, Prime Wave has even created and patented an invention to improve the performance of rice processing at the stage in which it is operating. These conclusions have a number of implications for policymaking and research in entrepreneurship and innovation.

[5] Speech by Nigeria's President Muhammadu Buhari during the Meeting with Key Stakeholders in the Rice Value Chain, 13 March 2018.

Implications for Policymaking

The findings of this chapter clearly highlight the role of government policy in opening up the opportunity for investment in rice processing. The opportunity is vast, spreading across the entire rice value chain. Banning the importation of rice, targeting the sector for development, and the provision of credit have proved decisive in changing the sector. Within the processing segment, the opportunity is further enhanced and sustained by shortages in capacity and expanding demand due to increase in population, which seems set to continue. However, there are challenges, especially with regards to weak linkages between the rice value chain actors (ECOWAS Factbook). There seems to be no deliberate design to link the 'actors' together in a 'formal' way such that supporting industries could develop within the value chain. A deliberate policy to create and sustain these linkages could lead to the elimination of bottlenecks. Accordingly, this finding, within a wider policy context, contributes to the debate on Ease of Doing Business at the national and subnational level. It shows that government policy does indeed improve business performance.

Implications for Rice Paddy Farmers

Although there is little competition between rice processors presently, in the near future, as processing capacity grows, there is likely to be competition between processors to get the right quantity and quality with the appropriate level of moisture. To obtain this on time and to build long-term beneficial relationships between the farmers and processors, competitive activities in the areas of farmer support (provision of improved seedlings, extension services, provision of fertiliser and other inputs such as lending or leasing planters, harvesters, etc.) are likely to emerge. Some form of government regulation is also likely. Both farmers and processors would seek information on how and where to obtain greater value that optimises their objectives. Creating a digital platform that makes this information available appears to be a natural next step for digital entrepreneurs in agri-business. In fact, this is already happening. A company called TechnoServe has created what it calls a 'Coalition'—a platform that supports innovation within smallholder sourcing schemes to expand the viability, reach, and value of smallholder sourcing schemes for both businesses and smallholder farmers.[6] A number of firms, such as Gulu Agricultural Development Company (GADC), a diversified commodity business operating in northern Uganda, have used the platform to improve business and farmer performance. A similar initiative is being contemplated by Olam, which recently opened a facility in Kaduna, northern Nigeria.

Implications for Digital Entrepreneurs

The opportunity opened up by government policy in rice production and processing would have come to nothing if entrepreneurs did not have the required disposition to act. That disposition feeds on learning, experience, exposure, and a 'compelling' circumstance. All of these add to the 'dynamic capabilities' of a firm, which are necessary for opportunity recognition and exploitation (Helfat et al. 2007). The actions of the two CEOs in this study have been informed by their past experience and business exposure. Both have been persuaded to do something based on 'compelling evidence'—they both operated in businesses that were threatened by the currency crisis. That learning helped them develop experience in risk-taking and being proactive in order to succeed (Collins and Hansen 2011).

The evidence also indicates that entrepreneurs could create a win–win situation through collaboration, which, as we have seen in the relationship between Prime Wave and Al-Wabel, is as important as competition. There is, therefore, the need for business owners to focus on common

[6] The Coalition is a partnership between TechnoServe, private agri-businesses, and a research partner to identify, co-finance, and pilot innovative approaches to address persistent challenges in smallholder sourcing. The Coalition supports rigorous analysis and impact evaluation of these approaches through a research partner, IDinsight. Once impactful innovations are identified, the goal of the Coalition is to support and encourage replication and scaling up in other relevant contexts. Read more about the Coalition at (http://www.technoserve.org/our-work/projects/technoserve-coalition-for-smallholder-sourcing).

areas to expand the opportunity rather than focusing on sharing what exists. More importantly, collaboration portends the need for a digital platform, as demonstrated by the TechnoServe example, for information sharing and flagging of problems and challenges to allow for faster response. While a telephone call now seems adequate, in future things will have to occur online in real time. This is one area with great potential for both good and evil—if Prime Wave ignores this, it is just as likely an Asian ICT company or TechnoServe will seize the opportunity.

Implications for Research in Digital Entrepreneurship

A major constraint to rice productivity in the Economic Community of West African States (ECOWAS) region—and hence in Nigeria—is the lack of linkages between firms in the value chain. The processes are also mechanical, involving manual operation and control. For example, soaking, heating, steaming, and draining of soaking tanks is performed manually. The taps to fill and drain the soaking tanks, the valve to let the steam in, and the testing of rice paddy moisture are performed manually in separate stages. These are some of the potential areas of research—determining the factors that facilitate or hinder linkages among actors in the value chain would help in the development of a platform for building a powerful network and the appropriation of benefits within the network. Just as research established the processes of pre-treatment, research should also establish what needs to be monitored and controlled, what digital technology is required, and how entrepreneurs could develop it.

9.7 Recommendations

Following the conclusions and implications for policymaking, entrepreneurs, and research, this chapter makes the following recommendations. Government should introduce targeted incentives to support research and development in innovation. Such support should be aimed at future upgrades in terms of automation and development and the use of appropriate digital technology for the monitoring and evaluation of processes.

There are many agricultural research centres and university agricultural faculties that could do this with appropriate funding and orientation.

The provision of loans to farmers to boost production could be extended to entrepreneurs such as Prime Wave to improve the quality and aesthetics of their products. In future, local manufacturers of tools and equipment should be able to meet global standards in order to empower them to compete more effectively in the local and international market, at least within the African continent in the first instance. So far, it appears that only the federal and Kebbi State governments have shown commitment to rice production. The federal government has also committed to rice processing through direct investment.

There is a need for other state governments to support the initiative in order to widen its scope and speed up development. Kano State government, for example, could set up an enterprise support fund to support firms such as Prime Wave. The more the government is involved at all levels, the greater the chances of policy stability.

Perhaps nowhere is the lack of linkages more glaring than in the relationship between the research centres, academia, and industry. Collaborative research between digital entrepreneurs and research centres and universities is a necessary requirement but one that is lacking. Prime Wave is already leading in this direction—engaging a PhD in Engineering in its activities. The government and the universities should enter into this with greater interest and vigour. Research should focus more on relevance in order to feed into industrial requirements in addition to rigour—satisfying academic pedagogy. A certain measure of deliberateness is required to create this linkage. Industrial attachment—the practice of sending students to work for three months in a factory—is simply not enough. Research that involves working directly with entrepreneurs and eventually feeds into the subject curriculum is required.

As is already emerging, in the near future entrepreneurs in the market, such as Prime Wave and Al-Wabel, should focus on finding ways to use the by-products of rice processing. There is already an ongoing initiative to use the rice husk as a source of energy.

For example, rice husk now meets 80% of the water boiling needs for soaking at Al-Wabel. There is a need to explore other by-products, such as broken rice, bran, and so on for other markets, such as animal feeds.

This requires collaboration with others outside the current network of relationships. The confidence earned by Prime Wave among investors should now be invested to build other relationships. Al-Wabel has proven skills to champion this initiative, as it provides another opening for pro-activeness to lead in another market. Again, the need for building a digital platform to support this is evident.

References

Christensen, C. M. (1997). *The Innovator's Dilemma*. New York: Harper Business.

Christensen, C. M., & Raynor, M. E. (2003). *The Innovator's Solution: Creating and Sustaining Successful Growth*. Boston, MA: Harvard Business School Press.

Collins, J., & Hansen, M. T. (2011). *Great by Choice*. New York: Harper Business.

Covin, J. G., & Lumpkin, G. T. (2011). Entrepreneurial Orientation Theory and Research: Reflections on a Needed Construct. *Entrepreneurship Theory and Practice, 1042*(1), 855–872.

Covin, J. G., & Slevin, D. P. (1991). A Conceptual Model of Entrepreneurship as Firm Behaviour. *Entrepreneurship: Theory and Practice, 16*, 7–25.

ECOWAS Rice Factbook. (2018). Grow Africa.

Garba, A. M., Ibrahim, M. A., Gorondutse, A. H., & Abubakar, A. A. (2018). Entrepreneurial Orientation: An Extended Model. *International Journal of Organizational and Business Excellence (IJOBE), 3*(1), 52–64.

Global Agricultural Information Network (GAIN) Report. (2017). United States Department of Agriculture, Foreign Agricultural Services.

Gudmundsson, S. V., & Lechner, C. (2014). Entrepreneurial Orientation, Firm Strategy and Small Firm Performance. *International Small Business Journal, 32*(1), 36–60.

Gupta, V. K., & Gupta, A. J. (2015). Relationship between Entrepreneurial Orientation and Firm Performance in Large Organizations Over Time. *Journal of International Entrepreneurship, 13*, 7–27.

Hamel, G. (2007). *Future of Management*. Boston, MA: Harvard Business Review Press.

Helfat, C., Finkelstein, S., Mitchell, W., Peteraf, M., Singh, H., Teece, D., & Winter, S. (2007). *Dynamic Capabilities: Understanding Strategic Change in Organizations*. Oxford: Blackwell Publishing.

Katsina State Agriculture Restoration Project. (2016). Katsina Government Printers.
Miles, M. B., & Huberman, A. M. (1994). *Qualitative Data Analysis*. Thousand Oaks, CA: Sage.
Miller, D. (1983). The Correlates of Entrepreneurship in Three Types of Firms. *Management Science, 29*(1), 770–791.
Pearce, J. A., & Robinson, B. R. (2011). *Strategic Management*. New York: McGraw-Hill/Irwin.
Peters, T. J., & Waterman, R. H., Jr. (1982). *In Search of Excellence*. Harper and Row.
Porter, M. E. (1980). *Competitive Strategy: Techniques for Analysing Industries and Competitors*. New York: The Free Press Macmillan Publishing Company.
Pratono, A. H. (2016). Strategic Orientation and Information Technological Turbulence Contingency Perspective in SMEs. *Business Process Management Journal, 22*(2), 1–15.
Punch Newspaper (2018, February 15). Anchor Borrowers' Scheme: CBN Disburses N55bn to Farmers.
Ridderstrale, J., & Nordstrom, K. (2007). *Funky Business Forever*. Stockholm: Book House Publishing/FT Prentice Hall.
Shehu, B., & Lolo, A. (2017). Promoting Rice Productivity in Kebbi State: Linking Data and Policy. State Policy Note 2, June 2017. Innovation Lab for Food Security Policy Nigeria Agricultural Policy Project FEED the FUTURE (The US Government's Global and Food Security Initiatives).
The Coalition. (2015). Retrieved from http://www.technoserve.org/our-work/projects/technoserve-coalition-for-smallholder-sourcing.
Thomke, S. H. (2003). *Experimentation Matters*. Boston, MA: Harvard Business School Press.
Van Maanen, J. (1988). *Tales of Field* (2nd ed.). Chicago: Chicago University Press.
WAAPP-Nigeria. (n.d.). *Rice Production, Processing, Utilisation and Marketing in Nigeria*. Extension Bulletin No. 230.
Wiersema, F. (1996). *Customer Intimacy: Pick Your Partners, Shape Your Culture, Win Together*. London: Harper Collins Business.

10

What Next for Digital Entrepreneurship in Sub-Saharan Africa?

Nnamdi O. Madichie, Nasiru D. Taura, and Elvira Bolat

10.1 Motivation

Digital Entrepreneurship in Sub-Saharan Africa is a collection of empirical evidence and narratives on the historical, contextual, and cultural nuances that are accompanying the digital entrepreneurial revolution in the sub-Saharan Africa region. The narratives in this book help readers develop a better understanding of what makes the region unique and the challenges and opportunities the digital entrepreneurship revolution offers.

Most countries in the sub-Saharan Africa region have had to, and continue to, deal with a plethora of complex and never-ending challenges including armed conflicts, political instability, unemployment,

N. O. Madichie
Centre for Research & Enterprise, Bloomsbury Institute London, London, UK
e-mail: nnamdi.madichie@bil.ac.uk

N. D. Taura (✉) • E. Bolat
Business School, Bournemouth University, Bournemouth, UK
e-mail: ntaura@bournemouth.ac.uk; ebolat@bournemouth.ac.uk

N. D. Taura et al. (eds.), *Digital Entrepreneurship in Sub-Saharan Africa*, Palgrave Studies of Entrepreneurship in Africa, https://doi.org/10.1007/978-3-030-04924-9_10

and gender inequality. Social issues are perhaps the most critical circumstances of all that drive new ways of surviving and hence new business models and approaches. However, innovation is not ubiquitous across the region, which creates significant disparities among and within countries in sub-Saharan Africa, with millions of people left at the margins and suffering from a range of crises—including food shortages, poor quality education, inadequate healthcare, and digital illiteracy (see Madichie 2016, p. 8).

One of the key observed reasons for the aforementioned negatives is the problem of project execution. For example, in their assessment of information and communication technology projects and project management in South Africa, Joseph, Erasmus, and Marnewick observed the need for more focus on product success rather than project management success, as well as the need for the development of more soft skills rather than technical skills (training and development) in order to achieve project outcomes. Furthermore, Asongu and Nwachukwu (2018) in their recent study on *Openness, ICT and Entrepreneurship in Sub-Saharan Africa* highlighted "substantial evidence that ICT complements openness to improve conditions for entrepreneurship, the effects [of which] are contingent on the dynamics of openness, ICT and entrepreneurship" (p. 293).

However, despite the region's economic and entrepreneurial performance being described as poor, progressive developments regarding entrepreneurial practice and ability in sub-Saharan Africa are inspiring (Kshetri 2011). In particular, *Digital Entrepreneurship in Sub-Saharan Africa* posits that digital technologies act as enablers of positive change within education systems, social mindsets, institutional governance structures, and most importantly business and self-employment practices—in other words, across all facets of the entrepreneurial ecosystem. Digital technologies, as described by Pijnaker and Spronk (2017), are means to express "aspirations and senses of being in the world". The adoption and use of digital technologies in sub-Saharan Africa enables social and economic change through the ability to capture cultural heritage and contextual complexities of the region and at the same time enable connectivity with much more developed practices and experiences elsewhere. Having said that, the limited amount of research on digital entrepreneurship in sub-Saharan Africa hinders a comprehensive understanding of its contribution to economic growth and positive impact on society (Dana et al. 2018).

In their recently edited book *African Entrepreneurship*, Dana et al. (2018, p. 2) point out that "whilst Africa's entrepreneurial performance has been described as weak, positive developments regarding entrepreneurship and entrepreneurial ability in Africa are encouraging". In Africa, the potential for self-employment abounds, but limited research on the subject of entrepreneurship in this region leaves a gap in the contribution of entrepreneurship to economic growth. Consequently, researching the opportunities and challenges of doing business in the region deserves further attention and exploration in the entrepreneurship literature. Furthermore, the dramatic changes in the global business environment, to which no industry is immune (Prahalad and Krishman 2008), demands that we investigate and develop a better understanding of not just the opportunities and challenges of doing business in Africa, but how this intersects with the dual forces of globalization and digitalization.

Digital Entrepreneurship in Sub-Saharan Africa aims to bridge the knowledge gap by highlighting the opportunities and challenges of doing business in sub-Saharan Africa. Both individual aspects of the role of entrepreneurs, as well as environmental conditions of institutional support, networks, and consumer dynamics are discussed and debated. This ten-chapter book covers a range of topics, sectoral evidence, and theoretical perspectives with a view to shed light on the idiosyncratic nature of "thinking" and "doing" among sub-Saharan African entrepreneurial practices, as well as suggest avenues for future research.

The book is split into five broad parts, covering fin-tech, media-tech, animation, and games, as well as inclusive-tech. As such, the chapters in the book have touched upon these broad spheres of activity in sub-Saharan Africa. These chapters also feature a distinctive perspective on digital entrepreneurship in sub-Saharan Africa, taking into account historical elements that have shaped current business practices. The changing nature of entrepreneurship is frequently discussed in the book, effectively building on earlier contributions edited by Dana et al. (2018), and Ndemo and Weiss (2017). The main empirical contributions provide interesting analysis of recent business developments in sub-Saharan Africa. This is useful in understanding the changing nature of business in Africa in terms of how it is progressing. Moreover, the contributions in this volume discuss the constraints and improvements confronting entrepreneurs in the sub-Saharan Africa region. The book altogether identifies broad aspects of entrepreneurship and focuses on specific enablers as well as barriers that limit opportunities for entrepreneurs to grow their businesses in this geographical space (Kolo et al. 2016; Madichie 2016; Madichie et al. 2017; Ahmed 2017; Ahmed and Nwankwo 2013; Akinyoade et al. 2017; Amankwah-Amoah 2018; Atiase et al. 2018). Ultimately *Digital Entrepreneurship in Sub-Saharan Africa* is a timely intervention to document different segments and shades of entrepreneurship in sub-Saharan Africa, which may be of value to scholars, policymakers, development partners, youth, institutions, and society at large.

10.2 African Entrepreneurship

Entrepreneurship is considered a solution to the economic and social problems in parts of Africa (Tvedten et al. 2014; Ratten and Jones 2018). There is growing recognition that entrepreneurship in sub-Saharan Africa is a way to enable financial independence and control over one's destiny. This is important for community development and improving the quality of life for people in Africa. According to Reid et al. (2015, p. 264), "while Africans display among the highest entrepreneurial intent globally, African countries are less well prepared than many other regions to capitalize on these motivations". The reason for this might be that there are more people being pushed into entrepreneurship due to lack of education and job opportunities (Ferreira et al. 2017). Entrepreneurship has been lower in sub-Saharan Africa than in other parts of the world due to the region's abundance of state-owned enterprises (Edoho 2016; Ratten and Jones 2018). This has discouraged small business activity and reduced incentives for individuals to engage in entrepreneurship. In addition, the emphasis on government-controlled businesses discouraged private investment in new start-ups. More recently there has been a shift towards entrepreneurship as a way to increase employment and economic growth Garba (2010; The Economist 2000, 2011; Nwankwo and Ibeh 2015; Nwankwo 2011, 2012; Kolo et al. 2016; Madichie et al. 2017). For example, Adenle et al. (2017, p. 94) states that in Africa, "entrepreneurship will play a critical role in tackling the youth unemployment that is growing at exponential rate in the continent". Education will play an important role in encouraging more entrepreneurship in sub-Saharan Africa, by teaching the business skills that can help empower people to start businesses.

Entrepreneurship in sub-Saharan Africa differs from that in other parts of the world due to cultural and historical factors. Moreover, the competitiveness of business in Africa has been limited by cultural barriers and the perceived ability to be entrepreneurial. Only recently has there been an increased interest in African entrepreneurship due to the economic growth in the region. George et al. (2016, p. 377) opine that "Africa is beginning to capture the imagination of entrepreneurs, corporate executives, and scholars as an emerging market of new growth opportunities". Despite the popularity of African entrepreneurship in the media, there is still a lack of understanding in the academic literature about how it differs from entrepreneurship in other geographical locations. For this reason, it is important to provide an overview of current research about sub-Saharan African entrepreneurship as a way to project future research intentions. This is due to the historical and institutional factors that have affected the performance of businesses in the region (Tvedten et al. 2014). Furthermore, within sub-Saharan Africa there are several diverse countries with different business systems that make it necessary to examine individual countries rather than categorize all countries as the same.

Jones et al. (2018), in their set of three interrelated special issues of *Journal of Small Business and Enterprise Development*, set out to provide novel and empirically rigorous insights into a range of under-reported and emerging topics in an African context, including: reporting aspects of entrepreneurial behaviour, described in Issue 1 as entrepreneurial dynamics; the development of entrepreneurial education and ecosystems to support entrepreneurial activity, in Issue 2; and entrepreneurial growth and diversity, in Issue 3. The special issue was arguably motivated by the desire to offer fresh insights into African entrepreneurship, and thereby provide a voice for African scholars doing research in entrepreneurship and small business development. Interestingly, research focusing on entrepreneurial behaviour and small business practices in sub-Saharan Africa has been scant in the literature published in leading international journals.

The entrepreneurial dynamic in Africa is rapidly evolving in the face of the continual socio-economic, political, technological, and cultural changes sweeping the continent. There is widespread recognition of the urgent need for effective entrepreneurial behaviour to alleviate a myriad of systemic problems, including high graduate unemployment, endemic poverty, economic growth inequality, corruption, excessive bureaucracy, ineffective infrastructure, and a lack of enterprise support mechanisms. Moreover, research into entrepreneurial behaviours remains limited in the complex and heterogeneous African cultural context. It is rewarding to note the range of entrepreneurial behaviour being reported, including social enterprise, the emergence and deployment of information and communication technology, and the use of microfinance to enable business start-ups. In addition, we note the significant investment in entrepreneurial education and ecosystems to encourage starts-ups and effective entrepreneurial learning, despite ongoing resource challenges and issues pertaining to business sustainability and failure.

In any case, the three-part special issue by Jones et al. (2018) has proved to be a considerable undertaking, with over 60 papers received during the call for papers. This statistic reflects the popularity of entrepreneurship in an African context. After a rigorous and lengthy review process, a total of 25 papers were accepted for publication. It was noteworthy to see that papers were submitted from all across the African continent, confirming the increased interest in entrepreneurial activity research. As a result, the special issue was split between three separate issues of the journal, for publication during 2018. This first issue, entitled "Entrepreneurial dynamics in Africa", includes nine articles which explore various aspects of entrepreneurial behaviour—from female entrepreneurship, to venture capital, information and communication technology, and the influence of entrepreneurial leadership.

Notably, the study by Nziku and Struthers (2018) presents the development of an innovative taxonomy which highlights the role of strength of weak ties (SWT) social networks in mitigating the principal–agent problem among African women entrepreneurs. The taxonomy presents new insights for understanding the constraints that inhibit women entrepreneurs in Africa. Embedding the SWT concept within a principal–agent framework will facilitate further research to understand African women entrepreneurs' attitudes towards risk and uncertainty. This will facilitate greater understanding of the importance that African women entrepreneurs attach to incentives within their businesses.

Gudeta and van Engen (2018) explore work–life boundary management experiences and the challenges women entrepreneurs in Ethiopia face in combining their work–life responsibilities. The study contributes to the work–family literature by highlighting contextual and environmental factors imposing work–family boundary management styles on women entrepreneurs in Ethiopia. The research underlines the requirement to recognise the work–life interface challenges faced by women entrepreneurs and to develop educational programmes and specific training to assist them in adopting better work–life boundary management tactics. The findings inform policies and female entrepreneurship development programmes designed by government, development partners, and other stakeholders.

Ukanwa et al. (2018) consider the problem of why the poorest, most disadvantaged groups such as rural African women benefit less from microfinance. The study focuses on the perceptions and experiences of rural entrepreneurial women of microfinance, in a context of extreme poverty and where family responsibility and economic activities are closely intertwined. The study offers a number of relevant insights. In terms of theoretical implications, existing theories, especially functionalist economic theory, do not take account of microfinance users' experiences. For practical implications, microfinance providers should note that the poorest perceive microcredit differently and seek to reduce the intimidating barriers. Instead of offering a process for the poor to alleviate poverty, or coping strategies to manage cash flows and risks, microfinance causes fear and anxiety by demanding high return rates in a short time period. Consequently, the poorest members of society, who should be the beneficiaries of microfinance, are less likely to benefit. Importantly, the condition of poverty creates different realities for those in severe poverty.

Hain and Jurowetzki (2018) highlight the patterns and characteristics of international financial flows into the emerging entrepreneurial ecosystems of sub-Saharan Africa, providing a novel taxonomy to classify and analyse them, and discuss how such investments contribute to competence building and sustainable development. The study observes a new group of mainly Western investors that support innovative ideas in sub-Saharan Africa by identifying and investing in domestically developed technical innovations with the potential to address global market needs. Such innovations are developed at the intersection of global and local knowledge. The study offers a novel taxonomy of technology investments in low-income countries, suggesting further research opportunities.

The study by Boojihawon and Ngoasong (2018) explores how context as an antecedent to entrepreneurial digital competencies (EDCs) influences digital entrepreneurship in a resource-scarce environment. The data comprises semi-structured interviews with digital entrepreneurs who are owner-managers of digital businesses in Cameroon. The results reveal the ways in which EDCs shape the entry (or start-up) choices and post-entry strategic decisions of digital entrepreneurs in response to context-specific opportunities and challenges associated with digital entrepreneurship. The study highlights important implications for encouraging digital entrepreneurship by focusing on institutional, technology, and local dimensions of context and measures to develop the entrepreneurial and digital competencies. This includes policy interventions to develop the information and communication technology infrastructure, transport and local distribution infrastructure, and training opportunities to develop the EDCs of digital entrepreneurs.

Shemi and Procter (2018) consider the application of mobile devices, and how social media networks (SMN), such as Facebook, have revolutionized the e-commerce adoption process in small and medium enterprises (SMEs). However, extant research into this area is nascent and there is a dearth of knowledge regarding how SMEs in developing countries enact and apply this phenomenon. The study explains how e-commerce entrepreneurship using SMN is conceptualized and applied in SMEs and highlights the factors that influence e-commerce innovation. The study provides a theoretical lens to increase the understanding of an e-commerce entrepreneurship process using a contextualism theory.

The study showcases how e-commerce using Facebook can be portrayed in a developing country context. Overall the special issue points to the need for further evaluation and interrogation of entrepreneurship ecosystems within sub-Saharan Africa, which is the focus of this book project.

10.3 Entrepreneurship Ecosystems

In their exploration of the present state of entrepreneurship ecosystems in selected countries in Africa, Sheriff and Muffatto (2015) argued that "entrepreneurship ecosystems could be useful road maps for the formulation of entrepreneurship policies for countries in Africa". According to these authors, the twenty-first-century economic development agenda heavily emphasized the pivotal role that entrepreneurship plays in the growth of economies, job creation, and poverty alleviation. But without the right entrepreneurial ecosystems to enhance the formulation of pertinent entrepreneurship policies, achieving entrepreneurial economic growth will be difficult. The existing frameworks for the development of entrepreneurship ecosystems are based on research that has been conducted elsewhere.

However, entrepreneurship research in Africa has rarely focused on understanding and evaluating the entrepreneurship ecosystems. Sheriff and Muffatto (2015) have attempted to examine the present state of the entrepreneurship ecosystems in four countries (Botswana, Egypt, Ghana, and Uganda) in Africa. Even though extant literature on the concept is limited, it has been reviewed to provide a picture of entrepreneurship ecosystems. Previously, Naudé and Havenga (2005) highlighted the paucity of research that has been published about entrepreneurship in Africa, especially in mainstream entrepreneurship journals. This position is also supported by Lingelbach et al. (2005), who state that specialist literature has focused more on the description of entrepreneurial attributes in developing countries rather than the provision of frameworks where entrepreneurs and policymakers can interact. The scholars further stress that even the existing models of entrepreneurship are based largely on research conducted in developed countries, which usually does not reflect the manner in which entrepreneurship is being practised both in the least developed and emerging economies. Sheriff and Muffatto (2015) conclude that the literature about entrepreneurship in Africa needs to be enriched and extended, especially with regards to recent emerging concepts such as national entrepreneurship ecosystems. These national systems of entrepreneurship involve many key players, their interconnectedness, and their interactions with the entrepreneurship environment. Understanding these systems could form a solid base for the formulation of entrepreneurship policies. But, to extend and enrich the literature with regards to entrepreneurship ecosystems, the first step is to examine the present state of entrepreneurship ecosystems in sub-Saharan Africa, which is the purpose of *Digital Entrepreneurship in Sub-Saharan Africa*. Indeed, Chaps. 3 to 5 in this collection capture these insights from the perspective of Nigeria.

The entrepreneurship ecosystem concept recently has attracted the interest of scholars, practitioners, policymakers, and leaders as entrepreneurship is being considered as playing a pivotal role in national economic growth. The reasons are not difficult to discern, as governments around the world are proposing or formulating policies for the creation of an enabling environment that will unleash productive entrepreneurship, which is viewed as an important contributor to a country's industrial and economic growth as well as one of the critical pillars germane to the commercialization of innovations in the new economic era (see, e.g., Archibong 2010). Since research on this topic in Africa is limited, *Digital Entrepreneurship in Sub-Saharan Africa* attempts to fill this chasm by examining and comparing the interactions between different entrepreneurial actors and the entrepreneurial environment in the selected countries. In Chap. 2, for instance, Friederici highlights the surge in innovation hubs across Africa.

The concept of entrepreneurship ecosystems has emerged quite recently as a benchmark for formulating and implementing entrepreneurship policies. As a consequence, governments in most countries are attempting to base the design of entrepreneurship policies on the entrepreneurship ecosystem approach, but there is a paucity of research on this topic (Kantis and Federico 2012), especially in emerging and less developed countries. Anecdotal evidence has shown that there are various types of entrepreneurship ecosystems in existence, but the most recognized one is that presented by the Babson Entrepreneurship Ecosystem Project, which has been applied in different regions of the world (Isenberg 2010). Maroufkhani et al. (2018, p. 545) make the point that:

> The literature on entrepreneurial ecosystems is fragmented, and yet, no studies have paid attention to integrating the available studies. The purpose of this study is to provide a systematic review of contributions related to entrepreneurial ecosystems.

These authors also highlight the recent state of research across industries, geographical scopes, and methodologies as they seek to extend Isenberg's (2011) model of entrepreneurial ecosystems. According to them (see Maroufkhani et al. 2018, p. 546):

> the entrepreneurial ecosystem is designed to deal with some of the policy faults resulting from the way the above-mentioned strategies are perceived and performed including—lack of public priority for entrepreneurship; ambiguity in entrepreneurship strategy objectives; unintentional undermining of entrepreneurship ambitions; inadvertent aversion of entrepreneurial finance providers; and distorted results of disorganized programs, such as an educational plan that prompts brain drain.

What makes *Digital Entrepreneurship in Sub-Saharan Africa* different from previous similar publications discussed in this section is that the entrepreneurship ecosystem approach underpins all the contributions, while the sectoral perspective is extended by including unique discussions on animation, gaming, and inclusive technology.

10.4 Animation and Games

Azi (2012, p. 37), in a study titled "Appraising the Role of Afrimation (African-Animation) in Promoting Africa's Rich Cultural Heritage in a Digital Age", opines that "Africa's animation industry's impact on its socio-eco-cultural development has been very inconsequential to say the least". He discusses "six contemporary 'indigenous' Afrimation projects that have potential of being highly innovative in the digital technology arena, as a medium for promoting the African Renaissance agenda" and notes that "repackaging relevant aspects of Africa's unique cultural heritage as animated digital contents, would in no small way be vital in preserving and promoting the culture both locally and internationally" (Azi 2012, p. 38).

Similarly, Pijnaker and Spronk (2017) provide some insights into the intersection of digital technologies and social class and contribute to the theorizing digital technologies as a means of expressing middle-class aesthetics, aspirations, and senses of being in the world. These authors set about showcasing how the production processes of "Africa's Legends" has been informed by historically embedded ideas about cultural heritage and notions of design and style in the subregion. The study explores and traces "how the upper middle-class background of the producers informs the production, distribution and reception of the app". According to the producers, digital technologies such as Adobe Photoshop and Adobe Illustrator allow "Africa's Legends" to be of the appropriate quality necessary to create a "new African" style and to reach a global audience. However, Ghanaians of a less privileged background do not share this interpretation, which suggests that digital technologies mediate specific class aesthetics and aspirations—which naturally leads to the discussion of inclusion.

Chapter 6 of *Digital Entrepreneurship in Sub-Saharan Africa*, authored by Paula Callus, expands all existing research in animation and gaming by bringing new insights to arts in digital spaces based on a case illustration from Kenya. In particular, Callus picks up on curatorial practice that defines animation and gaming entrepreneurship in sub-Saharan Africa.

10.5 Inclusive Technology

On the subject of inclusive technology, a recent International Finance Corporation (IFC) report titled "Digital Access: The Future of Financial Inclusion in Africa" sets a positive tone. In the report Reeta Roy, President and CEO of the Mastercard Foundation, and Philippe Le Houérou, CEO of the IFC, highlight the fact that "the launch and growth of digital financial services has led to an unprecedented increase in the number of people enjoying access to formal financial services". They also point out that "today, Africa is home to more digital financial services deployments than any other region in the world, with almost half of the nearly 700 million individual users worldwide" (Roy and Le Houérou 2018, p. 7).

This revelation is consistent with a decade-old scholarly article in which Mutula (2008, p. 468) opined that

> there is a link between bridging the digital divide and economic development. However, there is as yet no unanimity as to whether the digital divide is narrowing or widening in developing countries including those in sub-Saharan Africa. Nevertheless, countries in sub-Saharan Africa are making tremendous strides, especially in infrastructure development and mobile phone connectivity, to bridge the digital divide.

Irene, in Chap. 7 of *Digital Entrepreneurship in Sub-Saharan Africa*, throws additional light on the power of inclusive technology from the perspective of gender inequality and poverty through a discursive analysis of the impact of technology on the success of women entrepreneurs in South Africa.

Overall, this volume covers most of the topics discussed above in broad terms and extends the discourse beyond nomenclatures such as "Digital Kenya" (Weiss 2017), which is clearly missing the entrepreneurship component, and the work of Dana et al. (2018), with the obvious absence of the "digital" element. Arguably, *Digital Entrepreneurship in Sub-Saharan Africa* unites these perspectives within a single narrative cutting across the sub-Saharan Africa region.

Further Reading

Adusei, M. (2016). Does Entrepreneurship Promote Economic Growth in Africa? *African Development Review, 28*(2), 201–214.

Aglionby, J. (2016). Fintech Takes Off in Africa as Lenders Tap Mobile Technology. *Financial Times*, p. 17.

Aikhuomogbe, S. O. (2016). *Preparing Employees for Entrepreneurship in Retirement: A Case Study*. Doctoral dissertation, Walden University. Retrieved from https://scholarworks.waldenu.edu/cgi/viewcontent.cgi?article=4017&context=dissertations.

Aker, J. C., & Mbiti, I. M. (2010). Mobile Phones and Economic Development in Africa. *Journal of Economic Perspectives, 24*(3), 207–232.

Alexander, A. J., Shi, L., & Solomon, B. (2017). *How Fintech is Reaching the Poor in Africa and Asia (No. 30360)*. Washington, DC: The World Bank.

Amankwah-Amoah, J. (2015). Solar Energy in Sub-Saharan Africa: The Challenges and Opportunities of Technological Leapfrogging. *Thunderbird International Business Review, 57*(1), 15–31.

Collier, P., & Dercon, S. (2014). African Agriculture in 50 Years: Smallholders in a Rapidly Changing World? *World Development, 63*, 92–101.

Dana, L. P., & Ratten, V. (2017). International Entrepreneurship in Resource Landlocked African Countries. *Journal of International Entrepreneurship, 15*(4), 416–435. https://doi.org/10.1007/s10843-017-0211-6.

Davies, T. A. (2001). Entrepreneurship Development in South Africa: Redefining the Role of Tertiary Institutions in a Reconfigured Higher Education System. *South African Journal of Higher Education, 15*(1), 32–39.

Didenko, A. (2017). Regulating FinTech: Lessons from Africa. *San Diego International Law Journal, 19*, 311. Retrieved from https://digital.sandiego.edu/cgi/viewcontent.cgi?referer=https://scholar.google.co.uk/&httpsredir=1&article=1063&context=ilj.

Elkan, W. (1988). Entrepreneurs and Entrepreneurship in Africa. *The World Bank Research Observer, 3*(2), 171–188.

Elmawazini, K., & Nwankwo, S. (2012). Foreign Direct Investment: Technology Gap Effects on International Business Capabilities of Sub-Saharan Africa. *Thunderbird International Business Review, 54*(4), 457–467.

Engelmann, R. (1994). Entrepreneurship and Africa. In *African Development and Public Policy* (pp. 67–85). London: Palgrave Macmillan.

Gerguri-Rashiti, S., Ramadani, V., Abazi-Alili, H., Dana, L. P., & Ratten, V. (2017). ICT, Innovation and Firm Performance: The Transition Economies Context. *Thunderbird International Business Review, 59*(1), 93–102.

Gnyawali, D. R., & Fogel, D. S. (1994). Environments for Entrepreneurship Development: Key Dimensions and Research Implications. *Entrepreneurship Theory and Practice, 18*(4), 43–62.

Hisrich, R. D., & Peters, M. P. (1992). *Entrepreneurship: Starting, Developing, and Managing a New Enterprise*. Homewood, IL: McGraw-Hill/Irwin.

Ika, L. A., & Saint-Macary, J. (2014). Special Issue: Why Do Projects Fail in Africa? *Journal of African Business, 15*(3), 151–155. https://doi.org/10.1080/15228916.2014.956635.

Joseph, N., Erasmus, W., & Marnewick, C. (2014). The Idle State of Information and Communication Technology Project Management. *Journal of African Business, 15*(3), 184–196.

Juma, C. (2015). *The New Harvest: Agricultural Innovation in Africa*. Oxford: Oxford University Press.

Kelly, N., Bennett, J. M., & Starasts, A. (2017). Networked Learning for Agricultural Extension: A Framework for Analysis and Two Cases. *The Journal of Agricultural Education and Extension, 23*(5), 399–414.

Kiggundu, M. N. (2002). Entrepreneurs and Entrepreneurship in Africa: What Is Known and What Needs to be Done. *Journal of Developmental Entrepreneurship, 7*(3), 239.

Kshetri, N. (2014). Developing Successful Entrepreneurial Ecosystems Lessons from a Comparison of an Asian Tiger and a Baltic Tiger. *Baltic Journal of Management, 9*(3), 330–356. https://doi.org/10.1108/bjm-09-2013-0146.

Kuzilwa, J. A. (2005). The Role of Credit for Small Business Success: A Study of the National Entrepreneurship Development Fund in Tanzania. *The Journal of Entrepreneurship, 14*(2), 131–161.

Madichie, N. (2003). Afronomics: How Relevant is Economic Theory when Ceteris Is Not paribus? In S. Nwankwo, L. Montanheiro, J. Aiyeku, & A. Ogbuehi (Eds.), *Dimensions of African Business and Development* (pp. 127–137). Sheffield: Sheffield Hallam University Press.

Madichie, N. (2015). A Commentary on African Business & Economic Environment in 2015. *African Journal of Business and Economic Research, 10*(1), 5–24. Retrieved from https://journals.co.za/content/aa_ajber/10/1/EJC171072.

Marnewick, C., & Labuschagne, L. (2011). An Investigation into the Governance of Information Technology Projects in South Africa. *International Journal of Project Management, 29*(1), 661–670.

Nafukho, F. M., & Helen Muyia, M. A. (2010). Entrepreneurship and Socioeconomic Development in Africa: A Reality or Myth? *Journal of European Industrial Training, 34*(2), 96–109.

Naudé, W. (2010). Entrepreneurship, Developing Countries, and Development Economics: New Approaches and Insights. *Small Business Economics, 34*(1), 1.

Naudé, A., & Havenga, J. (2007). An Overview of Entrepreneurship and Small Business Research. In L.-P. Dana & R. Anderson (Eds.), *International Hand-Book on Indigenous Entrepreneurship* (pp. 28–45). Northampton, MA: Edward Elgar Publishing Ltd.

Nwankwo, S. (2000). Assessing the Marketing Environment in Sub-Saharan Africa: Opportunities and Threats Analysis. *Marketing Intelligence & Planning, 18*(3), 144–153.

Ohiorhenuan, J. F. (2009). Don't Cry for Me Africa: Preamble of a Memo to the African Prince. *Transition: An International Review, 102*, 140–155.

Pantaleo, D. R., & Ssegawa, J. K. (2014). The African Project Failure Syndrome: The Conundrum of Project Management Knowledge Base—The Case of SADC. *Journal of African Business, 15*(3), 211–224. https://doi.org/10.1080/15228916.2014.956645.

Rugumamu, S. M., & Mutagwaba, B. B. (1999). Entrepreneurship Development in Africa: Some Reflections from Tanzania. In *African Entrepreneurship and Small Business Development* (pp. 65–83). Dar es Salaam: DUP Ltd.

Starasts, A. (2015). Unearthing Farmers' Information Seeking Contexts and Challenges in Digital, Local and Industry Environments. *Library & Information Science Research, 37*(2), 156–163.

The World Bank. (2015, October 27). Doing Business 2016: Measuring Regulatory Quality and Efficiency. Retrieved from http://www.doingbusiness.org/reports/global-reports/doing-business-2016.

Tshikuku, K. (2001, December). Culture, Entrepreneurship and Development in Africa. In *International Conference on the Cultural Approach to Development in Africa* (pp. 10–14). Retrieved from http://unpan1.un.org/intradoc/groups/public/documents/IDEP/UNPAN003349.pdf.

Verhoef, G. (2018a). Entrepreneurship in Africa. *Canadian Journal of African Studies/Revue canadienne des études africaines*, 1–3. https://doi.org/10.1080/00083968.2018.1462975.

Verhoef, G. (2018b). Entrepreneurship in Africa. Book Review. In A. Akinyoade, T. Dietz, & C. U. Uche (Eds.), *Entrepreneurship in Africa* (Vol. 15). Boston, MA: Brill. https://doi.org/10.1080/00083968.2018.1462975.

References

Acemoglu, D., Egorov, G., & Sonin, K. (2010). Political Selection and Persistence of Bad Governments. *The Quarterly Journal of Economics, 125*(4), 1511–1575.

Acemoglu, D., & Robinson, J. (2008). *The Role of Institutions in Growth and Development*. The World Bank.

Adenle, A. A., Manning, L., & Azadi, H. (2017). Agribusiness Innovation: A Pathway to Sustainable Economic Growth in Africa. *Trends in Food Science & Technology, 59*, 88–104.

Ahmed, A. (2017). *Managing Knowledge and Innovation for Business Sustainability in Africa* (pp. 3–12). Cham: Palgrave Macmillan.

Ahmed, A., & Nwankwo, S. (2013). Entrepreneurship Development in Africa: An Overview. *World Journal of Entrepreneurship, Management and Sustainable Development, 9*(2/3), 82–86.

Akinyoade, A., Dietz, T., & Uche, C. U. (Eds.). (2017). *Entrepreneurship in Africa* (Vol. 15). Boston, MA: Brill.

Amankwah-Amoah, J. (2018). Cultivating Greater Self-confidence in African Management Research. *Thunderbird International Business Review, 60*(4), 511–522.

Archibong, C. A. (2010). Entrepreneurship as a Critical and Missing Factor in Economic Development of Poor Nations: A Systematic Analysis of Factors of Production. *The IUP Journal of Business Strategies, 7*(1/2), 1–2.

Asongu, S. A., & Nwachukwu, J. C. (2018). Openness, ICT and Entrepreneurship in Sub-Saharan Africa. *Information Technology & People, 31*(1), 278–303.

Atiase, V. Y., Mahmood, S., Wang, Y., & Botchie, D. (2018). Developing Entrepreneurship in Africa: Investigating Critical Resource Challenges. *Journal of Small Business and Enterprise Development, 25*(4), 644–666.

Azi, J. I. (2012). Appraising the Role of Afrimation (African-Animation) in Promoting Africa's Rich Cultural Heritage in a Digital Age. *International Journal of Computer Graphics & Animation, 2*(2/3), 37–54.

Boojihawon, D. K., & Ngoasong, Z. M. (2018). Emerging Digital Business Models in Developing Economies: The Case of Cameroon. *Strategic Change, 27*(2), 129–137.

Crissey, J. (2010). Any Value in the Chain. *Unpublished Working Paper*. Retrieved from https://www.academia.edu/637947/Any_value_in_the_chain.

Dana, L. P., Ratten, V., & Honyenuga, B. Q. (Eds.). (2018). *African Entrepreneurship: Challenges and Opportunities for Doing Business*. Cham: Springer.

Edoho, F. M. (2016). Entrepreneurship Paradigm in the New Millennium: A Critique of Public Policy on Entrepreneurship. *Journal of Entrepreneurship in Emerging Economies, 8*(2), 279–294.

Ferreira, J., Ratten, V., & Dana, L. (2017). Knowledge Spillover-based Strategic Entrepreneurship. *International Entrepreneurship and Management Journal, 13*(1), 161–167.

Garba, A. S. (2010). Refocusing Education System towards Entrepreneurship Development in Nigeria: A Tool for Poverty Reduction. *European Journal of Social Sciences, 15*(1), 140–150.

George, G., Corbishley, C., Khayesi, J., Haas, M., & Tihanyi, L. (2016). Bringing Africa In: Promising Directors for Management Research. *Academy of Management Journal, 59*(2), 377–393.

Gudeta, K. H., & van Engen, M. L. (2018). Work-Life Boundary Management Styles of Women Entrepreneurs in Ethiopia—"Choice" or Imposition? *Journal of Small Business and Enterprise Development, 25*(3), 368–386.

Hain, D. S., & Jurowetzki, R. (2018). Local Competence Building and International Venture Capital in Low-Income Countries: Exploring Foreign High-Tech Investments in Kenya's Silicon Savanna. *Journal of Small Business and Enterprise Development, 25*(3), 447–482.

Isenberg, D. (2010). The Big Idea: How to Start an Entrepreneurial Revolution. *Harvard Business Review, 88*(6), 40–50.

Isenberg, D. (2011). The Entrepreneurship Ecosystem Strategy as a New Paradigm for Economic Policy: Principles for Cultivating Entrepreneurship. In *The Babson Entrepreneurship Ecosystem Project*. Babson Park, MA: Babson College.

Jedlowski, A. (2016). Studying Media "from" the South: African Media Studies and Global Perspectives. *Black Camera: An International Film Journal (The New Series), 7*(2), 174–193.

Jones, P., Maas, G., Dobson, S., Newbery, R., Agyapong, D., & Matlay, H. (2018). Entrepreneurship in Africa, Part 1: Entrepreneurial Dynamics in Africa. *Journal of Small Business and Enterprise Development, 25*(3), 346–348.

Kantis, H. D., & Federico, J. S. (2012). *Entrepreneurial Ecosystems in Latin America: The Role of Policies Entrepreneurial Development Programme (PRODEM)*. Los Polvorines, Buenos Aries: Institute of Industry, Universidad Nacional de General Sarmiento.

Kolo, J., Madichie, N., & Mbah, C. (2016). *Commonomics: A Panacea for the African Growth Tragedy in the 21st Century*. Paper presented at the 18th EBES (EuroAsia Business and Economics Society) Conference. United Arab Emirates: American University of Sharjah. Retrieved from https://www.ebesweb.org/Portals/0/18th%20EBES%20Conference%20U.A.E.%20Program.pdf.

Kshetri, N. (2011). Institutional and Economic Foundations of Entrepreneurship in Africa: An Overview. *Journal of Developmental Entrepreneurship, 16*(1), 9–35.

Lingelbach, D. C., De La Vina, L., & Asel, P. (2005). What's Distinctive about Growth-Oriented Entrepreneurship in Developing Countries? *UTSA College of Business Center for Global Entrepreneurship Working Paper*, pp. 1–10.

Madichie, N. (2016). Editorial—Introduction to the Issue. *African Journal of Business and Economic Research, 11*(2/3), 5–8. Retrieved from https://search.proquest.com/docview/1877788794?pq-origsite=gscholar.

Madichie, N., Mpofu, K., & Kolo, J. (2017). Entrepreneurship Development in Africa: Insights from Nigeria's and Zimbabwe's Telecoms. In A. Akinyoade,

T. Dietz, & C. U. Uche (Eds.), *Entrepreneurship in Africa* (Vol. 15, pp. 172–208). Leiden, The Netherlands: Brill Publishing.

Maroufkhani, P., Wagner, R., Khairuzzaman, W., & Ismail, W. (2018). Entrepreneurial Ecosystems: A Systematic Review. *Journal of Enterprising Communities: People and Places in the Global Economy, 12*(4), 545–564. https://doi.org/10.1108/JEC-03-2017-0025.

Mutula, S. M. (2008). Digital Divide and Economic Development: Case Study of Sub-Saharan Africa. *The Electronic Library, 26*(4), 468–489. https://doi.org/10.1108/02640470810893738.

Naudé, W. A., & Havenga, J. J. D. (2005). An Overview of African Entrepreneurship and Small Business Research. *Journal of Small Business & Entrepreneurship, 18*(1), 101–120.

Ndemo, B., & Weiss, T. (Eds.). (2017). *Digital Kenya: An Entrepreneurial Revolution in the Making*. London: Palgrave Macmillan.

Nwankwo, S. (2011). Imagining Africa in the Global Economy. *Thunderbird International Business Review, 53*(1), 3–8.

Nwankwo, S. (2012). Renascent Africa: Rescoping the Landscape of International Business. *Thunderbird International Business Review, 54*(4), 405–409. https://doi.org/10.1002/tie.21472.

Nwankwo, S., & Ibeh, K. I. N. (Eds.). (2015). *The Routledge Companion to Business in Africa*. New York: Routledge. ISBN-10: 0415635454; ISBN-13: 978-0415635455. Retrieved from http://routledge-ny.com/books/details/9780415635455/.

Nziku, D. M., & Struthers, J. J. (2018). Female Entrepreneurship in Africa: Strength of Weak Ties in Mitigating Principal-Agent Problems. *Journal of Small Business and Enterprise Development, 25*(3), 349–367.

Pijnaker, T., & Spronk, R. (2017). Africa's Legends: Digital Technologies, Aesthetics and Middle-Class Aspirations in Ghanaian Games and Comics. *Critical African Studies, 9*(3), 327–349. https://doi.org/10.1080/21681392.2017.1371617.

Prahalad, C. K., & Krishnan, M. S. (2008). *The New Age of Innovation*. McGraw-Hill Professional Publishing.

Ratten, V., & Jones, P. (2018). Bringing Africa into Entrepreneurship Research. In L. P. Dana, V. Ratten, & B. Honyenuga (Eds.), *African Entrepreneurship* (Palgrave Studies of Entrepreneurship in Africa). Cham: Palgrave Macmillan.

Reid, M., Roumpi, D., & O'Leary-Kelly, A. M. (2015). Spirited Women: The Role of Spirituality in the Lives of Female Entrepreneurs in Ghana. *African Journal of Management, 1*(3), 264–283.

Roy, R., & Le Houérou, P. (2018). *Digital Access: The Future of Financial Inclusion in Africa*. Washington, DC: International Finance Corporation. Retrieved from https://www.ifc.org/wps/wcm/connect/region__ext_content/ifc_external_corporate_site/sub-saharan+africa/resources/201805_report_digital-access-africa.

Shemi, A. P., & Procter, C. (2018). E-commerce and Entrepreneurship in SMEs: Case of myBot. *Journal of Small Business and Enterprise Development, 25*(3), 501–520. https://doi.org/10.1108/JSBED-03-2017-0088.

Sheriff, M., & Muffatto, M. (2015). The Present State of Entrepreneurship Ecosystems in Selected Countries in Africa. *African Journal of Economic and Management Studies, 6*, 17–54.

The Economist. (2000, May 11). Hopeless Africa. *The Economist*. Retrieved from http://www.economist.com/node/333429.

The Economist. (2011, December 3). The Hopeful Continent: Africa Rising. *The Economist*. Retrieved from http://www.economist.com/news/special-report/21572377-african-lives-havealready-greatly-improvedover-past-decade-says-oliver-august.

Tvedten, K., Wendelboe Hansen, M., & Jeppesen, S. (2014). Understanding the Rise of African Business: In Search of Business Perspectives on African Enterprise Development. *African Journal of Economic and Management Studies, 5*(3), 249–268.

Ukanwa, I., Xiong, L., & Anderson, A. (2018). Experiencing Microfinance: Effects on Poor Women Entrepreneurs' Livelihood Strategies. *Journal of Small Business and Enterprise Development, 25*(3), 428–446.

Weiss, T. (2017). Entrepreneuring for Society: What Is Next for Africa? In B. Ndemo & T. Weiss (Eds.), *Digital Kenya. Palgrave Studies of Entrepreneurship in Africa*. London: Palgrave Macmillan. https://doi.org/10.1057/978-1-137-57878-5_15.

Index

A

African continent, 10–12, 126, 164, 218, 226

Authenticity, 6, 67, 71, 125, 126, 129–135, 140

C

Communities, 13, 18–23, 68, 71, 96, 128, 136–138, 181, 183, 191, 214, 224

Creativity, 13, 67

Cultural capital, 5–6, 125–140

Culture, 67, 69, 73, 80, 82, 83, 115, 125, 129, 131, 136, 137, 139, 140, 187, 214, 231

D

Digital artefacts, 10, 47

Digital distribution, 90, 92, 95–99, 117

Digital divide, 74, 126–127, 165–168, 180, 233

Digital entrepreneurship, 3–6, 9–15, 24, 34, 89, 140, 176, 217, 221–233

Digital innovation, 4

Digital landscape, 4

Digital marketing, 90, 92, 99–101, 117

Digital production, 11, 90, 92–95, 117

Dyadic view, 19, 21–23

E

Ecosystem, 4, 15, 22, 40, 41, 74, 83–84, 222, 225, 226, 228–231

N. D. Taura et al. (eds.), *Digital Entrepreneurship in Sub-Saharan Africa*, Palgrave Studies of Entrepreneurship in Africa, https://doi.org/10.1007/978-3-030-04924-9

Entrepreneur, 4–6, 9–24, 33, 36, 38, 41, 75, 83, 93, 95, 96, 128, 130, 147–169, 176, 177, 181–182, 185–187, 189–192, 199, 210, 215–218, 223–225, 227–229, 233
Entrepreneurial communities, 21–23
Entrepreneurial participation, 17, 22
Environment, 3, 4, 10, 18, 22, 24, 32, 45, 59, 72, 80, 83, 84, 95, 110, 114, 132, 139, 148, 164, 165, 168, 176, 180, 182, 209, 214, 223, 227, 228, 230

G
Ghana, 14, 34, 40, 126, 175–192, 229

I
Incumbent, 4, 5, 32–33, 41–43, 47–50, 52–53, 57–59, 182, 213
Infrastructure and poor institutional quality, 4

K
Kenya, 4, 11, 16, 126–128, 130–132, 134, 137, 140, 232

L
Legitimacy, 5, 31–33, 36–37, 41–42, 44–45, 52–59

M
Macro environment, 38

N
Nigeria, 4, 31–59, 67–84, 90–92, 94, 95, 97, 103–105, 107–116, 126, 199–219, 230
Nollywood, 5, 68, 70, 71, 89–117

P
Policy, 165, 168, 183, 199–202, 209, 214–216, 218, 228, 231

S
Social media, 57–59, 67–68, 70–73, 76, 79, 107, 126, 127, 138, 148, 151, 168
South Africa, 4, 6, 12, 80, 96, 126, 147–169, 222, 233
Startup, 33

The manufacturer's authorised representative in the EU is Springer Nature Customer Service Centre GmbH, Europaplatz 3, 69115 Heidelberg, Germany. If you have any concerns regarding our products, please contact ProductSafety@springernature.com

Printed and bound by CPI Group (UK) Ltd, Croydon, CR0 4YY
25/09/2026
02222859-0002